Thinking About Suicide: Perspectives on Suicide

THINKING ABOUT SUICIDE: PERSPECTIVES ON SUICIDE

DAVID LESTER

Nova Science Publishers, Inc.
New York

Editorial Production Manager: Donna Dennis
Senior Production Editor: Susan Boriotti
Production Editors: Marius Andronie, Rusudan Razmadze and Keti Datunashvili
Office Manager: Annette Hellinger
Graphics: Magdalena Nuñez
Editorial Production: Maya Columbus, Vladimir Klestov, and Lorna Loperfido
Circulation: Ave Maria Gonzalez, Vera Popovic, Luis Aviles, Alexandra Columbus, Raymond Davis, Cathy DeGregory, Melissa Diaz, Marlene Nuñez and Jeannie Pappas

Library of Congress Cataloging-in-Publication Data
Available Upon Request

ISBN: 1-59454-147-7

400 Oser Ave, Suite 1600
Hauppauge, New York 11788-3619
Tele. 631-231-7269 Fax 631-231-8175
e-mail: Novascience@earthlink.net
Web Site: http://www.novapublishers.com

Printed in the United States of America

CONTENTS

Chapter 1

INTRODUCTION

The study of suicidal behavior has been truly interdisciplinary. Scholarly papers on suicide have appeared in anthropological, biological, criminal justice, economic, law, literature, medical, nursing, pharmacological, philosophical, psychiatric, psychological, religious, social work, sociological and thanatological journals, as well as those devoted to specific topics such as drug addiction and gambling.

Over the course of my career in suicidology, I have tried to read all of the literature on suicidal behavior, in all of these disciplines, and I have endeavored to think and to write from each of the perspectives developed by these disciplines. This book is a compilation of some of my thoughts and theories from this undertaking.

Although the chapters in this book do not "explain" suicide, they may further our understanding of the behavior by portraying it in all of its complexities. By examining the behavior from different perspectives, perhaps we will be challenged to broaden our view and, thereby, devise new theories and research approaches for studying suicide. The goal of this book, therefore, is to challenge you, the reader, to think about suicide in ways you have not considered before. For example, in Chapter 6, the possibility that suicidal behavior might have a function for society is discussed, and the question of whether a society could ever have a zero suicide rate is posed, issues that perhaps you have not hitherto considered. My aim is that each chapter will raise questions and issues which will stimulate your thinking about suicide.

As a start, in this introductory chapter, let us look at how ideas from physics might stimulate our thinking about suicide. Two analogies can be drawn from the natural sciences which may have applicability to suicidology and provide important insights. The first concerns the differences in predicting the behavior of the individual versus the aggregate.

THE INDIVIDUAL VERSUS THE AGGREGATE

Radioactive atoms are unstable and decay into other atoms. The speed of decay is measured by *half-life*. The half-life is the time period required for half of the atoms in a sample of the element to decay into the new element. Half-lives of different atoms can vary from less than one second to over billion years. For example, after 29 years, half of the atoms of a sample of Strontium-90 will have decayed into Yttrium-90. After another 29 years, a half of the remaining atoms will have decayed, and so on (Shapiro, 1979).

Physicists cannot predict which particular atoms will decay during the half-life or when any particular atom will decay. At the beginning, those atoms which decay during the half-life look identical to those which do not decay.

The analogy with suicide is strong. While it is impossible to predict which 30,000 Americans will commit suicide next year, we do know that about 30,000 will do so. Predicting the behavior of the aggregate is possible while predicting the behavior of the individual is very difficult.

Actually, the task for the suicidologist is a little easier than that confronting the physicist for the potential suicides do differ from the potential nonsuicides at the beginning of the observation period. Various risk factors have been identified for suicide (such as the presence of an affective disorder, current substance abuse, and a history of loss and sexual and physical abuse), whereas none have been identified for the atoms which will decay in the near future.

INPUT-OUTPUT: WHAT MAKES SOMEONE COMMIT SUICIDE?

It may be surprising to find out that, for many phenomena, small differences in input can produce large differences in output (Gleick, 1987). In meteorology, Lorenz (1979, 1984) attempted to model climate change using a simplified mathematical model. The traditional view was that later conditions could be reasonably accurately predicted from an approximate knowledge of initial conditions. Small influences will not have large effects eventually. On one occasion, Lorenz tried to replicate the second half of a sequence of his artificial climate by entering the values obtained in the middle of a previous run. He found that the slight discrepancies initially grew larger and larger until the new sequence was completely unlike the original sequence. He had entered decimals rounded to three places rather than six. This small change proved to be catastrophic.

The interesting feature of weather prediction is that we can predict the obvious, for example, that next July will be sunny and hot (the periodic component), but this is uninteresting. What people want to predict is whether a particular July day will have rain, that is, it is the nonperiodic component that we want to predict.

In the prediction of human behavior, suicidologists can predict the regularities. For example, using Erikson's (1959) stages of human development, we can predict the normal course of development. However, that is uninteresting. We want to be able to predict the statistically rare and nonperiodic occurrence, that is, suicide.

What may make this difficult is not necessarily the complexity of the information we have to obtain about individuals throughout their lives in order to make the prediction, but that this catastrophic event -- suicide -- may be produced, not by some *major* event or events occurring at some prior point in time, but rather by some minor difference in an otherwise ordinary life course.

Lorenz speculated on the possibility that a butterfly stirring its wings in Brazil today may produce a tornado in Texas next month. Perhaps slightly too much or too little of some ordinary parental behavior may lead to suicide later in life? In suicidology, we expect and, therefore, search for major events which might lead to suicide subsequently, whereas perhaps the causes of suicide are more subtle.

Comment

It can be seen that ideas even from physics can suggest issues for our study and greater understanding of suicidal behavior. We will explore the contributions of other, more relevant, disciplines in the rest of this book.

References

Erikson, E. *Identity and the life cycle*. New York: International Universities Press, 1959.

Gleick, J. *Chaos*. New York: Viking, 1987.

Lorenz, E. Predictability: Does the flap of a butterfly's wings in Brazil set off a tornado in Texas? Paper presented at the American Association for the Advancement of Science, Washington, DC, 1979.

Lorenz, E. Irregularity: a fundamental property of the atmosphere. *Tellus*, 1984, 36A, 98-100.

Shapiro, G. *Physics without math*. Englewood Cliffs, NJ: Prentice-Hall, 1979.

Chapter 2

LITERATURE AND SUICIDE

There is a long history of using literature to illustrate and sometimes test psychological theories (Lester, 1987). For example, theories of suicide have been tested using the content of suicide notes (Leenaars, 1988). Occasionally, suicides (for example, Sylvia Plath) leave a book or poem describing their behavior, and this kind of material may be of use in exploring the unconscious psychodynamics of the suicidal act. In other fields of psychology, folk tales of primitive societies have been studied, for example, for evidence of the societal need for achievement or power (McClelland, Davis, Wanner and Kalin, 1966), and literary stimuli have been used in studies of people's preference for differing degrees of complexity (Kammann, 1966).

Before focusing on the use of literature in the study of suicide, let us explore a few of these general areas of interaction between psychology and literature in a little more detail.

PSYCHOLOGY AND LITERATURE

Understanding Human Behavior in Historical Times

The psychological study of history has created a new discipline, called psychohistory. Psychohistory seeks to enlarge our understanding of historical events and persons by applying psychological theory and knowledge (Hoffer, 1979). Crosby (1979) defined the field as "the form of history which makes explicit use of the concepts, principles, and theories of psychology in order to enhance our understanding of particular people and events in the past" (p. 6).

This joining of psychology and history had long been advocated (Barnes, 1925; Smith, 1913) but developed in depth only in the 1970s. The major psychological theory applied to history has been psychoanalysis (for example, Erikson's [1962] study of Martin Luther), but other theories, such as cognitive theory and trait theory, have been utilized. Although psychohistorians can use a variety of materials in order to make inferences about the psychological state of historical individuals and cultures, literature has occasionally been used.

For example, Hoffer (1974) analyzed school textbooks in the first half of the Nineteenth Century to show how threats to national unity appeared to influence school textbook writers to minimize divisive and unruly episodes in earlier American history, a decision consistent with Festinger's (1957) theory of cognitive dissonance.

McClelland (1958) illustrated the possibility of incorporating quantitative methods into psychohistory. For example, McClelland scored a variety of Greek writings for the need to achieve and found that this need declined steadily in Greece from 700 BC to 250 BC, which fits with the historical events of that period. Hull, Allen and Hoffer (1978) used the manuscripts left by loyalists and revolutionaries in revolutionary New York to identify differences in a variety of traits, including need for order, submissiveness, and conformity, and they related this to the writers' political affiliation.

History and psychology can also interact through literature in attempts to categorize historical events and epochs in psychological terms (rather than in political or economic terms). For example, Manuel (1967) took utopian novels from the last five hundred years and argued that they fall into three clear psychological periods: utopias of calm felicity (pre-Nineteenth Century), open-ended utopias of the Nineteenth Century, and contemporary utopias based on either on the hypothesis of a growing spiritualization of man (the humanistic psychology influence) or on a fantasy of greater sensate gratification (the psychoanalytic influence).

Psychological Analyses of Literature

Psychoanalytic theory (and other psychodynamic theories) have been applied in order to understand better the unconscious motivations of the fictional characters. For example, Antigone's motives in Sophocles' play of the same name (Sophocles, 1947) have been analyzed by Faber (1970).

Oedipus accidentally murdered his biological father and married his biological mother, without any conscious awareness of what he was doing. He had four children by his mother/wife, Jocasta: Eteocles, Polynices, Ismene and Antigone. When he found out what he had done, his mother/wife hung herself, and Oedipus took the brooches from her dress and blinded himself. Oedipus then went into exile.

Antigone was with Oedipus in his exile, helping to take care of him. After his death, his two sons fought against each other for the control of Thebes, killing each other in the process, leaving Oedipus's uncle, Creon, as King. Creon ordered that Eteocles should be buried with honor, but that Polynices, the rebel, should be left to rot without burial. He ordered that anybody who tried to bury Polynices would be executed.

In Sophocles's play, Antigone decides to bury Polynices, her brother. At first she tries to enlist the help of her sister Ismene, but Ismene refuses to go against the law. So Antigone decides to bury Polynices herself, knowing that the penalty is death. She says she will be happy to die if she is caught.

She buries him, covering him with a layer of dirt, and the fact of his token burial is reported to Creon. After Polynices's body is cleaned off, Antigone tries to bury him again, this time screaming as she does it, with the result that the sentries discover her in the act.

When Creon questions Antigone, she admits the act. There is the feeling that Creon would pardon her, but Antigone provokes his anger against her, so that he sentences her to be walled up in a cave to be left to die, even though she is engaged to his son, Haemon. Ismene tries to join Antigone in being blamed for the act, but Antigone now refuses to let Ismene accept any responsibility. She wants to be punished alone.

As Antigone talks to the chorus of her impending death, she compares herself to Niobe, the daughter of Tantalus, but the chorus reminds Antigone that Tantalus's daughter was a goddess whereas Antigone is a mortal. As she talks of her death, she refers to it as her bridal bower. She looks forward to seeing her father, mother and brothers again.

Creon orders her to be removed to a cave and sealed in it. Later he has a change of heart and rushes to the cave with his son to save Antigone. They find that she has already hung herself. Haemon tries to slay his father but, missing, turns his sword onto himself, killing himself in front of his father.

Antigone's death can be seen as a case of victim-precipitated homicide, a term coined by Wolfgang (1958). She, perhaps unconsciously, commits suicide by getting Creon to execute her. The penalty for burying Polynices is death, yet Antigone buries him while screaming so that the sentries discover her. When Creon looks as if he might pardon her, she seems to goad him into ordering her execution. It is by no means clear that these psychodynamic processes are conscious to Antigone, however.

Once Antigone is imprisoned in the cave, she hangs herself rather than die slowly of starvation. Interestingly, she chooses the method for suicide employed by her mother -- hanging.[1] The suicides of young people often show an imitation effect, much more so than the suicides of older people.

At the time of her death, Antigone has had a succession of losses. All of her family are now dead. The stain on the name of her family, beginning with the actions of Oedipus and ending with the civil war of her brothers, has grown enormously. Her family has lost its honor, and Antigone to a large extent does restore some honor to the family by her actions and death. Antigone is primarily concerned with her status after death, which makes sense given her psychological pain (shame, grief, and humiliation) on earth. Her death will restore her nobility. Interestingly, the Chorus tries to restrain her fantasies.

Although her death satisfies her general reunion fantasies, her reunion with Polynices seems to be the central goal. She refers to her death bed as her bridal bower. She says she can easily find a husband, but where could she find another brother like him. She does not mention Eteocles. Incestuous desires between brother and sister are not uncommon, especially when the two are separated during their childhood and adolescence (Lester, 1972a).

A frequent task in the psychological study of literature has been the tracing of a significance of a symbol or an idea through its many manifestations in literature, perhaps identifying in the process a Jungian archetype. For example, McClelland (1963) started with the idea that not all people fear death. Indeed, some people, often women, actually seem to look forward to death, with a sense of excitement as well as fear, as if death could be an unconscious equivalent for the final sexual union with the ideal mate (Bromberg and Schilder, 1933, 1936). McClelland's student, Greenberger (1965), found that dying women were more likely to gives stories involving illicit sexuality to cards from the Thematic Apperception Test than women who were not dying. Women students in his classes rated "a gay seducer" as more appropriate as a description of death than did the men.[2] Stimulated by these findings,

---

1 The men in Sophocles's plays use swords or other piercing instruments for their self-destructive acts.

2 It should be noted that subsequent research has not always confirmed these empirical findings (Lester, 1966; Lester and Schumacher, 1969).

McClelland traced the development of the Harlequin theme in literature. In the typical Harlequin story, Harlequin pursues Columbine, his love, despite obstacles placed in his way by her father, guardian or suitor, Pantaloon. In the dark scenes, Harlequin is definitely connected to underworld figures, and often Columbine dies at the end of the story.

The Harlequin figure seems to derive from an old French character called Herlequin, who is the devil (Driesen, 1904). In an Eleventh Century manuscript by Ordericus Vitalis, there is a Herlequin family in the underworld which sometimes appears on earth. In a play written in 1262 by Adan de le Hale, Herlequin is a single character and, in time, variants of the Harlequin story were acted in pantomime and danced in ballet, from the Arlecchino tradition in Italy to the bullfight tradition in Spain, all the way to modern equivalents, such as Agatha Christie's stories of love and death in *The Mysterious Mr. Quinn* (Christie, 1930) and the 1961 Hollywood film *The Last Sunset*.[3]

Literary styles have also been studied. For example, Skinner (1941) attempted to estimate whether the amount of alliteration in Shakespeare's sonnets exceeded chance expectations, and Rokeach, Homant and Penner (1970) analyzed the Federalist Papers to ascertain the authorship of the disputed papers.

Psychological Studies of the Author and the Reader

Psychoanalysis (and other psychodynamic theories) have often been applied to fictional works in order to better understand the author. The first example of the use of psychoanalysis to this end was by Freud (Niederland, 1960), who applied his theory to the novel *Die Richterin* by the Swiss writer, Conrad Ferdinand Meyer (1825-1898). Freud sent an essay to his friend, Wilhelm Fliess, on June 20, 1898, in which he suggested that the novel was an unconscious defense against the writer's memory of an affair with his sister (Freud, 1954). In the novel, a mother murders her husband and rules in his place until her stepson returns and unmasks his stepmother as the murderer. The stepmother thereupon commits suicide, but, in the course of the novel, the avenging stepson has an affair with his half-sister. Niederland notes that Meyer's father died when Meyer was fifteen. His early efforts to write were thwarted by his mother but encouraged by his sister. After his mother's suicide, Meyer lived with his sister in a close and personal relationship until he married in his late forties. She acted as his housekeeper, companion, secretary and advisor.

There have been many studies of the psychological state of individual authors. Bellak (1963), for example, treated the short stories of Somerset Maugham as if they were stories written to stimuli such as those in the Thematic Apperception Test, scoring the stories to measure the psychological needs of Maugham. For example, the *descriptive theme* in "Footprints in the Jungle" is that Bronson brings Cartwright home because he is temporarily in hard circumstances. Bronson's wife has an affair with Cartwright and persuades Cartwright to murder her husband. Though the police discover the crime, they do not have enough evidence to try the couple, who then live happily ever after. Bellak saw the *interpretive theme*

---

[3] Other manifestations of the Harlequin complex can be found in older times, as in the story of Hades coming up from hell to take Persephone off to the underworld and the fear of witches both in Europe and North America, and in modern times, as in the stories about the hypnotist Svengali, the mystique of the foreign psychoanalyst who allies himself with the dark side of the unconscious (Bakan, 1958), and most recently, Dr. Jack Kevorkian, the Doctor of Death, who initially helped mostly women commit suicide.

as that women can come between men and cause trouble and that sexual passion can motivate murder even in decent people, who may not even suffer remorse. At the *diagnostic level*, Bellak suggested that Somerset Maugham perceived, perhaps unconsciously, women as sources of trouble for men, separating them and destroying them. There is also an Oedipal theme here in which a man has to kill another man in order to obtain a mate; and, finally, passion can overpower the superego, leading to lack of control over aggression.

In general, after an analysis of ten of Maugham's ninety one short stories, Bellak suggested that Maugham had a continuous struggle with his sexual and aggressive impulses. To control them, Maugham tried for emotional isolation and detachment, playing the role of an onlooker toward others. His resulting self-image is that of a mildly ineffective person pushed around by external forces. Maugham saw women as domineering and demanding, leading men to feel inadequate, a view which is perhaps a projection of his own strong unconscious aggressive drives. Maugham suffered from a conflict between activity and passivity, conformity and nonconformity, and male and female identification, leading to embarrassment and shame, a feeling of inadequacy and a fear of failure. Bellak noted that his conclusions from his thematic analysis of Maugham's short stories was consistent with biographies of Maugham's life.[4]

Research on the impact of literature on the reader is illustrated by the studies stimulated by the Commission on Obscenity and Pornography (Anon, 1979) which produced a number of studies of the effects of pornography on people.

Other Points of Contact

Goodman (1963) has noted two other areas in which psychology and literature relate. First, psychologizing can be seen itself as a literary genre. A psychoanalytic case history is, for Goodman, a real novel or adventure story. A second relationship that Goodman saw between psychology and literature is in the way that writers have been affected by psychological thought. Goodman noted, for example, how contemporary writing takes into account such psychodynamic ideas as the continuity of dream life, daydreams, waking life, slips, fantasy, and wishful thinking.

A Dissenting Voice

Not everyone approves of this interaction between psychology and literature. For example, Jaffe (1967) has argued that a work of literature is contrived, serving only the writer's intent. The literary structure of the play forces the character into particular acts and mannerisms. Thus we cannot learn about real people from a study of literary characters. We can learn only about unreal people. For example, "responses in literature are not only responses *per se*, they are responses to stimuli which have been inserted, so to speak, *in order to* elicit them. It is precisely this which is not true of life" (p. 7). Jaffe pointed out that the situation which causes neurosis in a client was not designed in order to produce the neurosis.

---

4 Of course, Bellak's knowledge of Maugham's life may have affected the conclusions he drew from his thematic analysis of Maugham's short stories!

In Franz Kafka's *The Trial*, K refuses to kill himself. This, noted Jaffe, is not a sign of strength or of weakness. K cannot kill himself because of reasons which have nothing to do with some real person "K." K cannot kill himself because of the nature of suicide itself in the text and the way it functions in the text. In *The Trial*, suicide by an individual implies that the person has chosen to kill himself after considering, and rejecting, the alternative of continuing to live and because his experience in the course of the text indicates to him that death is the preferred alternative. The act of suicide is a symbol of redemption, postulates values to be redeemed and requires an agent who can assimilate experience and understand these values. K cannot assimilate experience because, in the text, he is the experience itself. He cannot be an agent because of his function in the novel. If K committed suicide, it would falsify the novel. The novel would be another novel, and *The Trial* would not exist. Suicide is not a choice which is open to K or even to Kafka, the novelist. Thus, we cannot learn about the reasons people may have for not committing suicide from *The Trial*.

Furthermore, we must beware of rediscovering "facts" from a study of literary works that incorporated those facts. For example, we would be fools indeed to use Huxley's novels to provide support for Sheldon's theory of the relationship of physique to temperament, since Huxley was well aware of Sheldon's theory and depicted his characters so as to be consistent with the theory.

However, perhaps we can demonstrate in this essay that, with care and forewarned, the psychologist can find a rich source of materials for the study of suicide in the realm of literature.

Studying Suicide (and the Unconscious) through Literature

Understanding Suicide

Faber (1970) has provided several examples of how an examination of suicide in literary characters can throw light on our understanding of suicide. In doing this, Faber explicitly states that he views literary suicides as case studies (though he places the words in quotes) which may serve as archetypes of suicidal behavior and which may provide insights into suicidal behavior. He states that he is not interested in how the suicides further the literary aims or "esthetic contraptions" of the authors, their esthetic implications or how they might throw light on the attitudes toward suicide of the society in which the play was written.

In Faber's analyses of the suicide of Haemon in Sophocles' *Antigone* and self-blinding of Oedipus in his the *Oedipus The King,* Faber provides good insights into the unconscious motivation for suicide, since Sophocles appears to have anticipated Freud's insights by some two thousand years. However, Freud's theory could just as easily have been illustrated with modern cases. On the other hand, many of the suicides in the plays of Euripides are altruistic suicides, and altruistic suicide is rare in modern times. Few case studies appear in print, and many suicidologists have suggested removing altruistic and fatalistic suicide from Durkheim's (1897) theory since these types of suicide are so rare in modern society (Johnson, 1965).

The suicide of Alcestis, Queen of Thessaly, illustrates some of the possible unconscious psychodynamics of voluntary altruistic suicide. Apollo learns that Alcestis's husband,

Admetus, is to die prematurely and makes a deal with the Fates to spare his life. The Fates demand another death in Admetus's place, and only his wife, Alcestis, volunteers to die in his place.

The central theme in the play appears not to be that Alcestis has offered to die in place of her husband, but that her husband has accepted her offer! After Alcestis realizes that her husband is going to accept her offer, she is filled with resentment toward him. She acts so as to induce guilt in him in order to punish him for accepting her offer. However, her aggression is expressed in part consciously and in part unconsciously.

On the day of her death, Alcestis does not emphasize the voluntary nature of her death. She speaks of herself as one who is about to be destroyed, implying that Admetus should have protected her from this destruction. She hints of betrayal and abandonment, focusing for example on her soon-to-be-motherless children. She expresses the hope that her daughter will marry a noble husband, implying that her own husband is not so noble.

In Admetus's presence, Alcestis breaks down and weeps, whereas with others she is more controlled. As soon as Admetus begins to experience the guilt and to suffer, Alcestis recovers her composure rapidly. She then extracts a promise from Admetus that he will not remarry, so that he will be less likely to forget Alcestis and her sacrifice.

Faber notes that Admetus is very dependent upon his wife, and it is this dependence that leads him in part to ask for and accept her sacrifice. However, his dependency on Alcestis makes her loss unbearable. He ends up begging her not to abandon him. We have, therefore, a relationship between a dependent person with few inner resources and a self-sacrificing person who resents being involved with a man who needs her in an infantile way, as an object. Admetus uses Alcestis's sacrifice to stop living rather than anticipating the construction of a new life without her.

So, a clinical hypothesis generated by Faber's analysis is that voluntary altruistic suicides stress that they are victims; in contrast, obligatory altruistic suicides tend to protect their egos by transforming the will of others into their own will, that is, they see themselves as martyrs. I doubt that this hypothesis could have been formulated using cases of suicidal behavior found among the clinical material in the files of psychiatric hospitals or psychotherapists' offices.

Understanding a Culture

Suicides in literature have also been used to study a culture. Lester (1972b) examined the suicides which occurred in the plays of the Norwegian Henrik Ibsen (1828-1906) to see if they conformed to the patterns described by Hendin (1964) for suicides in Norway, Sweden or Denmark. Hendin used his clinical judgment to argue that suicide in Sweden was usually the result of failure to achieve a high level of performance, suicide in Denmark was the result of the loss of significant others, and suicide in Norway was the result either of loss of a significant other upon whom the suicide was dependent or of guilt over transgressions.

Apart from a brief mention in *Cataline* of the suicide of a woman after rape, there are seven suicidal deaths in Ibsen's plays, five victim-precipitated homicides and two equivocal deaths. In general, Lester found that the suicides had suffered from dependency loss whereas the victim-precipitated murders were experiencing guilt over transgressions. The suicides also appeared to be motivated by the desire to preserve or restore an ideal self-image.

For example, in *The Wild Duck*, Hedvig is very attached to her parents, especially her father. Because of her poor eyesight, she does not go to school and has no friends her own age. Hedvig's suicide occurs after her father realizes that she is not his daughter, considers leaving home, and verbally rejects her. Hedvig shoots herself shortly after her father tells her to go away and not to come near him. Her suicide is clearly provoked by the rejection from her father. It would seem to be a dependency-loss suicide, which fits Hendin's description of Norwegian suicides.[5]

Understanding a Suicidal Writer

There are several suicidal writers whose fiction appears to be somewhat autobiographical and, therefore, provides us with some insights into their unconscious psychodynamics which increases our understanding of them, authors such as Ernest Hemingway and Cesare Pavese. However, Sylvia Plath (1981, pp. 183-184) wrote a single poem (*Daddy*) in the months prior to her suicide which provides a startling insight into the unconscious psychodynamics of her suicide.

In *Daddy*, Plath casts herself as a Jew in a concentration camp versus her father as a Panzer man and as a devil who bit her heart in two. She says that she has always been scared of him, and she calls him a bastard. Yet she says that her suicide attempt at age twenty was an attempt to be reunited with him. She then made of model of her father and married him, but she calls this person a vampire who drank her blood for seven years. Indeed, her marriage to the British poet, Ted Hughes, lasted about seven years. At the end of her poem, she tells her father that he can lie back now, perhaps because, as she says a few lines earlier, that she is finally through.

The Oedipal theme in the poem is clear. The motivation for her first suicide attempt was to be reunited with the father who died when she was eight (though the poem says ten). And, in case he is jealous of her marriage to Ted Hughes (why else is Daddy sitting up in his grave), she is now finally through and, presumably, going to be reunited with Daddy for sure this time (and so he can lie back down to await her).

In addition, though, there are other elements in the poem. The ambivalence toward her father is evident throughout the poem, but most exquisitely expressed in the final line where she writes, "Daddy, daddy, you bastard...," a juxtaposition of affection (daddy) and anger (you bastard). Plath also says that, "If I've killed one man, I've killed two." Who are these two? Daddy and her husband? Plath's father died of natural causes when she was eight, but perhaps Sylvia had wished his death when she was angry at him and believes, magically, that her death wish for him contributed to his death, a common belief in children. Or perhaps she feels guilty over other actions toward her father before he died? But then, how did she kill her husband? Perhaps psychologically as her stature as a poet grew to equal, and perhaps surpass, his?

There is an interesting feature to this poem in that Plath uses the word "black" six times, a frequency much higher than in her first book of poems (Lester, 1989). According to Piotrowski's (1974) method for interpreting the Rorschach ink-blot test, the use of dark

[5] Interestingly, Ibsen considered moving to Denmark, but never did so. Furthermore, according to Meyer (1971), Ibsen did contemplate suicide during one stressful period in his life.

shading predicts a tendency to act-out, rather than quieten down, when anxious or under stress.[6]

Does Creative Writing Harm Suicidal People?

Is writing therapeutic for creative writers or it is a stressor which contributes to their psychological disturbance? Silverman and Will (1986) analyzed the life and suicide of Sylvia Plath and concluded that, although she tried to control her suicidal impulses by means of her poetry, she failed in this endeavor. Silverman and Will argued that poetry is successful when it bridges the inner worlds of the creative person and the audience. (Presumably they mean critically successful, for even poor poetry can serve a useful psychological function for the writer, even if it is merely cathartic.) To be successful, poetry must first achieve a balance between the writer's use of the audience to serve his or her own narcissistic needs (a type of exhibitionism) and the desire to give others a way of structuring the terrors and anxieties that afflict us all.

The writer must also achieve a balance between the potentially destructive conscious and unconscious forces motivating the writing and the constructive desires to harness these forces for the purpose of writing creatively. Related to this, the writer must balance primary and secondary process mechanisms. The writer must also compromise between the fantasy permissible in writing and the acceptance of reality necessary for successful living.

When they apply their ideas to Sylvia Plath, Silverman and Will assert that the successful creative process is successful only when the unconscious forces in the writer operate silently and remain hidden from view. This assertion represents a rather traditional view of creative writing. It would seem to express a preference on the part of Silverman and Will for a particular type of literature rather than expressing a universal truth. For example, the unconscious forces motivating Ernest Hemingway may be under control in his writing, but they are certainly not hidden. More pertinently, the confessional style of poetry developed by W. D. Snodgrass and Robert Lowell and pursued by Anne Sexton is in direct opposition to Silverman and Will's view.

Silverman and Will see the transitional period in Plath's poetry as being her final years in the United States. Plath may have had her confidence undermined by the frequent rejections that writers must endure so that she changed her style. In her new style, she revealed her deepest feelings in her poems, using her experiences to create the poem rather than to simply transform it. Silverman and Will note that she described her early poems as "proper in shape and number and every part" but not alive. Her poems moved from being a reordering and reshaping of experience with a poetic purpose toward becoming expressions of herself. She identified with her poems, which made their rejection even more painful, and Silverman and Will label this change as a "narcissistic regression."

The causal sequence which Silverman and Will propose for Plath has no evidence for or against it. It is simply one reading of Plath's life. Other, equally plausible, alternative paths can be proposed. For example, it is quite likely that Plath's participation, along with Anne Sexton with whom she became very close, in a poetry workshop run by Robert Lowell had a major impact on her writing style. Several members of his workshop adopted a more self-

[6] Lester (1991) noted a similar tendency in the poems on Anne Sexton, who also committed suicide.

revealing content for their poems, and two received Pulitzer prizes for their work (Lowell and Sexton).

Furthermore, Plath, as she herself clearly recognized, was prone to recurring depressions. In all probability, Plath had an affective disorder, possibly bipolar, and her depressions were likely to reoccur periodically. It is evident from the severity of her depression in 1953 which led to a very serious suicide attempt that she would likely become suicidal again with each new depression (much as Virginia Woolf had).

What is interesting is that, whereas in the early 1950s, her writing may not have helped her cope with the stressors, external and intrapsychic, with which she was confronted, in the later 1950s her switch to a more revealing and personalized style of writing may have helped her survive. Silverman and Will claimed that her writing failed to prevent her suicide. Perhaps it may have postponed her suicide?

In the months prior to her suicide, Plath wrote feverishly, sometimes producing several poems in one day. (This feverish activity in the months prior to a suicide was apparent also in Anne Sexton's life.) What would Silverman and Will suggest as a more appropriate strategy for a person confronting intrapsychic turmoil who is not under professional care? It is very likely that the writing helped Plath control her inner turmoil, and some commentators think that the poems she produced were among her finest.

In seeking to formulate a *general* hypothesis about the role of writing for the depressed and distressed person, it is obviously important to discuss more than one case. In the present context, the life and suicide of the poet Anne Sexton is relevant.

Lester and Terry (1992) argued that writing poetry can be useful with suicidal clients. Writing poems *per se* may not be helpful to the client, but the revision of the initial drafts of poems may be therapeutically useful. Revising poems may serve a similar function for clients as the journal assignments devised by cognitive therapists by giving the clients intellectual control over their emotions and distance from the traumatic memories.

Sexton revised her poems extensively and, in the process of revision, had to concentrate on form rather than content. This allows for both the action that therapists deem to be therapeutic and the distancing of the self from one's problems. Because Sexton ultimately chose the moment of her death, one should not discount the therapeutic help her writing afforded her.

Anne Sexton illustrates the dialectic in poetry as therapy, between expression and catharsis on the one hand and cognitive control on the other. Sexton, as long as she was able to stay psychiatrically stable, was able to apply the craft of poetry to her creative productions. Both Sexton and Martin Orne, her first therapist, believed that her poetry had helped her recover. Only toward the end of her life, as her ability to craft her poems declined, so did her mental stability dissipate.

Interestingly, both Plath and Sexton showed manic trends prior to their suicides, writing poems furiously, poems with more emotional expression and less poetic crafting. Rather than arguing that writing poetry contributed in part to their suicides, it makes much more sense to say that, in their final breakdowns, poetry was no longer able to help them deal with the intrapsychic forces driving them as it had in the past. As their inner turmoil increased, both wrote feverishly, almost like a safety valve letting out the steam under pressure in a boiler, but to no avail since the pressure was building up faster than they could release it.

But this final failure of the craft of poetry to keep Sylvia Plath and Anne Sexton alive does not, as Silverman and Will argue, signify total failure. Both were outstanding poets and functioned quite well given their probable affective disorders. I would argue that the craft of poetry kept both poets alive for many years after their self-destructive impulses first manifested themselves and so signifies success.[7]

Discussion

This chapter has attempted to provide an overview of the ways in which psychology and literature can enrich each other's field. For pursuing the understanding of suicide, examples were given of studying suicides in literature in order to generate and confirm clinical hypotheses and of using the writings of suicidal authors to gain a deeper understanding of their motives for self-destruction. Although there are those who reject such uses for literature, a good test of these strategies is whether our understanding of suicide is increased, and I hope that the examples provided in this chapter have convinced the reader of their usefulness.

References

Andreasen, N. C. Creativity and mental illness. *American Journal of Psychiatry*, 1987, 144, 1288-1292.

Anon. *Report on the commission on Obscenity and Pornography*. New York: Bantam, 1970.

Bakan, D. *Sigmund Freud and the Jewish mystical tradition*. Princeton, NJ: Van Nostrand, 1958.

Barnes, H. E. *Psychology and history*. New York: Century, 1925.

Bellak, L. Somerset Maugham. In R. W. White (Ed.) *The study of lives*, pp. 142-159. New York: Atherton, 1963.

Bromberg, W., & Schilder, P. Death and dying. *Psychoanalytic Review*, 1933, 20, 133-185.

______ . The attitudes of psychoneurotics towards death. *Psychoanalytic Review*, 1936, 33, 1-128.

Christie, A. *The mysterious Mr. Quinn*. New York: Dodd Mead, 1930.

Crosby, F. Evaluating psychohistorical explanations. *Psychohistory Review*, 1979, 7(3), 6-16.

Driesen, O. *Der Ursprung des Harlekin*. Berlin: Alexander Duncker, 1904.

Durkheim, E. *Le suicide*. Paris: Felix Alcan, 1897.

Erikson, E. *Young man Luther*. New York: Norton, 1962.

Faber, M. *Suicide and Greek tragedy*. New York: Sphinx Press., 1970.

Festinger, L. *The theory of cognitive dissonance*. Palo Alto, CA: Stanford University Press. 1957.

Freud, S. *The origins of psychoanalysis: Letters to Wilhelm Fliess, drafts and notes, 1887-1902*. New York: Basic Books, 1954.

Goodman, P. The psychological revolution and the writer's life view. *Psychoanalytic Review*, 1963, 50(3) 17-24.

Goodwin, D. W. *Alcohol and the writer*. Kansas City, MO: Andrews & McNeel, 1988.

---

[7] It should be noted in passing that creative writing has been found to be strongly associated with both affective disorder (Andreasen, 1987; Holden, 1987) and with alcohol abuse (Goodwin, 1988), and these disorders may adversely affect the psychological health of writers.

Greenberger, E. Fantasies of women confronting death. *Journal of Consulting Psychology*, 1965, 29, 252-260.

Hendin, H. *Suicide in Scandinavia*. New York: Grune & Stratton, 1964.

Hoffer, P. C. A case study of the reduction of cognitive dissonance. Paper read at the Ohio Academy of History, April, 1974.

_____ . Is psychohistory really history? *Psychohistory Review*, 1979, 7(3), 6-12.

Holden, C. Creativity and the troubled mind. *Psychology Today*, 1987, 21(4), 9-10.

Hull, N. E. H., Allen, S. L., & Hoffer, P. C. Choosing sides: a quantitative study of the psychological determinants of political affiliation in Revolutionary New York. *Journal of American History*, 1978, 65 344-366.

Jaffe, A. *The process of Kafka's trial*. East Lansing, MI: Michigan State University Press, 1967.

Johnson, B. D. Durkheim's one cause of suicide. *American Sociological Review*, 1965, 30, 875-886.

Kammann, R. Verbal complexity and preferences in poetry. *Journal of Verbal Learning & Verbal Behavior*, 1966, 5, 536-540.

Leenaars, A. A. *Suicide notes*. New York: Human Sciences, 1988.

Lester, D. Checking on the Harlequin. *Psychological Reports*, 1966, 19, 984.

_____ . Incest. *Journal of Sex Research*, 1972a, 8, 268-285.

_____ . Suicide in Ibsen's plays. *Life-Threatening Behavior*, 1972b, 2, 35-41.

_____ . Psychology and literature. *Psychology*, 1987, 24(1/2), 25-27.

_____ . Application of Piotrowski's dark shading hypothesis to Sylvia Plath's poems written before her suicide. *Perceptual & Motor Skills*, 1989, 68, 122.

_____ . Dark-shading in the poems of Anne Sexton. *Perceptual & Motor Skills*, 1991, 73, 366.

Lester, D., & Schumacher, J. Schizophrenia and death concern. *Journal of Projective Techniques & Personality Assessment*, 1968, 33, 403-405.

Lester, D., & Terry, R. The use of poetry therapy. *The Arts in Psychotherapy*, 1992, 19, 47-52.

Manuel, F. E. Toward a psychological history of utopias. In F. E. Manuel (Ed.) *Utopias and utopian thought*, pp. 69-98. Boston: Beacon, 1967.

McClelland, D. The use of measures of human motivation in the study of society. In J. W. Atkinson (Ed.) *Motives in fantasy, action, and society*, pp. 518-552. Princeton: Princeton University, 1958.

_____ . The Harlequin complex. In J. W. White (Ed.) *The study of lives*, pp. 94-119. New York: Atherton, 1963.

McClelland, D., Davis, W., Wanner, E., & Kalin, R. A cross-cultural study of folk tale content and drinking. *Sociometry*, 1966, 29, 309-337.

Meyer, M. *Ibsen*. New York: Doubleday, 1971.

Niederland, W. G. The first application of psychoanalysis to a literary work. *Psychoanalytic Quarterly*, 1960, 29, 228-235.

Plath, S. *The collected poems*. New York: Harper & Row, 1981.

Piotrowski, Z. A. *Perceptanalysis*. Philadelphia: privately published, 1974.

Rokeach, M., Homant, R., & Penner, L. A value analysis of the disputed Federalist Papers. *Journal of Personality & Social Psychology*, 1970, 18, 245-250.

Silverman, M. A., & Will, N. P. Sylvia Plath and the failure of emotional self-repair through poetry. *Psychoanalytic Quarterly*, 1986, 55, 99-129.

Skinner, B. F. A quantitative estimate of certain types of sound-patterning in poetry. *American Journal of Psychology*, 1941, 54, 64-79.

Smith, P. Luther's early development in the light of psychoanalysis. American Journal of *Psychology*, 1913, 24, 360-377.

Sophocles. *The Theban plays*. Baltimore: Penguin. 1947.

Wolfgang, M. *Patterns in criminal homicide*. Philadelphia: University of Pennsylvania. 1958.

Chapter 3

BIOLOGY AND SUICIDE

Biology is the "science of life and life processes, including the study of structure, functioning, growth, origin, evolution, and distribution of living organisms" (Morris, 1976, p. 133). Biology has relevance to suicidal behavior in several ways. Can ethology, the study of animal behavior guided by instincts, be applied to suicidal behavior? Since suicide removes certain individuals from the population, could suicide have had an impact on evolution? Does the relatively new field of sociobiology have relevance for our understanding of suicide? And finally, can an animal commit suicide?

ETHOLOGY AND SUICIDE[1]

Ethology is the study of animal behavior, focusing on how and why animal behavior occurs.[2] Ethologists stress accurate observation and description of animal behavior, particularly in the animals' natural habitats, but also in experimental situations where the stimuli with which the animals are confronted can be presented in a systematic fashion. Ethology believes that the mechanisms behind animal behavior are programmed into the animal's neural networks and, thus, are determined largely by the genes and by the ways in which evolution has changed the characteristics of the animal.

It may not immediately be clear how ethological concepts could be applied to suicidal behavior, as some would argue that there needs to be evidence of conscious suicidal intent in order to classify a death as suicidal in nature (Goldstein, 1940). However, others, such as Menninger (1938), have disagreed with this narrow definition. Behavior which appears to be suicidal to an observer has been reported in dolphins (Amory, 1970), and biologists frequently use the term "suicide" to describe behavior in lower animals such as the pink bollworm moth (Bariola, 1978), butterflies (Trail, 1980), pea aphids (McAllister and Roitberg, 1987), birds (O'Connor, 1978) and bacteria such as motil aeromonads (Namdari and Cabelli, 1989). Therefore, there appears to be a sound basis for examining how an ethological approach could assist our understanding of suicidal behavior.

---

1 This section was co-authored with Robert Goldney.

2 This presentation of the principles of ethology is based on Gould (1982) and Immelmann (1980).

This section reviews basic ethological principles briefly and then draws analogies with suicidal behavior.

The Basic Concepts of Ethology

The basic concepts of ethology were developed by Konrad Lorenz and Niko Tinbergen who were awarded the Nobel Prize for Medicine for their work. Consider the following example, the egg-rolling response of the greylag goose. When a goose which is incubating eggs notices an egg near the nest, its attention is focused on this egg. It slowly rises, extends its neck over the egg and with the bottom of its bill rolls the egg back up into the nest. This behavior is called a *fixed action pattern*. The response appears to be innate rather than learned, the coordination and patterning of the behavior is stereotyped, and, once initiated, the pattern is completed without any further sensory input. The stimuli which release the fixed action pattern is called the *innate releasing mechanism*. Because the goose responds to only one aspect of the object, the stimuli are also called the *sign stimuli*. The fixed action pattern is turned off and on by *drives* or *motivation* which limits the behavior to a particular period of time, in this case incubation until hatching. Innate releasing mechanisms are thought to illustrate the innate, programmed nature of much of animal behavior. They focus the animal's attention and enable animals to respond quickly to stimuli without interference from thinking.

These stimuli appear initially to be discrete rather than more complex patterns. But, they can be modified over time so that the animal comes to substitute a rapidly acquired complex picture of the object for the innate releaser on which they depended initially.

Tinbergen experimented with the greylag goose's fixed action pattern and found that a variety of convex objects would trigger the egg rolling behavior in the goose. In fact, the goose preferred objects larger than eggs, preferring a volleyball over a goose egg, for example. The volleyball, in this instance, is a *supernormal stimulus*.

These behaviors are quite rigid. For example, the digger wasp catches crickets and returns them to its burrow, setting the cricket down about an inch from the burrow. The wasp then checks the burrow and returns for the cricket. If, while the wasp is checking the burrow, the cricket is moved by the experimenter further from the nest, the wasp moves it closer to the nest and then checks the burrow. If the experimenter keeps moving the cricket, the wasp never gets the cricket into the burrow.

Innate releasing mechanisms and fixed action patterns can be arranged in sequences so that one fixed action pattern involves stimuli which act as innate releasing mechanisms for the next fixed action pattern -- sequences most easily observed in the courtship patterns of animals.

Another example of behavioral programming is *imprinting*, a behavior in which, for example, for a few hours after hatching, a bird responds to particular stimuli presented to it and follows the object presenting these stimuli. The bird accepts this object as a parent and, still later, will court this object.

The amplitude of the stimulus necessary to release the behavior is called its *threshold*. Performance of a behavior sometimes increases the threshold required for a repeat performance, for example, in copulation behavior, a phenomenon called *action-specific fatigue*. The animal can also habituate to the innate releasing mechanism and fail to respond to the stimulus, a phenomenon called *stimulus-specific fatigue*. This fatigue is presumed to occur at the neural level.

Each fixed action pattern has its own reaction-specific energy, similar to Freud's hydraulic model of energy (Cofer and Appley, 1964, p. 597). If the behavior pattern has not occurred for some time, then the fixed action pattern can be released by simpler and less specific stimuli. For example, dogs who do not get the opportunity to break the necks of prey, will attempt to this with slippers or other household objects, *substitute objects*. In extreme circumstances, the fixed action pattern may occur without any external stimuli present, *vacuum behavior*.

Attempted Suicide as an Innate Releasing Mechanism

The first application of ethology to suicidal behavior was made by Stengel and Cook (1958). Referring to the work of Lorenz and Tinbergen, they suggested that "the suicidal attempt acts very much as a 'social releaser'" (p. 117). Stengel (1962) later wrote that "the suicidal attempt functions as an alarm system and an appeal for help. It does so almost with the regularity of an 'innate release mechanism'" (p. 726). It is of interest that these concepts are embodied in the title of Farberow and Shneidman's (1961) influential book, "The Cry for Help," where the suicide attempt, the innate releasing mechanism, is the stimulus which elicits a response, the fixed action pattern, in other people. The response elicited in others is evidently care-giving.

This notion was also suggested by Henderson (1974) who characterized attempted suicide as care-eliciting behavior and saw it as a developmentally primitive signal for care.[3]

Attempted Suicide as a Fixed Action Pattern

Attempted suicide can also be seen as a fixed action pattern. In Freud's early version of psychoanalytic theory, there was only one source of energy for human behavior, an energy which he called libido. In this version of the theory, the natural response to frustration is to aggress against the frustrating object, that is, to become assaultive. If this outward-directed aggression is forbidden or punished, then the aggression is blocked and turned inward onto the self, resulting in depression and self-destructive behavior (Henry and Short, 1954).

However, in the later version of his theory, Freud proposed two major motivations for humans, the life and death instincts, Eros and Thanatos, fueled respectively by libido and destrudo. In this latter theory, adopted by Menninger (1938) in his theorizing about suicide, self-destructive behavior becomes a basic pattern which, in order to survive, we must control. In this view, suicidal behavior is an innate pattern of behavior, a fixed-action pattern in ethological terms.

If suicidal behavior can be viewed as a fixed action pattern, two questions arise. First, what is the innate releasing mechanism that elicits this behavior? At the most general level, stressors could be seen as the stimuli which elicit the behavior, but research has shown that

[3] For such appeals to work, they must elicit altruistic or care-giving behavior in the significant others, but the lack of such behavior does not negate the ethological analogy.

the stressors which most commonly precipitate suicidal behavior vary with age, gender, and other personal characteristics (Lester, 1992).

More interestingly for an ethological perspective is the possibility that interpersonal stimuli are critical in eliciting suicidal behavior, a possibility most clearly illustrated in Richman's (1986) focus on the role of the family in both eliciting and reducing the occurrence of suicidal behavior. If this is the case, then we have sequencing, in which the behavior of one person releases the suicidal behavior pattern in another, which in turn releases care-giving behavior in the first person. Much more abstract analysis has been conducted on the dynamic interchange between the murderer and the victim (e.g., Luckenbill, 1977) than has been conducted on the interchange between the suicidal individual and his/her significant others, and this lacuna needs to remedied in future research on suicidal behavior.

The second question is, if suicidal behavior is a fixed action pattern, what will happen when no innate releasing mechanism appears? According to ethology, fixed action patterns must be expressed from time to time. As time passes without the occurrence of the fixed action pattern, the stimuli required to release the pattern become weaker and weaker, until the pattern can occur without any releasing stimulus, vacuum behavior.

In writing about outward-directed aggression, Lorenz (1966) addressed this problem by suggesting that socially acceptable outlets must be provided for the outward expression of aggression, outlets such as contact sports and paramilitary organizations. The same may, therefore, be true for suicidal behavior. The society must provide socially acceptable ways for self-destructive impulses to be safely discharged, for example, in death-risking activities such as mountain climbing or in chronic and focal suicidal activities, to use Menninger's (1938) terminology, such as drug use and self-mutilation. Just as the dog shakes a slipper rather than breaking the neck of its captured prey, perhaps people can abuse alcohol and other drugs rather than commit suicide with overdoses. From this perspective, therefore, drug abuse may be a means of preventing suicide!

EVOLUTION AND SUICIDE

It has long been noticed that animal populations adjust to the size and abundance of nutrients in the environment. When resources are abundant, the population grows; when resources are scarce the population shrinks.

Does the human animal fits this pattern? Many human practices can be viewed as serving to achieve population regulation. Infanticide, geronticide, and murder in general can be seen as reducing the population in times of scarce resources. Social regulations on marriage, taboos on child spacing, and homosexuality can also be seen as ways of controlling population size.

Addressing the problem of drug addiction, Jonas and Jonas (1980) noted that, although addiction to drugs initially seems gratifying to the individual, the addict eventually suffers from declining health and a disrupted social adjustment. The fertility of the addict is impaired, and his genes are typically removed from the gene pool. (Natural selection involves the survival of the genes of individuals who are fit while those of less fit individuals are weeded out over time.)

Jonas and Jonas speculated that the genes of the addict (and perhaps those with psychiatric illnesses) predispose them to be sensitive to external stimuli and group pressures.

These tendencies may have been adaptive when societies were smaller and when man had to be acutely sensitive to danger from the environment in order to survive. But in modern society, this sensitivity leads to discomfort which can sometimes be alleviated, for example, by the person blunting his perception by means of drugs.

Jonas and Jonas saw addicts today as forming an available pool of individuals readily amenable to a reduction in the population. (The large increase in stress diseases can also be seen as ways of reducing the population.) Jonas and Jonas noted that self-eliminatory behaviors have adaptive significance for the species. Addiction and similar behaviors are pathways along which some people move toward removing their genes from the gene pool.

Application to Suicide

Suicidal behavior fits well into this process. Suicide clearly removes the genes of those individuals from the gene pool and reduces the size of the population.

Furthermore, when we look at the kinds of individuals who complete suicide, we find that, typically, suicide rates are highest in those who are older and past child-bearing age, except in the poorest nations of the world where suicide rates are higher among the young and fertile female members of the society (15 to 24 year-olds) than among the older women (Lester, 1982). Thus, it seems that when resources are scarce, as in the poorest nations, it is the fertile who kill themselves at the highest rate, thereby reducing the potential for growth in the population.

The fact that suicide rates are much higher in those who are psychiatrically disturbed (Lester, 1992) can also be seen as genetically useful, for the suicide of these people removes their (possibly defective) genes from the gene pool in the society.

The existence of fatalistic suicide (Durkheim, 1897), in which people kill themselves in conformity to societal pressures, may also be seen as fitting the type of suicide necessary for this evolutionary view better than the suicides of the isolates and the alienated of the society (egoistic and anomic suicides). The ritualistic suicides, for example, suttee in Indian widows and seppuku in Japan, are suicides committed in response to social pressures. Mass suicide too can be seen as satisfying this evolutionary need.

Sociobiology and Suicide

Sociobiology is a relatively new field which is an "amalgamation of behavioral biology, modern population ecology, and evolutionary theory...Its central concern is to understand how and why animal social behavior has evolved" (Wittenberger, 1981, p. 6). Animal behavior orients the species toward maintaining and advancing its biological fitness, maintaining its existence and promoting its reproduction (DeCatanzaro, 1981).

DeCatanzaro (1981) noted that suicide appears to act contrary to this trend by removing the individual's genes from the population gene pool. However, DeCatanzaro noted that suicide occurs primarily in those who are under stress which reduces their biological fitness and who have a reduced capacity to promote their genes in future generations. Suicide has been more common in those who are older, who have no children, who are divorced, widowed and single, and in those who are psychiatrically disturbed, factors which reduce the capacity and ability to have children and pass on genes to future generations. Since suicide is related to decreased reproductive status, it does not necessarily remove genes from the population gene pool. Furthermore, the suicidal individual may, by committing suicide, support related individuals in their quest for survival and reproduction, individuals who share some of their genes because they are members of the same family by descent. For example, the suicide of the elderly in primitive societies removes a burden on the remaining members of the society who no longer have to feed the aged and infirm and whose migration is no longer hindered by the weak elderly.

Perhaps this made sense in 1981 when DeCatanzaro wrote his book. However, the rising youth suicide rate in the 1980s and 1990s in most nations of the world seems to argue against this point of view. The youths who are committing suicide would in all probability have children later had they not killed themselves. Furthermore, DeCatanzaro is very selective in his presentation of suicide statistics. For example, he notes that the high suicide rates in the widowed and divorced fits with his theory (since these individuals are presumably less likely to reproduce than married people), but he ignores phenomena such as the reduced suicide rate in women *after* they pass their period of child-bearing. Furthermore, the sociobiological perspective on suicidal behavior ignores nonfatal suicidal behavior. The sociobiological hypothesis about suicidal behavior thus seems to explain only some aspects of fatal suicidal behavior at some points in time and in some nations of the world.

Can Animals Commit Suicide?

We have seen above that biologists often use the word "suicide" to describe the behavior of animals which leads to their self-destruction. We have also seen that scholars such as Menninger (1938) use the term "suicide" in a broad sense which permits non-conscious intent and mildly self-destructive behavior to be included in the category. However, is it possible to *prove* that an animal can commit suicide?

There has been one approach to this problem that has potential for theory and research. Schaefer (1967) first identified the basic issues involved in deciding whether an animal can commit suicide. (1) Can the animal discriminate between life and death or, to be more specific, between a live animal and a dead animal? (2) Can an animal discriminate between a lethal and a nonlethal environment? (3) Under what circumstances will an animal choose to enter a lethal environment?

Schaefer demonstrated how these questions might be answered. To demonstrate that an animal can discriminate a dead animal from a live one, Schaefer used an operant conditioning technique in which one lever in a Skinner box produced food when a live mouse was the stimulus and a second level produced food when a dead mouse was the stimulus. Schaefer's mice learned this discrimination.

To demonstrate that mice can discriminate between a lethal chamber and a nonlethal chamber, Schaefer allowed mice to choose to enter one of two chambers. In one chamber they were electrocuted, while in the other they were allowed to live. The behavior of these mice was the stimulus for other mice. As long as the observed mouse was alive, one lever produced food. When the observed mouse was dead, a second lever produced food. The observing mice learned this discrimination. After learning the discrimination, the observing mice were allowed to enter the chambers. On test trials, the mice entered only the nonlethal chamber.

If these demonstrations can be replicated (no-one has pursued Schaefer's ideas in recent years), it would be possible to investigate under what circumstances an animal might choose to enter the lethal chamber.

In his demonstrations, however, Schaefer failed to include controls for several factors. For example, are the mice learning to discriminate between a dead and a live stimulus mouse or merely a non-moving and a moving mouse? Would the observer mouse respond differently if instead of observing mice killed, he observed mice waking from sleep. Perhaps it is the change in the state of the mice that led the observer mouse to avoid the lethal chamber rather than mice being killed? Many other methodological problems can be raised about these demonstrations. However, all of these problems could be overcome, and Schaefer's formulation of the problem enables us to plan a set of studies to explore whether an animal could commit suicide.

Discussion

Biological views are, of course, speculative and not amenable to empirical test. However, they serve to include suicide among other behaviors which have been seen as having evolutionary significance. Three factors have been identified as having possible evolutionary significance: the possible instinctual basis of suicide, suicide as a means of population control, and suicide as a means of removing the less fit individuals from a population.

References

Amory, C. After living with a man, a dolphin may commit suicide. *Holiday*, 1970, May, 16-18.

Bariola, L. A. Suicidal emergence and reproduction by overwintered pink bollworm moths. *Environmental Entomology*, 1978, 7, 189-192.

Cofer, C. N., & Appley, M. H. *Motivation*. New York: Wiley, 1964.

DeCatanzaro, D. *Suicide and self-damaging behavior*. New York: Academic, 1981.

Durkheim, E. *Le Suicide*. Paris: Felix Alcan, 1897.

Farberow, N. L., & Shneidman, E. S. (Eds.) *The cry for help*. New York: McGraw-Hill, 1961.

Goldstein, K. *Human nature in the light of psychopathology*. Cambridge, MA: Harvard University, 1940.

Gould, J. L. *Ethology*. New York: Norton, 1982.

Henderson, S. Care-eliciting behavior in man. *Journal of Nervous & Mental Disease*, 1974, 159, 172-181.

Henry, A. F., & Short, J. F. *Suicide and homicide*. New York: Free Press, 1954.

Immelmann, K. *Introduction to ethology*. New York: Plenum, 1908.

Jonas, D., & Jonas, A. A bioanthropological overview of addiction. In D. Lettieri, M. Sayers, & H. Pearson (Eds.) *Theories on drug abuse*, pp. 269-277. Rockville: NIDA, 1980.

Lester, D. The distribution of sex and age among completed suicides: a cross-national study. *International Journal of Social Psychiatry*, 1982, 28, 256-260.

Lester, D. *Why people kill themselves*. Springfield, IL: Charles Thomas, 1992.

Lorenz, K. *On aggression*. New York: Harcourt, Brace & World, 1966.

Luckenbill, D. Criminal homicide as a situated transaction., *Social Problems*, 1977, 25, 176-186.

McAllister, M. K., & Roitberg, B. D. Adaptive suicidal behavior in pea aphids. *Nature*, 1987, 328, 797-799.

Menninger, K. *Man against himself.* New York: Harcourt, Brace & World, 1938.

Morris, W. (Ed.) *The American heritage dictionary of the English language.* Boston: Houghton-Mifflin, 1976.

Namdari, H., & Cabelli, V. J. The suicide phenomenon in motile aeromonads. *Applied & Environmental Microbiology*, 1989, 55, 543-547.

O'Connor, R. J. Brood reduction in birds. *Animal Behavior*, 1978, 26, 79-96.

Richman, J. *Family therapy for suicidal people.* New York: Springer, 1986.

Schaefer, H. H. Can a mouse commit suicide? In E. S. Shneidman (Ed.) *Essays in self-destruction*, pp. 494-509. New York: Science House, 1967.

Stengel, E. Recent research into suicide and attempted suicide. *American Journal of Psychiatry*, 1962, 118, 725-727.

Stengel, E., & Cook, N. G. *Attempted suicide: Its social significance and effects*, Maudsley Monograph Number 4. London, UK: Oxford University Press, 1958.

Trail, D. R. Behavioral interactions between parasites and hosts. *American Naturalist*, 1980, 116(1), 77-91.

Wittenberger, J. F. *Animal social behavior.* Boston: Duxbury, 1981.

Chapter 4

NEUROPHYSIOLOGY AND SUICIDE

Two main issues arise in the study of the neurophysiology of suicidal behavior. First, is there a genetic contribution to suicide and, second, what is the neurophysiological basis for the behavior. Let us first look at the evidence for a genetic component.

THE INHERITANCE OF SUICIDE

There are only two sound methodological designs for exploring whether a behavior has a genetic component -- twin studies and adoption studies.

In twin studies, the similarity between identical twins for the behavior in question is compared to the similarity between non-identical twins. However, since identical twins are reared more similarly than non-identical twins, the identical twins have to be separated soon after birth and raised in different families. This methodology has been used, for example, for studies on intelligence test scores and schizophrenia.

Unfortunately, suicidal behavior has been studied only in identical twins raised together. A review of these studies does show an increased similarity (technically called the concordance rate) for identical twins over non-identical twins (Lester, 1986), but a sound conclusion must await the collection of data from a group of identical twins raised apart.

In adoption studies, babies from mothers who were suicidal and babies from mothers who were not suicidal would be adopted and raised by adoptive families the members of which are non-suicidal. Of course, this could not be done for mothers who had completed suicide (who would be deceased), but it could be done for mothers who had attempted suicide in the past, perhaps seriously. The study must also be done prospectively, identifying the babies and then following them up.

This methodology has never been followed. However, studies have appeared in which adult suicides are identified and, if adopted, suicidal behavior examined in their biological families and adoptive families. In the retrospective studies, suicides, identified as such as adults and who were adopted, do tend to have more suicide in their biological families than nonsuicidal people who were adopted (Schulsinger, et al., 1979). (They do not differ in suicidal behavior in their adoptive families.) Again, this evidence is suggestive, but not conclusive. Prospective studies are required for firm conclusions.

There is another problems with these studies, sound and unsound. Since suicide is associated with psychiatric disturbance, especially depressive disorders, investigators have to show also that the effects are not simply a side-effect of depressive disorders having a genetic component. Is it the suicidal tendency or a depressive disorder which is inherited? No investigation has yet addressed this issue, and indeed Wender, et al. (1986) failed to find the difference in suicidal behavior between biological and adoptive families of adopted suicides and nonsuicides who did not have a depressive disorder.

The Physiological Basis of Suicidal Behavior

Studies of the physiological basis of suicidal behavior have focused primarily on the brains, the cerebrospinal fluid, the blood and the urine of suicides. It has been difficult to draw firm conclusions from the brain studies because the sample sizes have been small, making the results unreliable and making it difficult to control for extraneous variables (such as the conditions in which the brains were stored, the methods of chemical analysis, the areas of the brain examined, the characteristics of the subjects and the medications they were taking).

There are many neurotransmitters in the brain, but research has identified serotonin as the neurotransmitter most likely to be involved in suicidal behavior. For example, Lester (1995) carried out a meta-analysis of all of the studies of the cerebrospinal fluid and found some consistency in the results of the diverse studies. People who had attempted suicide had lower levels of the breakdown product of serotonin (5-hydroxyindoleacetic acid) in their cerebrospinal fluid as compared to nonsuicidal psychiatric patients, and so did those completing suicide later.

However, more recent research has suggested that serotonin might be implicated also in behaviors such as violence, eating disorders, and obsessive-compulsive disorder. Thus, whereas it was originally thought that serotonin might be the basis for depression and suicide, it is now more likely that it is the basis for impulsive behavior, instability and the tendency to overreact to situations (Durand and Barlow, 1997).

Thus, at the present time, it is difficult to be sure of the reason why serotonin deficiencies in the brain might be associated with suicidal behavior and, furthermore, to what extent and in which ways other neurotransmitter systems might also be involved.

Impulsive Aggression

French (1991) has noted that violence is often associated with substance abuse, particularly with alcohol abuse, and that often there is evidence of the involvement of neurological factors. Violence can be a symptom of a clinical syndrome, and French suggested that violence could be the results of a general disorder of "impulsive aggression," in particular, the specific disorder "organic aggressive syndrome," a syndrome which is thought to have an innate biochemical etiology. This syndrome was called episodic dyscontrol by Menninger and Mayman (1956) and was called organic personality disorder -- explosive type in DSM-III. Another syndrome associated with violence, more commonly found in young people, is post-traumatic stress disorder linked to a physical trauma (which itself might also have caused brain damage). French noted that impulsive aggression is also common in those with abnormal brain scans, and especially epilepsy. According to French, impulsive aggressive disorders have an early onset, and recent research has shown that those who have such disorders were often victims of physical and sexual abuse. These early traumata may affect the levels of neurotransmitters in the brain, particularly, dopamine and norepinephrine, which may in turn lead to paranoid ideation and a flight-or-fight response mode in the central nervous system. These disorders are marked by unpredictable and unprovoked explosive rage. If substance abuse is present also, the drugs may act to lower the epileptic threshold, exacerbating both the onset and the intensity of the rage.

Nell (1990) described a syndrome which he called "rage dyscontrol," which consists of irritability, anger, and rage in response to relatively trivial stimuli, sometimes to the extent of assault and murder. The episodes of rage are sometimes precipitated by alcohol use. This pattern, often maladaptive, can become chronic and characteristic of the individual's life. Nell noted that the syndrome may be related to temporal lobe epilepsy, particularly with bilateral limbic system involvement. Limbic activation, often undetectable by surface electroencephalography, can cloud consciousness, diminish inhibitory controls and permit release of aggressive urges. Damage resulting from traumatic brain injury may also lead to the rage dyscontrol syndrome. Childhood minimal brain dysfunction may characterize the childhoods of those with the rage dyscontrol syndrome in adulthood, and those with the rage dyscontrol syndrome often have parents characterized by psychiatric illness, alcohol abuse and violence.

Ellis (1987) proposed a theory of crime and delinquency which in part focuses upon the contributing role of mild nonconvulsive brain seizures provoked under conditions of stress and alcohol consumption.

Application to Suicide

These syndromes have relevance to suicidal behavior because of some occasionally reported findings about suicidal people. For example, a recent review of research into suicide (Lester, 1992a) found that a history of physical and sexual abuse was more common in the childhoods of people who were later suicidal than in the childhoods of nonsuicidal individuals. For example, Smith and Crawford (1986) found that high school students who had attempted suicide had experienced a greater frequency of physical beatings, rapes and sexual abuse than the other students. In line with French's comment that these experiences may be associated with neurological impairment, Kenny, et al. (1979) found that adolescent suicide attempters performed worse on the Bender-Gestalt Visual Motor Test, under both normal conditions and with background interference, suggesting neurological dysfunction. It would be useful for future research to combine studies of both neurological impairment and physical and sexual abuse in the same group of adolescent suicide attempters.

Salk, et al. (1985) found that adolescent completed suicides were more likely to have mothers who sought little maternal care during pregnancy and who had chronic diseases during pregnancy. The adolescent suicides were more likely also to have suffered respiratory distress in the first few hours after birth. These factors lend support to the possibility of neurological impairment in these adolescent suicides.

Interestingly, the research reviewed in this section has been on adolescents who are suicidal, and it is adolescents who are typically described as showing the most unpredictable and the most impulsive suicidal behavior (Lester, 1992a).

Brain Damage

Epilepsy has been linked to suicidal behavior, particularly temporal lobe epilepsy (Barraclough, 1987; Lester, 1992a), and Barraclough has suggested that the increased risk of suicide in epileptics might be a result of the accompanying psychiatric disturbance, substance abuse or personality disorders caused by the epilepsy.

Related to this, Struve (1986) found that suicidal behavior was more common in patients with paroxysmal EEGs, and a connection may exist between paroxysmal EEGs and Nell's rage dyscontrol syndrome.

There have been cases of suicidal behavior reported in patients with minimal brain dysfunction (for example, Rourke, et al., 1989), though large-sample studies have not yet been conducted on this association.

Impulsivity

Several investigators have documented the impulsiveness that often characterizes suicidal behavior (Lester, 1992a), and Lester and Wright (1973) suggested that Megargee's (1966) typology of undercontrol and overcontrol of aggressive impulses may be relevant to the suicidal individual, with completed suicides resembling the overcontrolled person and attempted suicides who repeat their suicidal behavior resembling the undercontrolled person.

Substance Abuse

A recent review of the research on alcohol and drug abuse found evidence that suicidal behavior is much more common among substance abusers than among nonabusers and that substance abuse is much more common among suicidal individuals than among nonsuicidal individuals (Lester, 1992b).

Pernanen (1991), in a discussion of why alcohol intoxication is associated with externally-directed violence, suggested three main theories. The *severity* hypothesis argues that alcohol makes violence more extreme and more severe. Thus, more violent acts are committed, and the degree of injury should be greater. The *indiscrimination* hypothesis argues that alcohol reduces the attention of the violent individual to the social situation and norms governing it. Thus, the violence will be more inappropriate -- such as taking place in public and with unacceptable victims (for example, women and children). The *elicitation* hypothesis argues that alcohol makes violent behavior easier to instigate, that is, the intoxicated individual will become violent in response to a lesser provoking stimulus than will the sober individual.

These three hypotheses appear to be equally applicable to suicidal individuals who direct their aggression inwardly, and French's focus on the neurological etiology of violence suggests that alcohol may increase the likelihood of violence, both internally-directed and externally-directed, because of its effect on neurological structures and processes.

Violence in Suicidal Individuals

Although it has been tempting in the past to view suicidal individuals as not externally violent since they appear to be directing their aggression inwardly, research does not support this view. Lester (1987a) reviewed research which showed that suicidal individuals are typically more violent toward others than nonsuicidal individuals. Lester (1993a) reported the case of a teenager who committed suicide shortly after wrecking a house in which he had stayed. His mother reported that he had often been violent in the past, putting his brothers through the sheet rock walls of their home and injuring even his mother.

The role of testosterone in provoking violence in individuals, particularly as a result of its effect of the central nervous system, was suggested by Ellis (1987). Lester (1993b) has noted that the high completed suicide rate found in men in almost all nations of the world as compared to the low rate found in women is almost completely accounted for by the excess of "violent" suicidal acts (that is, those suicidal acts using firearms, hanging, cutting and jumping). Lester suggested that testosterone in men may be responsible for "violent" suicidal acts, a view consistent with Ellis's focus on the role of testosterone in eliciting externally-directed violence and criminal behavior.

Borderline Personality Disorder

Research has documented a high incidence of suicide attempts in those with a borderline personality disorder, a disorder also commonly associated with externally-directed violence (Lester, 1992a). For example, Wade (1987) found that female suicide attempters obtained higher scores on tests of borderline personality disorder than did nonsuicidal adolescents. Gibbs (1981) found the highest incidence of attempted suicide in female delinquents who were diagnosed as having a borderline personality disorder as opposed to other psychiatric disorders.

Theories of Suicide

Lester (1987b) presented a theory of suicide as the result of a failure in socialization. Suicide is a rare event, and so suicides are deviating from cultural norms. Durkheim (1897) also saw suicide as more likely in those who were not integrated into or regulated by the society, calling these types of suicide *egoistic* and *anomic* respectively. Philip and McCulloch (1966) found that areas of Edinburgh (Scotland) with the highest rates of attempted suicide also had higher rates of juvenile delinquency, children taken into government care and overcrowding. Thus, attempted suicide was more common in areas of the city where other kinds of deviant behavior were also more common. A later study showed that this association of deviant behaviors with attempted suicide was found in individuals too (McCulloch and Philip, 1967, 1972), and the association was especially strong in those who made repeated suicide attempts.

Comment

This section has suggested that the psychiatric syndromes (with their possibly neurological etiology) which French and Nell have described as characteristic of many externally-violent individuals are also possibly relevant to suicidal individuals (see also Lester, 1990; 1992c). In particular, the syndromes may be found more often in adolescent completed and attempted suicides and in those who make repeated attempts at suicide. There is good evidence for the role of psychological and physical traumata in the childhoods of these suicidal individuals, trauma which may also lead to neurological impairment. Furthermore, mild epileptic-type seizures have also been implicated in the etiology of suicidal behavior. Finally, the effects of testosterone on the brain may make this syndrome more common in males than in females.

This view suggests some important research which may further our understanding of suicide. First, it would be of interest to explore whether the different characteristics of the syndromes described here (paroxysmal EEGs and temporal lobe/limbic seizures, high testosterone levels, childhood learning disabilities, disturbed and violent parents, experience of childhood abuse, impulsiveness in the suicidal act and assaultive behavior) are associated in suicidal individuals. Do these traits cluster together so that it makes sense to speak of a syndrome?

Second, it would be of interest to explore how common these traits are and, if they cluster, how common is this cluster found in suicidal individuals. Finally, these research questions should be explored in completed suicides, one-time suicide attempters and attempters who make multiple nonfatal attempts.

There remains the question of why some individuals with these etiological factors choose externally-directed aggression while others choose internally-directed aggression. Here such factors as race (whether the individual is a member of the oppressed groups in the society or the oppressing groups) and educational level may play a role, with the oppressed and the less educated more likely to choose externally-directed aggression while the oppressors and the more educated are more able to inhibit the outward expression of aggression in conformity with society's laws and turn the aggression inward onto themselves.

The relevance of these factors is not yet well established for suicidal individuals, but the hypotheses explored here suggest that further research on these factors might be productive.

Discussion

The notion that our genes and our neurophysiology might be responsible for some of our behaviors and many of our psychiatric disorders has become popular in recent years. We must remember, however, that the research into these factors is in its early stages. After another decade of research, our theories as to how these factors might play a role will be much improved. At the present time, there are some clues as to what factors might play a role in the genesis of suicidal behavior, most likely the serotonergic system, but we cannot yet place much confidence in the relevance of these systems. Furthermore, it would be useful to explore the role of factors associated with impulsive aggression and rage dyscontrol for their relevance to suicidal behavior.

REFERENCES

Barraclough, B. M. The suicide rate of epilepsy. *Acta Psychiatrica Scandinavica*, 1987, 76, 339-345.

Durand, V. M., & Barlow, D. H. *Abnormal psychology*. Pacific Grove, CA: Brooks/Cole, 1997.

Durkheim, E. *Le Suicide*. Paris: Felix Alcan, 1897.

Ellis, L. Relationships of criminality and psychopathy with eight other apparent behavioral manifestations of sub-optimal arousal. *Personality & Individual Differences*, 1987, 8, 905-925.

French, L. Neuropsychology of violence. *Corrective & Social Psychiatry*, 1991, 37(1), 12-17.

Gibbs, J. T. Depression and suicidal behavior among delinquent females. *Journal of Youth & Adolescence*, 1981, 10, 159-167.

Kenny, T. J., Rohn, R., Sarles, R. M., Reynolds, B. J., & Heald, F. P. Visual-motor problems of adolescents who attempt suicide. *Perceptual & Motor Skills*, 1979, 48, 599-602.

Lester, D. Murders and suicide. *Behavioral Sciences & the Law*, 1987a, 5, 49-60.

Lester, D. Suicide as a failure in socialization. *Corrective & Social Psychiatry*, 1987b, 33, 199-200.

Lester, D. The relevance of Ellis's neurohormonal theory of crime and delinquency to suicide. *Personality & Individual Differences*, 1990, 11, 1201-1206.

Lester, D. *Why people kill themselves*. Springfield, IL: Charles Thomas, 1992a.

Lester, D. Alcoholism and drug abuse. In R. W. Maris, A. L. Berman, J. T. Maltsberger & R. I. Yufit (Eds.) *Assessment and prediction of suicide*, pp. 321-336. New York: Guilford, 1992b.

Lester, D. Rage dyscontrol and suicide. *South African Journal of Psychology*, 1992c, 22, 27-28.

Lester, D. *The cruelest death: the enigma of adolescent suicide*. Philadelphia: Charles Press, 1993a.

Lester, D. Testosterone and suicide. *Personality & Individual Differences*, 1993b, 15, 347-348.

Lester, D. The concentration of neurotransmitter metabolites in the cerebrospinal fluid of suicidal individuals. *Pharmacopsychiatry*, 1995, 28, 45-50.

Lester, D., & Wright, T. Suicide and overcontrol. *Psychological Reports*, 1973, 32, 1278.

McCulloch, J. W., & Philip, A. E. Social variables in attempted suicide. *Acta Psychiatrica Scandinavica*, 1967, 43, 341-356.

McCulloch, J. W., & Philip, A. E. *Suicidal behavior*. New York: Pergamon, 1972.

Megargee, E. Undercontrolled and overcontrolled personality types in extreme antisocial aggression. *Psychological Monographs*, 1966, 80, #3.

Menninger, K., & Mayman, M. Episodic dyscontrol. *Bulletin of the Menninger Clinic*, 1956, 20, 153-165.

Nell, V. Rage dyscontrol. *South African Journal of Psychology*, 1990, 20, 235-242.

Pernanen, K. *Alcohol in human violence*. New York: Guilford, 1991.

Philip, A. E., & McCulloch, J. W. Use of social indices in psychiatric epidemiology. *British Journal of Preventive & Social Medicine*, 1966, 20, 122-126.

Rourke, B. P., Young, G. C., & Leenaars, A. A. A childhood learning disability that predisposes those afflicted to adolescent and adult depression and suicide risk. *Journal of Learning Disabilities*, 1989, 22, 169-175.

Salk, L., Lipsitt, L., Sturner, W., Reilly, B., & Levat, R. Relationship of maternal and perinatal conditions to eventual adolescent suicide. *Lancet*, 1095, 1, 624-627.

Schulsinger, F., Kety, S. S., Rosenthal, D., & Wender, P. H. A family study of suicide. In M. Schou & E. Stromgren (Eds.) *Origin, prevention and treatment of affective disorders*, pp. 277-287. New York: Academic, 1979.

Smith, K., & Crawford, S. Suicidal behavior among normal high school students. *Suicide & Life-Threatening Behavior*, 1986, 16, 313-325.

Struve, F. Clinical electroencephalography and the study of suicidal behavior. *Suicide & Life-Threatening Behavior*, 1986, 16, 133-165.

Wade, N. L. Suicide as a resolution of separation-individuation among adolescent girls. *Adolescence*, 1987, 22, 169-177.

Wender, P. H., Kety, S., Rosenthal, D., Schulsinger, F., Ortmann, J., & Lunde, I. Psychiatric disorders in the biological and adoptive families of adopted individuals with affective disorders. *Archives of General Psychiatry*, 1986, 43, 923-929.

Chapter 5

PHILOSOPHY AND SUICIDE

INTRODUCTION

The word philosophy comes from Greek words meaning "loving wisdom" and so has come to mean a quest for wisdom and knowledge (Grassian, 1984). Philosophy endeavors to "come to grips with concepts and beliefs that underlie our understanding of things" (Grassian, 1984, p. 3). For example, if we inquire into the "meanings and interrelationships of the basic concepts of...science and the justifications of that science's most fundamental assumptions' (p. 3), then we are involved in the philosophy of science. Since philosophers always try to justify the positions that they take, *logic*, the study of the principles and methods for distinguishing correct from incorrect reasoning, is one branch of philosophy. Other branches include *metaphysics* (the study of the nature of reality), *epistemology* (the study of the nature, origin and limits of knowledge), and *ethics* (the study of moral and value judgments).

Philosophy has developed three major concerns with suicidal behavior -- the logic of the suicidal person's reasoning, the meaning of the concept of suicide, and the moral judgments we make about suicidal behavior. We will first look at problems concerned with the logic of suicide.

THE LOGIC OF SUICIDE

Logic may be defined as the study of the laws or thought or the study of reasoning, but such a definition fails to distinguish logic from psychology. Psychology describes the ways in which people actually reason. In contrast, logic sets standards for the ways in which people ought to reason if they wished to reason well. Logic evaluates the quality of the reasoning.

Sentences are said to be cognitive when they are used to express or assert something which may be true or false (Baum, 1974). The thought conveyed by a cognitive sentence is called a statement or proposition. The truth or falsity of some statements depends upon the truth or falsity of related statements -- these are called supported statements. Other statements can stand on their own -- they are self-supporting statements. The burden of proof for a statement being self-supporting falls on those who consider it false. Statements may be consistent (it is possible for both to be true at the same time) or inconsistent (it is impossible for both of them to be true at the same time). An argument is a set of statements which is such that one of them (the conclusion) is implied or supported by the others (the premises).

There are two critical evaluations in logic. Validity refers to arguments of which, if the premises are true, then the conclusion must also be true. Truth refers to whether the premises or the conclusions are true or false. A valid deductive argument is one where, if the premises are true, then the conclusion must be true. An argument whose premises provide some support, but not absolute support, for the conclusion is called an inductive argument.

Thus, analysis of the logic of suicide would entail first describing the reasoning engaged in by the suicidal person, then evaluating the validity of the reasoning, and finally evaluating the truth of the premises and conclusion. Arguments that are both true and valid may be considered sound.

Irrationality or Are the Premises True?

Wilber (1987) argued that suicides interpret their experiences differently from nonsuicidal people. They fail to realize that there are several options open to them and, as a result, see suicide as the only way to deal with their intolerable circumstances. Their hopelessness makes their evaluation of their circumstances astigmatic. But, given their astigmatic perception of reality, their decision to commit suicide appears to be a logically valid deduction. Wilber is, therefore, suggesting that the premises of the suicidal person are false, but the argument is valid.

This issue is dealt with in detail by cognitive therapists who view the thinking patterns of all distressed people as irrational. Irrational thinking about events leads to pathological emotions and behavior, whereas rational thinking about events leads to appropriate emotions and behavior.

These ideas were originally formulated by Ellis (1973) in his rational-emotive therapy. Ellis described several common irrational thoughts that often underlie irrational thinking, such as the idea that we should be thoroughly competent, adequate and achieving in all possible respects in order to consider ourselves worthwhile and the idea that certain people are bad, wicked and villainous and that they should be blamed and severely punished for their villainy.

Burns (1980) has described more general irrational thinking patterns such as overgeneralizing (in which one negative event is seen as a never-ending pattern of negative events) and catastrophizing (seeing a negative event as the worst thing that could ever happen to you).

Although in the United States, a defendant in a criminal trial is innocent until proved guilty, in France a defendant must be proved innocent. Therapists who view irrational thinking as the basis for pathological emotions and behavior take the French position. They place the burden of proof on the client whom they believe is thinking irrationally. If after your marriage breaks up, you say, "I will never find happiness with a lover," the therapist asks "Where is the proof that you will never find happiness with a lover?" You are required to prove your belief. The therapist, who obviously is implying the opposite, is not required to prove his or her belief. I have known people who have never found someone to love them and who have never been in a happy long-term relationship. Some are in their sixties and probably will never find anyone. Had they made those statements, labelled irrational by Ellis, they would in fact have been correct.

Furthermore, though logicians define inductive arguments as those in which the premises provide some support, but not absolute support, for a conclusion, they do not define the word "some." Suppose I have been rejected by one lover, two, or perhaps three. How many must reject me to meet the criterion for "some support" for an inductive generalization? Conclusions are often judged to be irrational by cognitive therapists because the person has overgeneralized, but cognitive therapists, like logicians, do not propose how many occurrences permit generalization.

The fact that inductive reasoning may sometimes lead to false conclusions is no argument against it. The possibility of drawing false conclusions is inherent in the definition of inductive reasoning. But sometimes it is the only form of reasoning available to us.

Is Suicide the Result of a Decision?

Before examining whether a decision to commit suicide can be logical or rational, it is worth while considering whether suicide is the result of a decision. For example, if a schizophrenic hears a voice commanding him to jump from a building and fly, and if he obeys, his resulting death is not the result of a reasoned decision. In this context, Goldstein (1940) proposed strict criteria for judging a death to be suicidal which are pertinent here. Goldstein said that the person must have a mature concept of death and must consciously choose death. Only suicidal deaths which meet these criteria may be viewed as decisions.

The more determinants researchers identify for a behavior, the less easy it is to postulate that the behavior was a result of a decision. If schizophrenia is really the result of a genetically-programmed defect in the dopamine and norepinephrine neurotransmitters in the brain, then it makes less sense to talk about a decision to be schizophrenic. Similarly, if suicide can be shown to have biochemical and early event precursors, then the behavior appears to be more determined and less of a decision. However, it has been impossible so far to identify necessary and sufficient determinants for suicidal behavior.

Despite these caveats, suicidal individuals usually feel subjectively that they are making a decision, and so asking whether the decision can be logical and rational remains reasonable.

Can Psychiatrically Disturbed People Have Rational Premises?

Some writers on this topic have used the psychiatric disturbance present in most suicides as evidence that they could not have been thinking rationally. Pretzel (1968), for example, noted that we often endorse four types of suicide as rational: suicides carried out for some cause (such as martyrdom), suicide as a reaction to a lingering pain or to a painful and incurable illness, suicide where the individual is not receiving any pleasure from life, and love-pact suicides. Pretzel selected an example of each of these types of suicides and demonstrated some degree of psychiatric disturbance in the people involved. He concluded that in each case there were psychopathological factors at work in the motivation of the suicide, and therefore, that the suicide was irrational. This approach is biased, of course, because he could have selected a nondisturbed case for each type of suicide since not all suicides are demonstrably disturbed. Although some psychiatrists have found almost all suicides to be psychiatrically disturbed in retrospect (Robins, 1981), not all psychiatrists agree, and estimates of the percentage of the psychiatrically disturbed in samples of suicides range from 5 to 94 percent (Temoche, et. al., 1964).

Rationality and the Statistical Rarity of Suicide

The statistical rarity of suicide means that only a small proportion of people experiencing any trauma kill themselves. For example, even for those diagnosed with an affective disorder or who have attempted suicide, only about fifteen percent of their deaths are from suicide. The statistical rarity of suicide means that the precipitating conditions can never be considered *necessary* or *sufficient*. This factor makes suicide appear irrational to many observers.

Others, however, may view suicide committed as a result of particular precipitants as rational. This typically means that the observer thinks that he or she might also have committed suicide under such circumstances. If we think that we might kill ourselves if we were dying from cancer, then suicide under those circumstances is judged to be rational. If we would never immolate ourselves on the steps of the Capitol Building in Washington, DC, in order to bring peace to the world, then we probably view such suicides as irrational. The judgement of suicide as rational on this basis is an example of the subjective definition of normality.

Nevertheless, when we feel that a suicide was precipitated by sufficient stressors, we may view the suicide as understandable, and Margolis (1975), for example, equates understandable with justified. In recent years, suicide committed by people dying from painful incurable cancers or AIDS-related infections has been widely viewed as rational.

Do Unconscious Forces Make Suicide Irrational?

As Leenaars (1988) has noted, some theories of suicide, Freud's for example, stress the role of unconscious forces in the motivation of suicide, and Leenaars (1986) has documented the existence of unconscious determinants in suicide notes. Since the Freudian unconscious is typically viewed as using irrational thinking patterns, suicide motivated by unconscious forces may appear to be irrational. Kelly (1955), however, has argued that unconscious determinants of behavior are usually proposed only when psychologists fail to understand the person's behavior, and so he denied the usefulness of the unconscious as an explanatory variable.

Further Definitions of Rationality?

The word rational is used in many ways, and it is important to distinguish the various meanings and explore the implications of each for viewing suicide as rational or irrational. We have already discussed rationality viewed from the viewpoint of truth and validity in logic, psychiatric disorder, necessary and sufficient causes, and unconscious motivation. Other viewpoints are possible.

Empirical Judgements of Rationality

We might look at the outcome of the suicidal action as a basis for deciding whether the suicidal action was rational or not. For example, if the suicidal action changes the person's life for the better, perhaps it was a rational action? Certainly, as Nietzsche is commonly quoted as saying, the thought of suicide helps many people through a crisis. The person can say that, if things get worse, he can always kill himself, a thought that gives him enough energy and motivation to live another day during which, perhaps, the strength of the suicidal impulse decreases. To take another example, one patient who, when assured that no one would interfere if she tried to kill herself, decided not to since now she felt back in charge of her life.

Attempted suicides are often pleased with the changes in interpersonal relationships brought about by their suicide attempt. But can we say that the completed suicide ever changes one's life for the better? This of course depends on how one evaluates the quality of life which the suicide is leading as compared to death. Was death worse than life in a concentration camp under the Nazis? Surprisingly few inmates of those camps committed suicide. Perhaps they viewed their life as better than death. Yet a few did commit suicide, directly or indirectly, and so presumably they viewed their death as better than continued life. The judgement here is subjective.

Rational versus Autonomous

Beauchamp and Childress (1979) have noted that suicide can be an autonomous act by a person, and suicide by an autonomous individual which also meets utilitarian criteria (maximizing good and minimizing harm) is acceptable. Hauerwas (1981) felt that autonomous individuals could commit rational suicides, though he found such suicides to be not morally justified.

Can suicide be the action of an autonomous individual? The right of people to refuse extraordinary medical treatment has been viewed as acceptable by the federal courts in America, and suicide differs from this only in the activity (versus the passivity) of the behavior. Suicide is not illegal in any state and so, as least by implication, individuals have the legal right to commit suicide.

Rational versus Emotional

Hauerwas (1981) contrasted rational suicide (which he defined as cool and unemotional) with (by implication) emotional and impulsive suicide. He gave the Stoics as examples of rational suicide using these criteria. Can suicide be the action of a cool and unemotional person? Such suicides probably exist, though we would prefer neutral observers to be present to witness the death in order to be sure. Some of the suicides by terminally-ill individuals probably meet this criterion. As far as we can tell, Freud's physician-assisted suicide, for which he had made arrangements many years earlier, may well have met this criterion.

An Economic View of Suicide

Economists define rational behavior as maximizing some variable such as utility or profit. Can suicide ever be rational using the criteria of economists? Yeh and Lester (1987) presented a cost-benefit analysis of suicide in which the individual is assumed to weigh the costs and benefits of suicide as a strategy as compared to the costs and benefits of other alternatives. Clarke and Lester (1989) have also presented such an analysis. Thus, if these analyses have merit, it may be that suicide maximizes utility.

In psychoanalytic theory, desires, both conscious and unconscious, motivate all behavior, and all behavior is a compromise of conflicting desires. Thus, choices in this perspective can always be seen as maximizing psychological utility. The fact that some of the desires may be unconscious has no relevance to this criterion.

Shneidman's Views on the Logic of Suicide

Shneidman (1970) noted that the formal logic of suicidal reasoning is not as interesting as the actual style of reasoning used by the individual, what he termed *concludifying*, that is, how the individual reaches conclusions, thinks, reasons, and infers. Shneidman called the individual's style of concludifying his or her *idio-logic*. Idio-logic includes both the aspects of reasoning which might be subsumed under the traditional fallacies of reasoning and the cognitive maneuvers which describe the cognitive style of the individual.

Logic versus Psychologic

In several papers, Shneidman makes a distinction between pure logic and the logic that ordinary people use, that is, *psychologic*. As an example of this, Shneidman (1982a) considered the use of the word "therefore". He argued that people use the word in ways that do not imply "always" or "under all circumstances". Shneidman suggested that the mind does not syllogize in a logical sense, but rather "concludifies" (comes to conclusions) in a psychological sense. "....therefore, I must commit suicide" may mean a variety of things to the individual, such as I may commit suicide, I ought to commit suicide, I should commit suicide, I might commit suicide, I shall commit suicide, and I must commit suicide. The thought may refer to the present time or the future. It may refer to all circumstances or only to some circumstances. Shneidman warned psychotherapists to be aware of this flexible usage of the word "therefore" and take care to understand precisely what the client means rather than simply assuming that the client is using the word in a formal logic sense.

Indeed, Shneidman noted that the use of the word "therefore" by people is closer to the Persian logic of centuries ago which included the temporal dimension of ubiquity versus occasionality as well as a dimension of necessity/certainty versus probability.

Fallacies

Shneidman and Farberow (1970) suggested one fallacy that suicidal individuals may make in their reasoning. Although they called this type of reasoning "catalogic", since it destroys the reasoner, they described it more accurately as a *psychosemantic fallacy*. They suggested that some suicidal individuals confuse the self as experienced by themselves with the self as experienced by others. If the suicidal individual reasons thus -- If a person kills himself, he gets attention; I will kill myself, therefore I will get attention -- the I that kills is the self as experienced by self while the I that gets attention is the self as experienced by others. This fallacy is present in the statement often found in suicide notes, "Don't think too badly of me". This fallacy is called by logicians the fallacy of equivocation (Engel, 1986). Shneidman and Farberow noted that this fallacy is avoided if the suicidal individual believes in a life after death in which he or she will be able to watch the reaction of others.

Shneidman (1970) gave other examples of fallacies in suicidal thinking. One very brief suicide note read as follows: "I love everybody but my darling wife has killed me." Shneidman noted the suppressed premise -- therefore, I kill myself. The man's logic is: If X loves Y and Y kills X, then X must kill X. Once this suppressed premise is added to the argument, then the fallacy of equivocation in the use of the word kill is apparent. Kill is used figuratively in the overt premise to mean betray or violated, while in the suppressed premise it is used literally.

The Idio-Logic of Cesare Pavese

Shneidman (1982b) examined the diary of Cesare Pavese, the Italian writer who killed himself in 1950, and identified two styles of thinking in Pavese.

(1) A style of combining opposites, juxtaposing assertions with denials and contradictory ideas. For example, "The richness of life lies in memories we have forgotten" (February 13, 1944) or "The unique event which you find so exciting can only have its full value if it has never taken place" (February 13, 1945).

(2) A constricting style of thinking so that he limited his options to a narrow few. For example, "To choose a hardship for ourselves is our only defense against that hardship...This is how we can disarm the power of suffering, make it our creation, our own choice; submit to it" (November 10, 1938). Pavese perceived only one option here, whereas in fact there were many strategies open to him.

In addition, Shneidman observed the particular form of illogical reasoning which he had called catalogic. An example from Pavese's diaries is the following: "...If I were dead, she would go on living, laughing, trying her luck. But she has thrown me over and still does all those things. Therefore, I am dead" (February 25, 1938).

"If A, then B" does not imply "If B, then A". This error in propositional logic is commonly called affirming the consequent (or consequence). "If I drop objects, they fall to the ground" does not imply. "This object fell to the ground (imagine a meteor), therefore I dropped it". The word "as" in the phrase "I am as dead" possibly makes Pavese's argument literary rather than (il)logical, but using such phrasing may well have shaped Pavese's reasoning.

Shneidman noted that suicide may not be due to faulty logic. Rather Pavese's style of thinking and reasoning directly predisposed him to make a suicidal decision when the stress he felt was great.

DISCUSSION

What we have tried to do in this section is to lay out a set of definitions to clarify the question of whether suicide can be logical or rational. Irrationality can refer to (1) the degree of psychiatric disturbance of the individual, (2) the statistical rarity of a behavior, (3) whether there are unconscious processes motivating the behavior, at least in part, (4) whether the behavior improved the state of the person, (5) whether the behavior was that of an autonomous individual, (6) whether the decision was affected by emotional states, (7) whether the behavior maximized utility, and (8) whether we find the reasons for the behavior acceptable. Of course, some of these criteria might be judged more salient to the decision to commit suicide than others.

Questions concerning whether the decision to commit suicide is illogical center around (1) the truth of the premises and (2) the validity of the logic involved in the reasoning.

Obviously suicide can be irrational and illogical. The critical question, therefore, is whether suicide can ever be rational and logical. Since we are rarely around the individual who is about to commit suicide and since there are few standardized psychological tests to measure the variables involved in the criteria listed above, the questions may be unanswerable. Some investigators do find some suicides to be free of psychiatric illness, and some suicides meet the criteria for being autonomous individuals. Occasional suicides do seem to improve the state of the person and maximize utility (both for the suicide and the society). And, unless one thinks that suicide is never acceptable, most of us could find acceptable reasons for suicide. However, suicide is always statistically rare and, if one accepts the existence of the unconscious, is probably always motivated in part by unconscious forces.

Finally, there may be some suicides for whom their premises are true or, at least, not demonstrably false, and whose reasoning is valid and free from the many kinds of fallacies which logicians have described (Engel, 1986), and this might be most easily demonstrated by those suicides who meet the economists' criteria for maximizing utility.

Recently, I have studied the lives of thirty suicides sufficiently interesting and famous for biographies and autobiographies to have been published (Lester, 1991). Do any of those lives fit the criteria above? The presence of psychological disturbance in many of the suicides makes it difficult to be sure without an interview with the person prior to their death in order to explore whether some of the criteria listed above could be met. However, the physician-assisted suicide of Sigmund Freud, who was in the end stages of a painful cancer (Gay, 1988), comes closest to meeting many of the criteria, and one example is sufficient to establish the possibility of rational suicide.

PHILOSOPHERS EXAMINE A SUICIDE

In order to illustrate how philosophers explore a concept, we will examine what they have said about the suicide of Socrates. Socrates was tried for treason in Athens and found guilty. Stone (1988) has argued that he provoked his judges into ordering his execution, refused to escape from prison when his followers urged him to do so, and then acquiesced in the sentence by drinking a poison. Thus, suicidologists would view Socrates's death as, in part, a victim-precipitated homicide, where a person, consciously or unconsciously, plays some role in his own murder by provoking another into killing him. Then, by taking the poison voluntarily, his death is clearly a form of suicide.

A number of philosophers, however, have raised the question of whether Socrates did indeed commit suicide. Their ideas will be discussed here, and I will comment on these ideas from the perspective of a suicidologist.

It has been argued either that his death was really a state-ordered execution, and therefore a form of murder, or that he did not intend to die. Frey (1978) argued that Socrates did indeed commit suicide because his death satisfied the two main criteria for suicide: he *killed himself* and he did so *intentionally*. Frey examined a number of objections to this conclusion, and we amplify his discussion of these here.

"Who" Committed Suicide?

Peterman (1984) suggested that we must distinguish between the man Socrates and the character named Socrates created for the story related by others. The question of why Socrates the man committed suicide may have a different answer from that to the question of what was Plato's purpose in presenting Socrates's death in the way that he did. Peterman suggests that Plato used Socrates's death to show that a teacher must die in his role as a teacher, must cut the umbilical cord of teaching, in order for his students to truly find life. Eckstein (1981) made a similar point, suggesting that Plato was writing a dramatic play with the intention of discrediting Socrates's arguments.

The Role of Intent

Did Socrates want to die? It is often possible to argue that a person did not want to die despite the fact that he or she killed himself. For example, a person may be seeking escape from pain and may view death as similar to a long sleep. Or a person may seek to be reunited with a loved one who is already dead. *Death* may be only a means to an end. Indeed, there is some evidence that those about to kill themselves purposefully avoid thinking about death, perhaps because the realization that death is imminent may make them too anxious (Spiegel and Neuringer, 1963).

Duff (1982-1983) suggested that perhaps Socrates wanted to obey the law and, in his case, the court's verdict. Had he been reprieved, he would not have killed himself. We may take a modern example here of a patient with a terminal illness who plans to kill himself, as did Percy Bridgman, the Nobel Laureate in physics. If the disease was to unexpectedly abate, perhaps disappear completely, would such a person then kill himself. Almost certainly not.

But since the illness did not abate and since the person did take his own life, we may still call it suicide.

Still Duff argued that Socrates did not drink the hemlock in order to avoid execution (in the way that Herman Goring took poison to avoid execution after the Nuremburg trials), but that drinking hemlock was the method of execution. Cooperation with this custom does not, therefore, mean that Socrates intended his own death. Holland (1980) agreed. I think that they are wrong. Socrates may not have *wanted* to die, but he certainly *intended* to die, that is, he knew that his acts would lead to his death and he carried out those acts. Lesser (1980) agreed that intention to do something does not require wanting to do it.

The problem with bringing in the reason for the suicidal act as a criterion for calling the act suicide is that it would become possible to view no deaths as suicidal in the narrowest sense of the word. This person killed herself in order to escape from the unbearable pain of cancer. Her aim was not death. This person killed himself to make his wife feel guilty for leaving him. His aim was not death. This man killed himself to be reunited with his wife in Heaven. His aim was not death and, for him, there is no death since life continues.

Menninger (1938) classified the motives for suicide as *to die* (to escape from unbearable pain), *to kill* (to aggress against frustrating others), and *to be killed* (to punish oneself for real or imagined sins). Note that none of these motives involve seeking death *per se*. The more we examine the reasons for a person's suicidal act, the more likely (perhaps inevitably) we will find justification for saying that *death* was not intended.

Smith (1980) drew a bizarre analogy. He asked us to suppose that a person attends a lecture about the way in which large objects can move air molecules. When she walks out of the lecture, does she intend to move air molecules? He says, "Of course not." Since Socrates did not intend to move air molecules out of the way when he raised the cup of hemlock to his lips, he did not intend to die. This seems to be an odd argument. Socrates's intentions regarding air molecules have no relevance to his intent to die. Using Smith's example, expressing actions in molecular (and, even better, in atomic terms) we can prove that no one ever intends anything!

Did Socrates Want to Die?

Walton (1980) rendered much of this discussion irrelevant by documenting that indeed Socrates may have consciously wanted to die. Socrates implied that life was not worth living when the body was ruined and that one should not cling to life in greed. Only a noble life was worthwhile, suggesting that, when such nobility was no longer possible, death was appropriate.

Suicide under Duress

Since Socrates was forced to drink the hemlock, does this make his death nonsuicidal? Frey (1978) said that this is not so. Socrates did not take the cup reluctantly, nor throw it to the ground. It was not force-fed to him. Socrates was, however, under duress and, related to this, under sentence of death. (Frey argued that duress does not vitiate choice, although legal precedents would take issue with this. For example, prisoners are no longer able to "volunteer" to be subjects in medical experiments in return for reduced sentences.)

More pertinently, the suicide rate on death row in America is extremely high, 146 per 100,000 per year as compared to a rate of only 25 among prisoners in general (Lester, 1987a). The fact that the death-row inmates are under sentence of execution does not change the certification of the cause of death.

Consider again the suicide of Percy Bridgman, mentioned above. The disease from which he was dying (Paget's disease) made it very difficult to have freedom of action. He killed himself at a time which he thought was the last possible opportunity he would have to do so. If had waited any longer, he would not have been able to commit suicide. Could not Bridgman be considered to have been under duress? And do the pressures on him make his death nonsuicidal? I think not.

Or consider a *kamikaze* pilot. Does he act freely or under duress? A member of the military is no more "free" to volunteer for duties than is a prisoner. (A kamikaze pilot also illustrates the relevance of desire. Does he want to die or rather to attack and kill the enemy?) What we must conclude from these examples is that not all suicides are alike and that different *types* of suicides are worthy of study. But they remain types of *suicide*.

Choosing the Time of Death

Socrates did not choose the time of his death, and some think that this makes his death nonsuicidal. Frey (1978) gave an example of someone who sets up a method of suicide for which the timing is uncertain, as in the case of a bomb which will explode and kill the person whenever someone makes a call to his house. The fact that the timing of death was uncertain has no relevance to labeling the death as suicide.

Other examples can be given. Consider a person like Percy Bridgman who decides that, when he or she has developed cancer which has progressed to the later stages, he or she will commit suicide, and in fact does so. The person did not choose the timing of their death. It was determined by forces outside of their control, namely the occurrence and development of the disease. In such cases, the choice of the timing of death is irrelevant to its classification as suicide.

Does Suicide Rule out Murder?

Walton (1980) phrases the issue as whether Socrates committed suicide or was murdered? This phrasing makes it an either/or situation and eliminates the possibility that he did commit suicide *and* that he was murdered. There is no reason that both labels may not apply. In cases of victim-precipitated murder (where the victim plays a role in his or her own murder), the fact that there was a real murderer does not prevent us for discussing the suicidal intent of the victim.

Lesser (1980) asserted that suicide means "self-murder," and went on to argue that Socrates did not murder himself in the sense in which "murder" is typically used. This definition of suicide is not used by suicidologists.

A companion question is whether murder rules out suicide? Sigmund Freud, typically ahead of his time, had his physician administer a lethal dose of morphine to him as he lay dying in pain from cancer. This physician-assisted suicide has elements of murder, but the presence of those elements does prevent us from classifying Freud's death as a suicide.

That the criminal justice system requires a single category of death (so that it may assign responsibility and decide upon the culpability of others) does not force us to be so limited, especially since our aim is to understand behavior rather than assigning moral and criminal responsibility.

The Justifiability of Suicide

Duff (1982-1983) raised the issue of the morality of suicide. There are many possible issues here. We may ask whether suicide in general or whether this particular suicide was morally right, rational (a term best reserved for judgments about the premises underlying the person's reasoning), logical (a term best reserved for the soundness of the reasoning process given the premises), and legal. The answer to each of these questions may affect how we view the suicide, but they do not affect whether he is classified as a suicide. The justifiability of suicide has no relevance to an accurate certification of death.

Was Socrates Wise to Take Hemlock?

Anderson (1972) asked a different question, one of wisdom rather than definition. Anderson noted that Socrates advocated two principles: employ the best possible reasoning (think rightly) and avoid wrong-doing (act rightly). Socrates felt that his thinking was right, and so the death sentence was wrong. Therefore, Socrates should not have poisoned himself for that would be wrong-doing. In order to explain Socrates's choice to drink hemlock, Anderson suggested that Socrates might have considered disobedience a worse wrong-doing or that he might have felt that death was not a punishment.

Anderson noted, but rejected, other explanations of Socrates's choice to drink hemlock: that he drank hemlock because he was weary of fighting the status quo or that his death would remind his followers of how faulty the Athenian state was.

Anderson's arguments, however, ignore the fact, later raised by Stone (1988), that Socrates could, in all likelihood, have avoided death by proposing a reasonable alternative to death. The choice of whether to drink hemlock arises only because of decisions made earlier.

Comment

In my opinion, Socrates's death was certainly a suicide. It was also an execution. One label does not rule out the other. Making these judgments does not, however, prevent us from deciding what type of suicide was Socrates's death.

We have noted that there is good evidence that Socrates, like Antigone, provoked his judges into condemning him to death. Socrates then took hemlock as instructed (or as expected) whereas Antigone hung herself rather than dying slowly of starvation. Both can be seen to have elements of victim-precipitated homicide in their behavior, committing suicide by getting others to kill you. Indeed, the suicidal impulse is perhaps of greater interest in its impact on Socrates's behavior during his trial than in the mere act of drinking the hemlock because its influence in the trial is more subtle, less obvious.

In deciding to go along with the Athenian system of justice, by being a good citizen, Socrates's suicide also has other elements. In Durkheim's (1897) typology, his suicide is that of a person fully integrated into and regulated by the society and thus is both *altruistic* and *fatalistic*.

Interestingly, Socrates, like Antigone, achieved something noteworthy by his death, namely changing the image left behind. Their suicides changed the way in which we view them. Antigone achieved a certain degree of nobility in her stand against Creon and in her death. How does Socrates's suicide change our image of him?

Duff suggested that Socrates's actions show that he saw citizens, not merely as servants of the state, but rather as *participants* in the state's lawful activities. He drank hemlock because it was his duty to play his part in his execution. His suicide illustrated his ideological position.

Perhaps I can suggest another way in which Socrates's suicide might affect our image of him. There is Zen parable in which a young pregnant girl accuses a Zen monk of being the father. After the child is born, the villagers take the baby to him and tell him that, since he fathered it, he must raise it. He takes the baby and thanks them. A year later, the girl confesses that the monk was not the father of her child, but that a boy in town was the father. The villagers go back to the monk, apologize and ask for the baby back. The monk gives them the baby and thanks them.

What is, is. One can rail against the way in which one's life turns out, or one can accept it. Perhaps Socrates in, almost cheerfully, going along with the trial and sentence, showed that he too was as enlightened as any Zen master?

The Morality of Suicide

There are two major ways of deciding whether suicide is morally right or wrong (Beauchamp and Childress, 1979). The first uses absolute principles, the *deonotological* position. One major principle advocated by people in our society is "Thou shalt not kill." This position leads to choices such as opposition to capital punishment, opposition to abortion, and, therefore, opposition to suicide.

The problem of absolute principles is that they sometimes compete with one another and, furthermore, people sometimes act against them. Those firmly opposed to abortion and capital punishment often go off to war quite willingly, believing that "God is on our side." If you break an absolute principle in any way, then it is no longer an absolute principle. Furthermore, some of those advocating this principle of not killing often do not worry about killing certain organisms, such as animals, and so their application of the principle sometimes seems arbitrary.

Contrasting with this absolute principle is another -- the *principle of autonomy*. Autonomous individuals have the right to behave in any non-criminal way they choose. The difficulty here is agreeing upon who is autonomous. This label is typically not granted to the psychiatrically disturbed, the retarded, children, and those suffering from extreme stress. This is why federal courts typically grant adults the right to refuse blood transfusions and surgery if their religion forbids this but will authorize such treatment for their children.

The alternative position to deontology is the *utilitarian* position. Here, among the various criteria proposed for morality are maximizing good and minimizing harm. The best options are those which achieve these goals. The problems here are twofold. First, the judgments of good and harm are subjective, and different people weight them differently. Second, the question arises of good and harmful for whom.

Although the basic positions are easily laid out, the morality of suicide has been the subject of much scholarly debate.

Is Suicide Intervention Moral?

Although some practitioners argue that suicide (and, indeed, all suicides) should be prevented (Pretzel, 1968), others argue that suicide prevention is not always appropriate (Szasz, 1986). If the right to commit suicide exists (and it is certainly not illegal in most jurisdictions), what is the justification for suicide intervention (Lester, 1989). The suicidal person may be acting willingly and autonomously, thereby not permitting others to intervene in a paternalistic fashion.

Macks (1971) argued that the goal of suicide prevention centers should *not* be to prevent suicide but rather to help clients find other alternatives. Suicide prevention is suitable only if the client is ambivalent, and clients must have the right to informed consent over any actions taken with them as the target. Szasz (1971) noted that labeling clients as psychiatrically disturbed is sometimes used simply to justify forcible intervention into their lives.

However, if a client voluntarily seeks advice and help, then not to respond would be unethical. Since almost all suicide prevention centers are passive, waiting for clients to contact them, then their responding is morally correct More active suicide prevention, however, does run the risk of being oppressive. To force counseling on those who do not request it is demeaning and can be life-threatening. As Szasz (1971) and Lester (1987b) have noted, Ernest Hemingway committed suicide partly to avoid ever have to return to the Mayo Clinic for further treatment.

References

Anderson, A. Was Socrates unwise to take the hemlock? *Harvard Theological Review*, 1972, 65, 437-452.

Baum, R. *Logic*. New York: Holt, Rinehart & Winston, 1974.

Beauchamp, T., & Childress, J. *Principles of biomedical ethics*. New York: Oxford University Press, 1979.

Burns, D. *Feeling good*. New York: Morrow, 1908.

Clarke, R. V., & Lester, D. *Suicide: Closing the exits*. New York: Springer-Verlag, 1989.

Duff, R. A. Socratic suicide. *Proceedings of the Aristotelian Society*, 1982-1983, 83, 35-47.

Durkheim, E. *Le Suicide*. Paris: Felix Alcan, 1897.

Eckstein, J. *The deathday of Socrates*. Frenchtown, NJ: Columbia Publishing, 1981.

Ellis, A. *Humanistic psychotherapy*. New York: Julian, 1973.

Engel, S. M. *With good reason*. New York: St. Martins, 1986.
Frey, R. G. Did Socrates commit suicide? *Philosophy*, 1978, 53(203), 106-108.
Gay, P. *Freud*. New York: Norton, 1988.
Goldstein, K. *Human nature in the light of psychopathology*. Cambridge, MA: Harvard University Press, 1940.
Grassian, V. *Perennial philosophical issues*. Englewood Cliffs, NJ: Prentice-Hall, 1984.
Hauerwas, S. Rational suicide and reasons for living. *Progress in Clinical & Biological Research*, 1981, 50, 185-199.
Holland, R. F. *Against empiricism*. London: Blackwell, 1980.
Kelly, G. *The theory of personal constructs*. New York: Norton, 1955.
Leenaars, A. A. A brief note on latent content in suicide notes. *Psychological Reports*, 1986, 59, 640-642.
Leenaars, A. A. *Suicide notes*. New York: Human Sciences Press, 1988.
Lesser, H. Suicide and self-murder. *Philosophy*, 1980, 55, 255-257.
Lester, D. *The death penalty*. Springfield, IL: Charles Thomas, 1987a.
_____ . *Suicide as a learned behavior*. Springfield, IL: Charles Thomas, 1987b.
_____ . *Can we prevent suicide*? New York: AMS, 1989.
_____ . The study of suicidal lives. *Suicide & Life-Threatening Behavior*, 1991, 21, 164-173.
Macks, V. Suicide prevention. *Social Work*, 1971, 16, 102-104.
Margolis, J. *Negativities*. Columbus, OH: Merrill, 1975.
Menninger, K. *Man against himself*. New York: Harcourt, Brace & World, 1938.
Peterman, J. E. The Socratic suicide. In E. Kelly (Ed.) *New essays on Socrates*, pp. 3-15. Lanham, MD: University Press of America, 1984.
Pretzel, P. W. Philosophical and ethical considerations of suicide prevention. *Bulletin of Suicidology*, 1968, July, 30-38.
Robin, E. *The final months*. New York: Oxford University Press, 1981.
Shneidman, E. S. Content analysis of suicidal logic. In E. S. Shneidman, N. L. Farberow, & R. E. Litman (Eds.) *The psychology of suicide*, pp. 73-93. New York: Science House, 1970.
Shneidman, E. S. On "Therefore I must kill myself". *Suicide & Life-Threatening Behavior*, 1982a, 12, 52-55.
_____ . The suicidal logic of Cesare Pavese. *Journal of the American Academy of Psychoanalysis*, 1982b, 10, 547-563.
Shneidman, E. S., & Farberow, N. L. The logic of suicide. In E. S. Shneidman, N. L. Farberow, & R. E. Litman (Eds.) *The psychology of suicide*, pp. 63-71. New York: Science House, 1970.
Smith, M. Did Socrates kill himself intentionally? *Philosophy*, 1980, 55, 253-254.
Spiegel, D., & Neuringer, C. Role of dread in suicidal behavior. *Journal of Abnormal & Social Psychology*, 1963, 66, 507-511.
Stone, I. F. *The trial of Socrates*. Boston: Little Brown, 1988.
Szasz, T. The ethics of suicide. *Intellectual Digest*, 1971, 2, 53-55.
_____ . The case against suicide prevention. *American Psychologist*, 1986, 41, 806-812.
Temoche, A., Pugh, T. F., & MacMahon, B. Suicide rates among current and former mental institution patients. *Journal of Nervous & Mental Disease*, 1964, 138, 124-130.
Walton, R. E. Socrates' alleged suicide. *Journal of Value Inquiry*, 1980, 14, 287-299.

Wilber, C. G. Some thoughts on suicide: is it logical? *American Journal of Forensic Medicine & Pathology*, 1987, 8, 302-308.

Yeh, B. Y., & Lester, D. An economic model for suicide. In D. Lester, *Suicide as a learned behavior*, pp. 51-57. Springfield, IL: Charles Thomas, 1987.

Chapter 6

SOCIOLOGY AND SUICIDE[1]

INTRODUCTION

Sociology may be defined as the "study of human behavior, of group life, and the societies created by human beings" (Hess, et al., 1982, p. 3). It differs from anthropology, which on the whole has focused on prehistoric and preliterate societies, in its focus on modern societies. It also differs from psychology in studying the group rather than the individual and by stressing the importance of situational, interpersonal and environmental factors rather than intrapsychic factors. The study of suicide by sociologists has focused on two major issues, one of which is well-studied (the impact of society on suicide) and one of which has been relatively ignored (the impact of suicide on society).

Let us first examine the impact of society on suicide. There have been two major sociological theories of suicide, as well as many minor theories. Here we will describe briefly the two major theories, those of Durkheim and of Henry and Short.

DURKHEIM'S THEORY OF SUICIDE

There are two basic concepts in Durkheim's (1897) theory of suicidal behavior -- *social integration* and *social regulation*. A society is integrated insofar as its members possess shared beliefs and sentiments, interest in one another, and a common sense of devotion to common goals (Johnson, 1965). Other attempts to define exactly what Durkheim meant by the concept of social integration state that a society is integrated to the extent that its members possess durable and stable social relationships (Gibbs and Martin, 1964). However, it should be noted that Durkheim himself did not provide a specific explicit definition of the concept (Douglas, 1967).

Suicidal behavior was hypothesized to be more common in societies where there is a high degree of social integration (*altruistic* suicide) and in societies where there is a low degree of social integration (*egoistic* suicide). Societies with a moderate degree of social integration have the lowest incidence of suicide. Egoism results from excessive individualism, and the individual is protected from egoism by religions with strong group ties, family ties especially

---

[1] This chapter was co-authored by Bijou Yang.

where children are involved, or political affiliations. When the ties in a society are minimal, then suicide becomes more likely. At the other extreme, the individual can be too closely integrated and identified with a particular group. He may take his life, for example, as a religious sacrifice or as a result of political or military allegiances.

The second social variable that Durkheim defined was social regulation. A society is regulated insofar as the society has control over the emotions and motivations of the individual members. Suicidal behavior is common in societies with a high degree of social regulation (*fatalistic* suicide) and in societies with a low degree of social regulation (*anomic* suicide). Societies with a moderate degree of social regulation have the lowest incidence of suicidal behavior.

Johnson (1965) noted that it was possible to assume from Durkheim's writings that the incidence of suicide in a society is determined by the degree of social integration and the degree of social regulation acting *independently* upon the members of the society.

To What Entities Can Durkheim's Theory Be Applied?

An important issue to consider before we examine the extent to which we may consider Durkheim's theory confirmed or disconfirmed by empirical evidence is to what may the theory be applied. A good deal of sociological research is conducted on nations. Can we legitimately distinguish different levels of social integration and social regulation in different nations? This seems possible. For example, if one nation permits divorce while another does not, we may conclude that, at least in this respect, the two nations differ in the degree of social integration. Similarly, a totalitarian nation differs from a democratic nation in the degree of social regulation.

Can the concepts be applied to regions within a nation? Again, the different states of America, for example, differ in such social variables as divorce rates and church membership, variables which may affect the levels of social integration and regulation. Thus, the concepts may be applicable to regions within a nation.

Third, within a society there are different groups -- men and women, blacks and whites, and young and old, for example. These groups may also differ in ways which impinge upon the levels of social integration and social regulation.

Finally, there are individuals. Might individual suicides be classified as anomic, egoistic, altruistic and fatalistic? Although the classification of individuals moves to the psychological level of analysis, it may be possible. For example, Faber (1970) has conceptualized the suicides in some Greek tragedies as altruistic, and Lester (1994b) classified cases of celebrity suicides into the four Durkheimian types.

Is It Legitimate to Look at Overall Suicide Rates?

Since Durkheim proposed four types of suicide, it could be argued that it is crucial to examine the rates of each type of suicide. For example, societies with low levels of social integration are expected to have high rates of *egoistic* suicide. To test predictions based on the concept of social integration, therefore, requires measurement of *egoistic* suicide rates. This, of course, has never been done. Researchers use the overall suicide rate of the society. Thus, failures to confirm Durkheimian hypotheses may result from this failure to measure suicide rates appropriately.

Typical Tests of Durkheimian Hypotheses

Almost all sociological studies of suicide cite Durkheim and purport to be tests of his theory. It is interesting to examine whether such studies do in fact test Durkheim's theory. To do this, let us examine one methodologically sound sociological study.

Breault (1986) sought to examine the effect of religious integration and family integration on suicide in the United States. Breault examined the effects of church membership, divorce, and inter-region migration on the suicide rates of the states (and of counties) at various times during the period 1933 to 1980 by means of multiple regression analyses. In general, suicide rates were higher where divorce rates were higher, inter-region migration higher, and church membership lower.

Breault noted that Durkheim argued that religion reduced the likelihood of suicide because it promotes shared values, intense interactions, and strong social bonds. First of all, we may note that this statement implies both social regulation (shared values) and social integration (intense interactions). Thus, we may question Breault's assertion that he is examining the effects of social integration on suicide. This is especially relevant since most religions view suicide as immoral and thereby introduce regulatory elements.

Secondly, is there any evidence that those who are religious are in fact more socially integrated? The evidence that Breault cites in his paper is concerned only with whether religious behavior in a social group is associated with the rate of suicide. It would be useful, if not critically necessary, to show that those who attend church are more socially integrated than those who do not attend church, for we cannot simply assume that those who do not attend church engage in fewer activities which promote social integration. Given the large amount of attention given to the validity of official suicide rates, the failure to explore the validity of measures of social integration and social regulation is noteworthy.

Lester (1994a) factor-analyzed a number of social variables over the states of America. He found that divorce rates, interstate migration and church membership all loaded on the same factor. However, the variables of longitude (east-west), the ratio of men to women and the strictness of state handgun control laws also loaded on this factor. Thus, because of the complex associations between social variables, we cannot always be sure which is the critical social variable in the association with (and more importantly the cause of) our target variable, in this case the rate of suicide.

Breault next examines Durkheim's assertion that Jews are more socially integrated than Roman Catholics who, in turn, are more socially integrated than Protestants. Research on suicide rates has not always produced results consistent with this assertion of Durkheim's. Perhaps Durkheim's theory is incorrect? Here we confront a common problem in sociological research, which finds a parallel in psychological research. Just as clinical psychologists feel free to assert what is going on in the mind of their patient (after all, they are experts), sociologists often feel free to assert what is going on in a particular social group (after all, they are experts too). More skeptical commentators would prefer to see evidence that Jews are more socially integrated *because of their religion* than are Roman Catholics. And this evidence cannot be tautological. The evidence from suicide rates cannot be used to prove the difference in social integration which is then used to explain the suicide rates.

Then again, could we not predict that Jews should have high rates of altruistic suicide because of their high level of social integration, while Protestants (or perhaps atheists) should have high levels of egoistic suicide? Breault, himself, adopts the position that altruistic suicide is not generally applicable to modern society, but he presents no evidence for this position.

Improved Tests of Durkheim's Theory

The operational measurement Durkheim's concepts of social integration and social regulation remains a problem, as does our inability to distinguish between Durkheim's four types of suicide However, one study has been reported which attempts a more appropriate test of Durkheim's theory by measuring social integration and social regulation independently and by classifying a number of nonliterate societies into the nine-fold typology that results:

social regulation	**social integration**		
	high	**moderate**	**low**
high	A	B	C
moderate	D	E	F
low	G	H	I

It can be seen that Durkheim's theory would predict highest suicide rates for societies in cells A, C, G, and I, moderate rates in cells B, D, F and H, and lowest rates in cell E. We might note that suicides in each cell are hard to classify. Suicides in cell B, for example, are fatalistic since social integration is high and social regulation moderate. However, suicides in cell A, for example, are fatalistic/altruistic since both social regulation and social integration are high. It is clear that Durkheim's four types of suicide do not adequately encompass the nine cells demanded by his theory.

To illustrate this sound methodology, Lester (1989a) studied suicide in nations of the world in 1980. Data were available for 53 nations. Several measures of social regulation were included in the data set: a political rights index and a civil rights index from Taylor and Jodice (1983), and measures of political freedom, religious liberty for Christians, and a political freedom index from Barrett (1982). The marriage rate and the birth rate were used as measures of social integration and obtained from the United Nations (1986).

The seven measures were subjected to a factor analysis (with a principal components extraction and a varimax rotation), and two orthogonal (that is, independent) factors identified:

	Factor	
	I	II
political rights index	0.95*	-0.06
civil rights index	0.97*	-0.04
political freedom	0.90*	0.01
religious liberty	0.71*	0.24
political freedom index	-0.97*	0.09
birth rate	0.46	-0.66*
marriage rate	0.28	0.83*

* a high loading (> 0.50).

It can be seen that Factor I appears to tap social regulation while Factor II may tap social integration. However, a high birth rate (which was expected to increase social integration since it would lead to a large number of children and larger families) was loaded negatively on Factor II, opposite to expectations. This illustrates the need for empirical investigation of the relationship of social indicators to the concepts supposedly underlying them.

It should be noted that the factor scores were completely independent. Their correlation was zero. Thus, it is possible to assess the two concepts (social regulation and social integration) separately and independently.

The nations were divided into three groups on each factor score -- high moderate and low. The nations were then sorted into the nine cells (see Table 1), and their suicide rates examined. It can be seen that the data provide some support for Durkheim's theory. Nations high on both dimensions (cell A) and low on both (cell I) did have the highest suicide rates. Those moderate on both (cell E) had low suicide rates. However the results are not in complete support of Durkheim's theory; for example, societies high in social regulation and low in social integration (cell G) had very low suicide rates rather than the very high suicide rates that the theory would predict.

It can be seen that, although Durkheim's theory of suicide has been very influential in subsequent research on suicidal behavior, a great deal more thought must be given to designing adequate tests of his theory. In particular, some thought must be given as to how to measure the different types of suicidal behavior inherent in Durkheim's theory.

The Theory of Henry and Short

Henry and Short's (1954) theory of suicide departs to some extent from the basic ideas of Durkheim's theory because it incorporates the frustration-aggression hypothesis developed by Dollard, et al. (1939), explains the societal level of murder as well as suicide, and integrates psychological perspectives.

Henry and Short assumed that the basic and primary target of aggression is another person rather than the self. They then attempted to identify the sociological and psychological bases of the legitimization of other-oriented aggression. What enables the child to develop so that his primary response to frustration, that of other-oriented aggression, is seen as legitimate, while other children develop in such a way that this primary response is inhibited and self-directed aggression becomes legitimate?

Table 1. Suicide Rates of Nations with Varying Level of Social Regulation and Social Integration

Social Integration	Social Regulation: high	Social Regulation: moderate	Social Regulation: low
high	Bulgaria 13.5 Czechoslovakia 19.9 Egypt 0.1 Hungary 45.0 Korea, South 20.6 Poland 11.7 Singapore 9.8 Yugoslavia 14.8 mean 16.9	Israel 6.0 Japan 17.6 Portugal 8.3 Sri Lanka 29.2 USA 12.0 mean 14.6	Australia 11.3 Canada 14.1 New Zealand 10.2 UK 8.6 mean 11.0
moderate	Argentina 7.1 Brazil 3.4 Chile 5.5 Syria 0.4 mean 4.1	Greece 3.2 Spain 4.4 Trinidad & Tobago 4.8 mean 4.1	Austria 26.0 Belgium 21.8 Costa Rica 4.4 Denmark 29.1 Finland 24.7 France 19.2 Germany, West 21.4 Ireland 6.2 Italy 7.1 Netherlands 10.2 Norway 12.4 mean 16.6
low	Honduras 1.2 Jordan 2.8 Mexico 1.6 Panama 1.9 Philippines 8.3 mean 3.2	Colombia 3.5 Dominican Republic 2.0 Ecuador 3.2 El Salvador 12.1 Guatemala 1.0 Paraguay 2.7 Peru 1.2 Thailand 7.1 Turkey 1.8 Venezuela 4.6 mean 3.9	Sweden 19.1 Switzerland 24.7 mean 21.9

Sociologically, the strength of external restraint was seen as the primary basis for the legitimization of other-oriented aggression. When behavior is required to conform rigidly to the demands and expectations of others, the share of others in the responsibility for the consequences of the behavior increases, thereby legitimizing other-oriented aggression. When external restraints are weak, the self must bear the responsibility for the frustration generated, and other-oriented aggression fails to be legitimized.[2]

Henry and Short found two psychological correlates of other-oriented aggression in people, low superego strength (or low guilt), and a specific type of cardiovascular reaction during stress similar to the effects of norepinephrine. They presented evidence to indicate that in the male child, these two factors are associated with the use of physical punishment as opposed to love-oriented punishment and punishment by the father rather than punishment by the mother.

Henry and Short then sought to show how experience of love-oriented punishment dealt out by the parent who is the source of nurturance and love leads to the development of tendencies to inhibit the primary other-oriented expression of aggression. The argument centers around the idea that when the source of nurturance and love also administers the punishment, then the primary other-oriented expression of aggression threatens to end the flow of love and nurturance. If the child retaliates, he will receive no nurturance. Therefore, the child develops habits of inhibiting this primary other-oriented aggression. Inhibition of other-oriented aggression will also occur if the parent punishes the child by threatening to withdraw and withhold love and nurturance.

Empirical Evidence for Henry and Short's Theory

Gold (1958) examined predictions based on the assumption of a relationship between socialization experiences and the expression of aggression. Henry and Short had argued that experience of physical punishment led people to develop habits of expressing aggression outwardly whereas experience of psychological punishment led people to develop habits of expressing aggression inwardly. Gold argued that females were more likely to have experienced psychological punishment than were males, officers more than enlisted men, whites more than blacks, and urban dwellers more than rural dwellers. Thus females, officers, whites, and urban dwellers should all prefer inward-directed expression of aggression (including suicide) over outward-directed expression of aggression (including homicide) as compared to males, enlisted men, blacks, and rural dwellers respectively.

Gold felt that Henry and Short had been mistaken to use absolute rates of homicide and suicide since the use of absolute rates did not allow a control to be applied for the total number of aggressive acts committed by a societal group. Gold suggested that a better measure was the suicide rate divided by the combined suicide and homicide rate. When Gold tested his predictions using this measure of the preference for suicide as compared to homicide in the groups under investigation, his predictions were confirmed for all four pairs of groups.

It can also be predicted from Henry and Short's theory that groups within a society exposed to more external restraint would be more homicidal and less suicidal than groups

[2] The reasoning in this part of their theory resembles Durkheim's use of the concept of social regulation.

exposed to less external restraint. Lester (1971) showed that the suicide and homicide rates of whites and blacks in both the United States and South Africa (before liberation) fitted this prediction.

Common sense suggests that, as we improve conditions in the world, people should be much happier. If we can eliminate poverty and oppression (such as sexism and racism), if we clean up the environment, if we improve the educational and cultural offerings for our citizens, if we do all this, then we should be much happier. Then, as the quality of life increases, life should be more worth living and suicide less common.

In contrast, using Henry and Short's theory, it can be argued that when external conditions are bad, we have a clear source to blame for our own misery, and this makes us outwardly angry rather than inwardly angry or depressed. When times are good, there is no clear external source of blame for our misery, and so we are more likely to become inwardly angry or depressed and less likely to be outwardly angry. Henry and Short would argue that a higher quality of life would lead to higher rates of suicide and lower rates of homicide, whereas a lower quality of life would lead to lower rates of suicide and higher rates of homicide. Lester (1989a) reviewed several studies he had conducted which supported the hypothesis derived from Henry and Short's theory.

One obvious prediction from Henry and Short's theory is that suicide and murder are opposite behaviors -- societies with high rates of one behavior should have low rates of the other. Lester (1987) reviewed research on the sociological correlations between suicide and homicide rates, and several studies report opposite associations between social characteristics and suicide and homicide rates. For example, as noted above, societies with a higher quality of life had higher suicide rates but lower homicide rates than societies with a worse quality of life. For other variables, however, the patterns of correlations were quite different for homicide and suicide, but not opposite.

Pokorny (1965) looked at self-directed and other-directed aggression when complete and when partial, by examining data about murderers, people who assaulted others (but did not kill them), completed suicides, and attempted suicides in one city. He examined differences in place of occurrence of the act, the census tract of residence, the hour, day, and month of the act, the age of the individual, the race of the person, and the sex of the person. He found that the murderers were similar to the assaulters in all characteristics. The murderers and the completed suicides differed in all characteristics except that of sex. The completed suicides differed from the attempted suicides in hour and day of the act, age and sex. Pokorny concluded that homicide and suicide are committed by different types of people. Attempted suicides appeared to be a mixed group. They resembled the completed suicides in place of occurrence of the act, their race, and the census tract in which they dwelt, but they resembled the murderers in the hour and day of the act and in age. They were different from all three other groups in having a the high proportion of women.

Henry and Short's theory is provocative because it integrates psychological ideas with sociological ideas and because it introduces murder into the theory, broadening its range. The theory has stimulated a great deal of research, not all of which, however, supports the theory.[3]

---

3 For a fuller discussion of these issues see Lester (1989a).

Concrete versus Abstract Social Characteristics

Recently, two critiques of the sociological approach to the study of suicide have appeared (Taylor, 1990; Moksony, 1990) which are remarkably congruent. They both suggest that sociologists have failed to demonstrate the influence of the *society* on suicide. Taylor (1990) argued that, while Durkheim did demonstrate associations between social variables (such as religious affiliation and marriage) and societal suicide rates, he did not mean to suggest that religious affiliation or marriage in themselves caused the differences in suicide rates. Rather, Durkheim used these associations to reveal a common underlying cause of suicide -- the extent to which people are integrated and regulated by the society. Durkheim was searching for underlying and unobservable mechanisms and causal processes.

Later sociologists have forsaken the task of searching for invisible but real forces acting upon individuals in a society and have pursued instead a more empirical study of the relationships between observable social phenomena and suicide. They then view suicide as caused by these external social factors.

Moksony (1990) critiqued recent ecological studies of suicide, particular the spatial differences in suicide rate over the different areas of cities. The early studies of this by Cavan (1928) and Schmid (1928) attributed the spatial pattern of suicide in cities to their location in the ecological structure of the city. For example, those areas of the city with higher suicide rates tended to have an increased turnover in their population which Cavan saw as impeding the development of both a coherent system of norms and values governing behavior and stable social relationships.

Moksony argued that recent studies, such as Maris's (1969), use aggregate data to describe relationships between various characteristics of the population in each area of the city to the suicide rate. These studies tend to explore the effects of the *composition* of the population in an area on the suicide rate rather than the area as an *environment*. For example, if areas have high numbers of migrants, then the suicide rate is predicted to be high because migrants have higher suicide rates. Cavan and Schmid, according to Moksony, would instead have treated the high proportion of migrants as a characteristic of the area and sought to show that this characteristic of the area impeded the development of a stable social life for everyone in the area, newcomers and old-timers alike.

Moksony felt that his characterization of modern ecological studies was correct because the investigators often cast their studies as a preliminary step leading to a study in which the individuals would be directly observed. For example, if areas with many socially deviant individuals have higher suicide rates, the next step is usually to study suicidal behavior in the socially deviant and non-deviant people without regard to where they live (McCulloch and Philip, 1972).

Both Taylor and Moksony have made the point, then, that sociologists have not studied the effect of society *qua* society on suicide rates. Rather, sociologists have studied the impact of social variables as causal agents in themselves on the suicide rate of individuals in the society. Is there any research which might satisfy Taylor and Moksony?

Lester (1988a) suggested that social variables could be subjected to a factor analysis in order to identify factors, or clusters, of related variables. The factor scores can then be correlated with the suicide rates. Lester found that a cluster of variables including divorce rates, rates of interstate migration, and church attendance correlated most strongly with the suicide rates of the states of America. Lester's study does not imply that any of these three variables is more important than the other two in this association. It also does not imply that these three social variables cause the state suicide rates. Rather the study implies that there is a broader social characteristic, manifested perhaps in the states' divorce rates, migrant composition and religious patterns, which is associated with suicide rates. This higher order characteristic, whatever it may be called (though low social integration seems a good possibility) seems close to satisfying Taylor's and Moksony's requirement for a *societal* or *areal* effect.

More detailed analysis of the data in the study above (Lester, 1994a) has shown that the higher order characteristic (perhaps indicating low social integration) is associated with the suicide rate of males and females, whites and blacks and those of all ages. Thus, the association has generality.

The Impact on the Society versus the Individual

Lester and Yang (1991) noted that the social context of suicide can be examined from both the interpersonal and the social perspectives. An analogy here is economics where microeconomics is concerned with the behavior of individual economic units and macroeconomics with the economy as a whole. Lester and Yang suggested parallel terms for sociology, with *macrosocionomics* examining the impact of the society on the members of the society as a group while *microsocionomics* examines the impact of individuals on one another.

They explored the impact of divorce on suicide. In the microsocionomic perspective, divorce has a dramatic impact on the individuals involved. A person who was living with a spouse is now without that partner. The loss often leads divorced people to attach themselves impulsively to other, often inappropriate, individuals. Divorced people sometimes find that former friends have taken the side of their ex-spouse, and they often feel lonely. Divorced persons typically feel angry, depressed and anxious, and they are preoccupied with thoughts about the past and the future. From Durkheim's perspective, divorced people are less well socially integrated than those who are married.

To illustrate a macrosocionomic perspective, Lester and Yang compared those who get divorced in Ireland (where the divorce rate is very low) versus the United States (where the divorce rate is very high). How might the macrosocionomic variable of the divorce rate of the society affect the individual? In Ireland where divorce is rare, the divorced person may feel stigma, and for a person to get divorced in such a society implies a low degree of social regulation. In contrast, in the United States where divorce is common, there is less stigma to being divorced, and divorce does not imply less social regulation in those divorcing.

Furthermore, as we noted in the previous section, the divorce rate of the society may also be an indicator of a more abstract characteristic of the society, a characteristic which may affect all members of the society. For example, societies with low levels of social integration, indicated by a high divorce rate among other variables, may have a high suicide rate in all groups of the society. Lester and Yang showed that, in the United States in 1980, states with high divorce rates had high suicide rates in the single, married and widowed as well as in the divorced.

OTHER ISSUES

Criticisms of Sociological Research on Suicide

Sociological research into suicide relies heavily upon official statistics of suicidal behavior in the communities studied. Douglas (1967) has attacked the use of these official statistics in a powerful critique. Douglas documented in detail the different ways in which the collection of official statistics leads to errors in the actual number of suicidal deaths reported by a community and how these errors could lead to the observed associations between social variables and suicide rates. His criticisms, if valid, pose problems for the sociological study of suicide.

Douglas noted that in addition to a lack of agreement on the definition of the word suicide, there were two further sources of differences between communities: (a) the objective criteria used to classify a death as suicidal, and (b) the search procedures used to determine whether these criteria are met. For example, one coroner in the United States insisted on the presence of a suicide note with the body before he classified the death as suicidal, although not all suicides leave notes. With regard to the problem of the search procedures, it is obvious that coroners will differ in the number of witnesses that they interview in the course of their decision making, and they may differ in the kind of witnesses that they interview. A minister may give very different information about a man's background than will his estranged wife or his close friend in business.

As an example of the issues raised by Douglas, let us look at the association of Catholicism with low suicide rates. Douglas noted that there may be subcultural differences in the attempts to conceal suicidal deaths. For example, suicide is condemned more severely by Catholics than by Protestants, and so one would expect the reported suicide rate among Catholics to be lower than the reported rates among Protestants because Catholic communities will be more likely to conceal a suicidal death. It is this differential concealment which may result in the observed association between religious affiliation and suicide rates.

Although Douglas made a strong case for the lack of validity of official suicide rates, his arguments would have been more persuasive had he produced research data to support his hypotheses. But he carried out no research to test his hypotheses, and so his arguments remain *not-proven*. There is, however, research which contradicts Douglas's arguments. For example, Sainsbury and Barraclough (1968) noted that the correlation between the suicide rate in 1950 and 1960 in forty countries was 0.95, indicating a great deal of consistency over a ten-year period. Lester (1987) in fact reported a correlation of 0.42 between the suicide rates of fourteen European in 1875 and 1975, a span of one hundred years![4]

Furthermore, Sainsbury and Barraclough (1968) also correlated the suicide rate in eleven countries in 1959 with the suicide rate of the immigrants from those countries in the United States. Since the reporting of suicide rates in the United States should differ considerably from that in the countries from which the immigrants came, the correlation should be low. Although all eleven immigrant groups had higher suicide rates in the United States than the suicide rates of their home countries, the correlation between the two sets of rates was 0.87 (and highly significant). Both Lester (1972) and Sainsbury (1973) found that the suicide rates

[4] The stability of societal suicide rates means that sociologists are studying a *reliable* phenomenon.

of immigrant groups in Australia were also strongly associated with the suicide rates in the home countries.

As for whether differences in the certification in suicides might affect research results, Pescosolido and Mendelsohn (1986) studied the predictors of suicide rates in American counties and found that introducing medical examiner characteristics into the multiple regression equations had minimal impact on the associations between social variables and suicide rates.

Thus, despite the arguments made by Douglas in his critique of official suicide statistics, many sound studies find no evidence of systematic bias in the rates.[5]

The Generalizability of Secular Trends in Suicide

Individual nations are often concerned with recent secular trends in their suicide rate. A rise in the rate (or a fall) suggests the need to examine possible causes for the change, especially if the change occurs in special groups of concern in the population -- the young, aboriginals, or prison inmates, for example. Such papers are usually published in national journals, but have little interest outside of the nation concerned unless the changes can be shown to have some widespread generality.

For example, the rise in American youth suicide rates in the 1970s was widely noted, and Lester (1988c) found that this increase was found in twenty-three nations while only six experienced a decline in youth suicide rate during the same period. In contrast, Huchcroft and Tanney (1989) reported a trend in Canada for the ratio of the male/female suicide rate to increase from 1970 to 1984, but Lester (1990) found this to be so for only seven of the twenty-three nations which he studied. Thus, this secular trend had little generality for nations in general.

It is important, therefore, to explore the degree to which secular trends in suicide have worldwide generality. Once the generality of a trend has been explored, it is of interest and importance to discover why some nations show one trend while other show a different trend. Experience has shown so far that this is a very difficult task.

For example, in his study of changing youth suicide rates in the 1970s, Lester (1988c) found that the increase in the total suicide rates of nations was greater during the 1970s in those nations with higher suicide rates in 1970. This was not, however, true for youth suicide rates. He further found that changes in the youth suicide rates from 1970 to 1980 was not associated with changes in ratings of the quality of life in those nations from 1970 to 1980.

Similarly, while Pritchard (1992) found that elderly suicide rates were rising at a fast rate in many developed nations of the world, Lester (1993) found that the magnitude of these changes was not related to socioeconomic characteristics of the nations such as divorce rates, the percentage of elderly or the gross national product per capita.

The efforts may not, however, be doomed to failure. Sainsbury, et al. (1980) found that the proportion of young people in a nation and the divorce rate were positively associated with changes in the suicide rates of European nations. Similarly, Lester (1989b) found that, while urbanism and religiosity did not predict the suicide rates of industrialized nations in 1970, these social indicators did predict changes in the suicide rates from 1970 to 1980.

---

[5] For a fuller discussion of these issues see Lester (1989a).

Time Series versus Regional Studies

It has been noted that societal variables which are associated with, and which may therefore cause, societal suicide rates appear to differ for regional studies of suicide rates and for time-series studies of suicide rates. For example, while unemployment rates appear to be associated with the suicide rate in the United States over time (Yang and Lester, 1990), they do not appear to be associated with the suicide rates of the states (Lester, 1988a). This raises the possibility that different sociological theories may needed to account for the results of the two types of studies.

Predicting the Smoothed Trend in the Suicide Rate versus Deviations

In time-series studies of the societal suicide rate, the departure from the smoothed trend in the suicide rate is often viewed as "random noise" in the data. Thus, it of interest to ask whether theories which account for the smoothed-trend in the societal suicide rate over time might also account for these fluctuations. Yang and Lester (1990) found in the United States that the unemployment rate predicted both the smoothed trend in the suicide rate and the fluctuations from this trend. In contrast, the divorce rate predicted only the smoothed trend. Again, different sociological theories may be required to account for these two phenomena.

The Ecological Fallacy

There are two major errors commonly made in discussions of the results of sociological research. The first has been called the *ecological fallacy*. Robinson (1958) noted that, if it is found, for example, that the suicide rate is high in the states of America where the proportion of divorced people is high, then it is easy to assume that this association is a consequence of the divorced people in those states killing themselves at a high rate. Although this may true, it is not a necessary consequence of the sociological association. The ecological fallacy occurs when we make generalizations from ecological associations (over regions) and assume that the same association is true for individuals. Associations between variables over individuals have to be tested independently from associations between variables over regions.

A second fallacy which occurs frequently is when researchers assume that the results of correlational studies imply cause-and-effect relationships. Correlational studies, and the majority of sociological research is correlational in nature, do not permit conclusions about cause-and-effect. If variables A and B are found to be associated, then three possibilities exist: (1) A causes B, (2) B causes A, and (3) some third variable, C, causes both A and B which end up associated because of their association with C.

THE IMPACT OF SUICIDE ON THE SOCIETY

The impact of suicide on the society has been rarely studied by scholars, yet suicide must be presumed to have an impact on the society for suicide has often been made illegal (as in the United Kingdom prior to 1961 and in Canada prior to 1972), condemned as immoral and sinful, and been the focus of strenuous prevention efforts. Perhaps in these three areas respectively, suicide is viewed as a negative comment on the state, upon organized religion and on the competence of the mental health profession. In each case suicide undermines the power of the social system (political, religious and mental health).

Many communist nations in the past (including China, East Germany, Romania, and the USSR) refused to report suicide rates, possibly because they felt that suicide was an index of the misery experienced in those societies as a result of the communist dictatorships. Suicide also emphasizes the rights of the individual over those of the larger society, and many societies have asserted that the lives of its citizens belong to the state. Even the humanitarian trend in the Netherlands recently for providing a mechanism for citizens to apply for assisted-suicide can also be seen as a way for the state to regain control over the decision of people to commit suicide.

Viewed as an index of misery, suicide serves to draw attention to the social ills affecting a group, whether it be the youth, native Americans and other aboriginal groups, or the elderly. In addition, suicide, like all deviant behaviors, serves to define normality for the society.

There have been occasional suggestions by others for the impact of suicide on society. For example, suicide has an economic impact on the society, and this issue is reviewed in Chapter 9. Other possible impacts are discussed in the following sections.

Population Longevity

Waigandt and Phelps (1990) noted that 51,147 people died from suicide and homicide in the United States in 1980. They calculated that this reduced the life expectancy of men by 0.705 years and of women by 0.261 years. A total of 1,305,805 person years per decade are irretrievably lost from suicide and homicide. Waigandt and Phelps did not calculate these figures separately for suicide.

The Centers for Disease Control (1984) calculated that suicide accounted for 645,680 years of potential life lost in 1984, with seventy one percent of the total attributable to suicide among white males. Homicide accounted for an additional 609,678 years of potential life lost.

Suicide and Political Protest

Occasional suicides have an impact on society because of the political motivation behind the death. For example, the Buddhist monk, Thich Quang Duc, immolated himself in Saigon on June 11, 1963, as a protest against the regime of Ngo Dinh Diem in South Vietnam, following which other people immolated themselves in Vietnam, the United States and elsewhere to protest the political situation in Vietnam (Coleman, 1987). It is difficult to assess the impact of such acts quantitatively, and they are quite rare.

Societal Approval of Suicide

Schelling (1978), an economist, has noted that people's behavior often depends upon how many other people are behaving in the same way. An activity becomes self-sustaining (and may increase in incidence) once the frequency of that activity increases beyond a certain level. If this idea is applied to national suicide rates, it can be hypothesized that a given suicide rate creates a certain amount of publicity about suicide and a particular likelihood that a person in the society knows someone who has committed suicide. Once the suicide rate reaches a critical level, the publicity and probability of knowing suicides increase to such an extent that the effect of suggestion (or imitation) makes the behavior self-sustaining, and perhaps accelerates it, and may also increase the society's tolerance for and approval of suicide.

Lester (1989a) had conducted several tests of this hypothesis and shown that, both for nations of the world and for the states of America, those regions in 1970 with higher suicide rates experienced greater absolute increases in the suicide rate by 1980. However, Lester (1995) found that the nations with the *lower* suicide rates in 1980 experienced the larger increases during the 1980s, opposite to his finding for the 1970s.

Celebrity Suicides Leading to Further Suicides

Related to this last point, Phillips (1974) and Stack (1990) have documented that suicides reported by the media, especially of celebrities, are followed in the next week by an increase in the suicide rate, especially among those similar in age and sex to the celebrity suicide. The existence of suicide clusters (Coleman, 1987) illustrates a similar suggestion effect. Thus, it appears that a suicide stimulates, and perhaps creates, more suicides.

What is the Function of Suicide for Society?

In his discussion of crime, Durkheim (1895) argued that crime was necessary. It was linked to the basic conditions of social life. If one form of crime disappeared, other forms would develop to fill the void. If serious crimes were to be viewed sternly by society, they may be reduced in frequency. But the stern values would then lead people to view the hitherto minor crimes more seriously, making them now major crimes.

Durkheim also noted that not everyone in a society shares the same moral values, and so some people will always offend against the moral and legal rules of the society. Furthermore, some behaviors which were once labelled as criminal later prove to be important for the society. Today's traitors may be tomorrow's heroes, today's terrorists tomorrow's rulers.

What then might the social function of suicide be? To date, this question has not been addressed. Lester (1988b; see also Chapter 3) has explored this question at the biological level, suggesting that suicide may function to remove the genes of defective people (those who are psychiatrically disturbed, for example) and those past child-bearing age from the society and may also serve to reduce the size of the population. But we have little to suggest for the *social* function of suicide.

Is There a Natural Suicide Rate?

If crime serves a function for society, this raises the question of whether suicide is normal in the sense that it is impossible for a society to be free from suicide.

Lester and Yang (1997) mathematically analyzed theories of the relationship between economic conditions (x) and the suicide rate (y) and concluded that all theories predict that the curve has a positive intercept on the y-axis during normal economic conditions and that, therefore, there is an inevitable non-zero suicide rate for every society, the "natural" suicide rate of the society.

Durkheim's theory of suicide implies a non-zero suicide rate for societies since he argued that suicide was more likely at both high and low levels of social integration and social regulation. A moderate level of social integration and social regulation would not necessarily result in an absence of suicide. Maris (1981) also suggested that no society could be free from suicide because of the inherent harshness of the human condition.

Yang and Lester (1991) tested this idea by examining several multiple regression analyses in which the suicide rates of the states of America in 1980 were regressed on several sets of socioeconomic variables. Setting the socioeconomic variables to zero (that is, for example, a zero divorce rate and a zero unemployment rate) still left the suicide rate as non-zero and positive. They concluded that if social conditions were made ideal from the point of view of producing a low suicide rate, the suicide rate of Americans would still be non-zero and positive.

SUMMARY

In this brief chapter, we have introduced the major sociological theories of suicide, and we have highlighted several issues which merit thought and research in the future. Can we identify and show the impact of broad societal characteristics on suicide? Are different theories required for the regional variation in suicide rates and for the variation of societal suicide rates over time; and in time-series studies, are different theories required for predicting the smoothed trend and for predicting fluctuations from this trend?

We have also tried to identify some ways in which suicide might impact upon a society. We noted the economic costs of suicide and the impact of suicide on life-expectancy, and we also mentioned the possible impact of political suicides on the society. We also asked two questions which we hope will stimulate sociological research: what is the social function of suicide for a society and could there be a natural (non-zero) suicide rate for societies?

REFERENCES

Barrett, D. B. *World Christian Encyclopedia*. Nairobi: Oxford University Press, 1982.

Breault, K. D. Suicide in America. *American Journal of Sociology*, 1986, 92, 628-656.

Cavan, R. S. *Suicide*. Chicago: University of Chicago, 1928.

Centers for Disease Control. Premature mortality due to suicide and homicide. *Morbidity & Mortality Weekly Report*, 1987, 36(32), 531-534.

Coleman, L. *Suicide clusters*. Boston: Faber & Faber, 1987.

Dollard, J., Doob, L., Miller, N., Mowrer, O., & Sears, R. *Frustration and aggression*. New Haven: Yale University Press, 1939.

Douglas, J. D. *The social meanings of suicide*. Princeton: Princeton University Press, 1967.

Durkheim, E. *Les règles de la méthode sociologique*. Paris: Felix Alcan, 1895.

______. *Le suicide*. Paris: Felix Alcan, 1897.

Faber, M. D. *Suicide and Greek tragedy*. New York: Sphinx, 1970.

Gibbs, J. P., & Martin, W. T. *Status integration and suicide*. Eugene, OR: University of Oregon, 1964.

Gold, M. Suicide, homicide, and the socialization of aggression. *American Journal of Sociology*, 1958, 63, 651-661.

Henry, A. F., & Short, J. F. *Suicide and homicide*. New York: Free Press, 1954.

Hess, B. B., Markson, E. W., & Stein, P. J. *Sociology*. New York: Macmillan, 1982.

Huchcroft, S. A., & Tanney, B. L. Sex-specific suicide trends in suicide method. *Canadian Journal of Public Health*, 1989, 80, 120-123.

Johnson, B. D. Durkheim's one cause of suicide. *American Sociological Review*, 1965, 30, 875-886.

Lester, D. Suicide and homicide in open and closed societies. *Psychological Reports*, 1971, 29, 430.

Lester, D. Migration and suicide. *Medical Journal of Australia*, 1972, 1, 941-942.

_____ . Murder and suicide: are they polar opposites? *Behavioral Sciences & the Law*, 1987, 5, 49-60.

_____ . A regional analysis of suicide and homicide rates in the USA. *Social Psychiatry & Psychiatric Epidemiology*, 1988a, 23, 202-205.

_____ . *The biochemical basis of suicide*. Springfield IL: Charles Thomas, 1988b.

_____ . Youth suicide. *Adolescence*, 1988c, 23, 955-958.

_____ . *Suicide from a sociological perspective*. Springfield, IL: Charles Thomas, 1989a.

_____ . National suicide and homicide rates. *Social Science & Medicine*, 1989b, 29, 1249-1252.

_____ . Changes to suicide rates unique to Canada? *Canadian Journal of Public Health*, 1990, 81, 240-241.

_____ . *Why people kill themselves*. Springfield, IL: Charles Thomas, 1992.

_____ . Attempts to explain changing elderly suicide rates. *International Journal of Geriatric Psychiatry*, 1993, 8, 435-437.

_____ . *Patterns of suicide and homicide in America*. Commack, NY: Nova Science, 1994a.

_____ . Applying Durkheim's typology to individual suicides. In D. Lester (Ed.) *Durkheim's Le Suicide 100 hundred years later*, pp. 224-236. Philadelphia: Charles Press, 1994b.

_____ . Changes in national suicide rates, 1980-1990. *Psychological Reports*, 1995, 77, 906.

Lester, D., & Yang, B. Microsocionomics versus macrosocionomics as a model for examining suicide. *Psychological Reports*, 1991, 69, 735-738.

Lester, D., & Yang, D. *The economy and suicide*. Commack, NY: Nova Science, 1997.

Maris, R. W. *Social forces in urban suicide*. Homewood, IL: Dorsey, 1969.

_____ . *Pathways to suicide*. Baltimore: Johns Hopkins University, 1981.

McCulloch, J. W., & Philip, A. E. *Suicidal behavior*. Elmsford, NY: Pergamon, 1972.

Moksony, F. Ecological analysis of suicide. In D. Lester (Ed.) *Understanding suicide*, pp. 121-138. Philadelphia: Charles Press, 1990.

Pescosolido, B. A., & Mendelsohn, R. Social causation or social construction of suicide? *American Sociological Review*, 1986, 51, 80-101.

Phillips, D. P. The influence of suggestion on suicide. *American Sociological Review*, 1974, 39, 340-354.

Pokorny, A. Human violence. *Journal of Criminal Law, Criminology & Police Science*, 1965, 56, 488-497.

Pritchard, C. Changes in elderly suicides in the USA and the developed world 1974-87. *International Journal of Geriatric Psychiatry*, 1992, 7, 125-134.

Robinson, W. S. Ecological correlations and the behavior of individuals. *American Sociological Review*, 1958, 15, 351-357.

Sainsbury, P. Suicide. *Proceedings of the Royal Society of Medicine*, 1973, 66, 579-587.

Sainsbury, P., & Barraclough, B. M. Differences between suicide rates. *Nature*, 1968, 220, 1252.

Sainsbury, P., Jenkins, J., & Levey, A. The social correlates of suicide in Europe. In R. Farmer & S. Hirsch (Eds.) *The suicide syndrome*, pp. 38-53. London, UK: Croom Helm, 1980.

Schelling, T. C. *Micromotives and macrobehavior*. New York: Norton, 1978.

Schmid, C. F. *Suicides in Seattle, 1914-1925*. Seattle: University of Washington, 1928.

Stack, S. Media impacts on suicide. In D. Lester (Ed.) *Current concepts of suicide*, pp. 107-120. Philadelphia: Charles Press, 1990.

Taylor, C. L., & Jodice, D. A. *World handbook of political and social indicators*. New Haven: Yale University, 1983.

Taylor, S. Suicide, Durkheim and sociology. In D. Lester (Ed.) *Understanding suicide*, pp. 225-236. Philadelphia: Charles Press, 1990.

United Nations. *Demographic yearbook*. New York: United Nations, 1986.

Waigandt, A., & Phelps, L. The effects of homicides and suicides on the population longevity of the United States. *Journal of Traumatic Stress*, 1990, 3, 297-304.

Yang, B., & Lester, D. Time-series analyses of the American suicide rate. *Social Psychiatry & Psychiatric Epidemiology*, 1990, 25, 274-275.

Yang, B., & Lester, D. Is there a natural suicide rate for a society? *Psychological Reports*, 1991, 68, 322.

Chapter 7

ANTHROPOLOGY AND SUICIDE

INTRODUCTION

Anthropology has been defined as "the study of humankind everywhere" (Haviland, 1993), and most anthropologists admit that anthropology is a diverse field, difficult to define precisely. In general, "culture" is the focus of study, but the term "culture" is also hard to define. Haviland (1993, p. 30) has defined it as "a set of rules or standards shared by members of a society, which, when acted upon by the members, produce behavior that falls within a range of variation the members consider proper and acceptable."

There are, however, several clearly defined fields within anthropology. *Physical anthropology* is concerned with the differences in physical and physiological traits between people from different cultures and with the evolution of humans. *Cultural anthropology* explores the cultures that people establish, that is, the standards and norms for behavior and the customs that guide the behavior in the culture. One branch of cultural anthropology, *archeology*, studies the material remains of cultures in order to gain clues as to how ancient civilizations lived. Another branch, *linguistic anthropology*, studies the languages that different cultures employ. Finally, *ethnography* focuses on the study of present-day cultures by means of first-hand observation. Physical anthropology, archeology and linguistic anthropology have little to say about suicidal behavior; ethnography is the field which has insights to offer about suicidal behavior.

Besides these attempts at formal definitions, ethnography has been characterized by the study of primitive societies (sometimes called nonliterate societies) in which the anthropologist becomes a participant observer in the culture. In contrast, sociology involves the study of modern societies in recent times, usually with quantitative data and well-designed research methodology. In recent years, however, the distinction between these two disciplines has become blurred. Anthropologists have applied their techniques of study to cultural (and subcultural) customs in modern societies, and they have introduced quantitative techniques, usually based on formal codings of aspects of culture and behavior in samples of primitive societies. Sociologists, on the other hand, have acted as participant observers, a field that has come to be called ethnomethodology.

The aim of this chapter is to present an overview of some of the topics and issues which are present in the interaction of suicide and culture. A major dichotomy here, of course, is the level of analysis. The interaction can be explored for the aggregate suicide rate of a culture and for the individual suicide living in a particular society or culture. Let us first look at the interaction at the aggregate level.

SOCIETAL AND CULTURAL SUICIDE RATES

It is an obvious fact that societal suicide rates differ widely. In a data set of world suicide rates for 1979-1981 (Lester, 1996), the range of suicide rates was from 0.1 (per 100,000 per year) in Egypt to 45.0 in Hungary. Suicide rates also vary widely over the different geographic regions of a nation (for example, over American states and Canadian provinces, suicide rates increase toward the west [Lester, 1985]) and over the different social groups within a nation (for example, some groups of both native Americans and native Canadians have very high suicide rates). Although societies or nations are not necessarily homogeneous cultures, the members of different nations often do differ culturally, hard though it may be to define precisely in which ways.

An obvious explanation of such variations in the aggregate suicide rate is that the reporting and counting of suicides in different nations and cultures differs greatly in accuracy (Douglas, 1967). Indeed, it has been easy to document serious official under-reporting of suicides, for example, in Newfoundland (Malla and Hoenig, 1983) and for Native Americans in Alaska (Hlady and Middaugh, 1988).

Nevertheless, it is very unlikely that completely accurate reporting of suicides would eliminate the national and cultural differences. For example, Sainsbury and Barraclough (1968) for the United States and Lester (1972) for Australia have shown that the suicide rates for immigrant groups to those nations are in the same rank order as (though higher than) the suicide rates in the home nations. Hungarians have one of the highest suicide rates in the world, both in Hungary and after emigration to the United States.

Different cultural groups differ, of course, in social and cultural habits, beliefs, customs and practices. However, before exploring these a little, we must remember also that cultural groups may also differ physiologically. There is some evidence, for example, that the suicide rates of nations are associated with the proportion of people with Type O blood (Lester, 1987a) and that the suicide rates of cultures are associated with the degree of ectomorphy (thinness) of the members (Lester, 1981).

However, typically researchers look for social and cultural characteristics which might explain the differences in social and cultural suicide rates. Although the culture may affect the incidence of suicide, the circumstances and the methods, the extent of the societal disapproval of suicide and the reasons and meaning of suicide, most researchers have focussed on the association between culture and the incidence of suicide. For example, Conklin and Simpson (1987) found that Islam and economic under-development were associated with lower suicide rates among nations of the world.

As mentioned above, culture can also affect the methods chosen for suicide. DeCatanzaro (1981) noted that it easy to find culturally unique methods for suicide, such as hanging by tying a noose around one's neck and running to another part of the house in Tikopia. *Suttee* (suicide by burning on the husband's funeral pyre) in India and *seppuku* (ritual disembowelment, followed by beheading by an assistant) in Japan are famous examples of culturally determined methods (with culturally determined motives as well) for suicide.

Firearms are the most common method for suicide in the United States and Canada presently, while in Switzerland (whose residents typically own firearms) hanging is the most common method for suicide (Lester, 1990). Indeed, a method may come to symbolize the act of suicide, as in England earlier this century when "to take the pipe" meant to commit suicide. Burvill, et al. (1983) have shown that immigrants to a nation gradually shift to the methods of suicide used in their new culture.

SUICIDE IN ONE CULTURE: THE CHINESE

Studies by Lester on suicidal behavior in Chinese illustrates the role of culture, a culture of particular interest because the Chinese are native to many nations (such as mainland China and Hong Kong) and have emigrated in large numbers to nations such as America.

The suicide rates of Asian Americans are relatively low compared to whites in the United States. For example, in 1980, the suicide rates were 13.3 per 100,000 per year for Native Americans, 13.2 for white Americans, 9.1 for Japanese Americans, 8.3 for Chinese Americans, 6.1 for African Americans and 3.5 for Filipino Americans (Lester, 1994a).

Lester noted that the patterns of suicide also differed for these ethnic groups. The ratio of the male to female suicide rates was much larger for whites and African Americans than for Asian Americans and, whereas suicide rates increased with age for Asian Americans, the suicide rates peaked in young adulthood for African Americans and Native Americans. Asian Americans used hanging for suicide much more often that whites and African Americans, and they used firearms relatively less often.

Lester concluded that the epidemiology of suicide in Asian Americans in America showed similarities to the results of epidemiological studies of suicide in their home nations, indicating that cultural factors have an important influence on the circumstances of suicidal behavior.

Lester (1994b) then examined the epidemiology of suicide in Chinese in Hong Kong, Singapore, Taiwan, mainland China, Hawaii and the United States as a whole. A couple of examples here will illustrate the results. The ratio of the male to female suicide rates in 1980 were 1.2 for Chinese Americans, 1.2 for Hong Kong residents, 1.2 for Taiwanese residents and 1.2 for Singapore Chinese, identical gender ratios. Suicide rates peaked in the elderly in all the nations: for those 65 and older in Chinese Americans, 75 and older in Hong Kong and Taiwan and 70 and older in Singapore Chinese.[1]

As suggested by Burvill, et al. (1983), the methods used for suicide did differ for the different groups of Chinese: jumping was more common in the Chinese in Singapore and Hong Kong, hanging in Chinese Americans and poisons in Taiwan, probably a result of the difference between the nations in the availability of methods for suicide. For example, Lester (1994c) showed that the used of jumping for suicide in Singapore was strongly associated with the development of high rise apartments. Furthermore, the suicide rates differed: in 1980 the suicide rates were 13.5 in Singapore and Hong Kong Chinese, 10.0 in Taiwan and 8.3 for Chinese Americans.

[1] The nations used different classifications by age.

Thus, gender and age patterns in Chinese suicide seem to be affected strongly by culture, while the absolute suicide rates and methods used are affected by the nation in which the Chinese dwell.

Culture, Linguistics and Suicide

As Douglas (1967) pointed out, a shared linguistic terminology for suicidal behavior is associated with shared meanings of the behavior, and there are also shared associated terms and phrases, such as despair, hopelessness, and "life isn't worth living." Douglas emphasized that these terms are not the phenomenon itself but rather are adopted by members of the culture (or subculture) to construct meanings for suicidal behavior. However, since the terms are rarely clearly defined or detailed and since there is often disagreement among commentators on their meaning, it follows that the meaning of suicide is ambiguous. Furthermore, since the terms are used to construct meanings for suicidal behavior, then estimates of the incidence and circumstances of suicidal behavior are in part a social construction.

For example, according to the Mohave, a Native American tribe in the southwest of the United States, a fetus which presents itself in the transverse position for birth, leading to its own death and that of its mother, is viewed as having intended to commit suicide and to murder its mother so that they can be together in the spirit world (Devereux, 1961). Medical examiners and coroners in the rest of the United States would not view such a still-born infant as a suicide.

Counts (1980), who has studied the suicidal behavior of women in the Kaliai district of Papua New Guinea, noted that in the past elderly widows sometimes immolated themselves on their husband's funeral pyre. The German and Australian colonial governors considered this behavior to be a form of ritual murder rather than suicide, and they outlawed it. Counts, however, saw neither term (suicide or murder) as appropriate for this custom since it differed so much from what North Americans and Europeans regard as either suicide or murder. Neither term describes the behavior, the interpersonal relationships involved, or the attitudes toward the widow and those assisting in her death, nor do they predict how the community will respond to her death.

Recently, some scholars, especially in Europe, have expressed doubts that people engaging in nonfatal suicidal behavior have self-destruction as their aim, and they have moved to calling the behavior "self-poisoning" or "self-injury" (e.g., Ramon, 1980). The semantic implication is that nonfatal suicidal behavior is not "suicide." Since in most cultures women engage in more nonfatal suicidal actions than do men, this renaming of nonfatal suicidal behavior as self-injury makes "suicidal behavior" less common in women than it was hitherto.

Other suicidologists, on the other hand, include a wider range of behaviors under the rubric of "suicidal behavior." For example, Menninger (1938) classified such behaviors as alcoholism, drug abuse and anorexia as *chronic suicide* since such individuals were shortening their lives by their behaviors. Menninger also classified such behaviors such as polysurgery, self-castration, and self-mutilation as *focal suicide*, in which the self-destructive impulse is focused on one part of the body. These behaviors are often gender-linked. For example, anorexia is more common in women whereas illicit drug abuse is more common in men. Canetto (1991) has speculated that adolescents may respond differentially when under stress, with girls choosing nonfatal suicidal behavior more while boys choose drug abuse more. The use of Menninger's categories would change greatly the relative incidence of nonfatal suicidal behavior in women and men.

CULTURE AND THE INDIVIDUAL SUICIDE

Culture can obviously affect the suicidal behavior of its individual members. The reasons for committing suicide and the circumstances can be determined by the culture. The best documentation of this comes from the few anthropologists who have studied suicide. For example, Firth (1961) documented that the traditional method for suicide in Tikopia was swimming out to sea and drowning, with the timing of the act chosen so as to minimize, maximize or leave to chance the prospects of rescue.

Suicidal behavior may be quite differently determined and have different meanings in different cultures. The classic comparative study which demonstrated this was Hendin's (1964) study of suicide in Scandinavia. In Denmark, Hendin noted that guilt arousal was a major discipline technique used by Danish mothers, especially to control aggression, resulting in extremely strong dependency in their sons. This marked dependency was the root of depression and suicidality after adult experiences of loss or separation, and reunion fantasies were common in suicides.

In Sweden, there was a strong emphasis on performance and success by parents, resulting in ambitious children for whom work was central to their lives. Suicide typically followed failure in performance which had damaged the men's self-esteem. In Norway where, when Hendin conducted his study, the suicide rate was much lower than the rates in Denmark and Sweden. Hendin found a strong dependency of the sons on their mothers, but Norwegian children were less passive and more aggressive than Danish children. Alcohol abuse was more common, and Norwegian men were more open about their feelings -- able to laugh at themselves and cry more openly. Norwegian boys please their mothers by causing no trouble, and they do not worry unduly about failure, typically blaming others and retreating into alcohol abuse.

Counts (1988) illustrates the ways in which a culture can determine the meaning of the individual suicidal act in her account of suicide among females in Papua-New Guinea where female suicide is a culturally-recognized way of imposing social sanctions, with political implications for the surviving kin and for those held responsible for the events driving the woman to suicide. In one instance, the suicide of a rejected fiancée led to sanctions being imposed on the family which had rejected her. Counts noted that the woman's suicide was a political act which took her from a position of powerlessness to one of power.

Closer to home, it has been argued that part of the explanation for the low suicide rate in African Americans as compared to white Americans is that suicide is a less acceptable behavior for African Americans. Homicide rates are much higher in African Americans, both as murderers and as victims, and a large proportion of murders are victim-precipitated, that is, the victims played some role (conscious or unconscious) in precipitating their own demise. Perhaps African American culture deems a victim-precipitated murder as a more acceptable method of dying than suicide?

Subcultures

It is also well-known that subcultures exist within a dominant culture. The southern states of the United States have been said to have a "southern subculture" (Gastil, 1971). Wolfgang and Ferracuti (1969) have argued that some groups have a "subculture of violence." Lester (1987b) has applied this concept to suicide by examining possible subcultural factors in teenage suicide.

Cultural Anthropology's Role in Challenging Myths

Many theories of human behavior, including suicidal behavior, are based on physiological factors. For example, the role of estrogen in attempted suicide is sometimes stressed since the incidence of attempted suicide of women does appear to vary over the menstrual cycle. Cultural anthropology helps challenge such theories by showing, for example, that behaviors which we consider gender-specific are not found in every culture. As we have noted above, in the United States and in European nations, nonfatal suicidal behavior appears to occur at a higher rate in women than in men; as a result it is has come to be viewed as a "feminine" behavior by the general public (Linehan, 1973) and by suicidologists as well. Other cultures, however, provide examples where nonfatal suicidal behavior, often carried out in front of others, is more common in men rather than women. The Nahane (or Kaska), a Native Canadian tribe located in British Columbia and the Yukon, provide a good example of this.

> .....observations and communications agree that attempted suicide by men is of frequent occurrence and very likely to appear during intoxication. There is a general pattern for such attempted self-destruction. In the two cases of the sort observed during field work, the weapon selected was a rifle. As he brandishes the weapon the would be suicide announces his intention in an emotional outburst. This becomes the signal for interference to block the deed. One or more men leap forward to wrest the gun from the intended suicide's possession and toss it out of sight. The would be victim is now usually emotionally overwhelmed by his behavior. This pattern is illustrated by Louis Maza's behavior during intoxication. Several times during the afternoon, Louis had manifested aggression toward himself, crying: "I don't care if I'm killed. I don't care my life." After several hours of such emotional outbursts interspersed with quarreling and aggression toward his companions, he seized his large caliber rifle and threatened to kill himself. Old Man threw himself on the gun and as the two men grappled for the weapon, Louis succeeded in firing one wild shot. John Kean and the ethnographer ran to the camp and together wrenched the gun from the drunken man. John fired the shells in the chamber and Old Man tossed the gun half-way down the cutbank. No punishment or other discrimination is reserved for attempted suicides. The individual is comforted and in the future, while intoxicated, he is watched lest he repeat the attempt. (Honigmann, 1949, p. 204)

Among the Washo, located in Nevada and California, nonfatal suicidal behavior seems to be equally common in men and women.

> In one case, a man had been having difficulty with his wife; she was interested in another man. The husband ate wild parsnip, but was saved. As a result his sons brought pressure

> on the wife and made her behave. The couple stayed together until the husband died.....Pete also says that men attempt suicide more than women, who just leave home when interpersonal difficulties arise. The destruction of the self is an ultimate, and the fact that men are more likely to invoke it than women indicates a lack of male authority in Washo culture. (D'Azevedo, et al., 1963, p. 50-51)

The Washo man is described as lacking authority and lacking in self-confidence, perhaps because the Washo man has had more difficulty adapting to the changing culture in this century than has the Washo woman. Interestingly, the explanation provided by these Western anthropologists for the occurrence of nonfatal suicidal behavior among Washo men may be generalizable to societies where nonfatal suicidal behavior is more common in women. It may be that nonfatal suicidal behavior is not simply a "feminine" behavior, but rather a behavior found more commonly in those who are oppressed in a society, perhaps because the oppressed have fewer options for expressing their discontent.

Culture Conflict

Cultures often come into conflict. For example, the conflict between the traditional Native American culture and the dominant American culture has often been viewed as providing a major role in precipitating Native American suicide. May and Dizmang (1974) noted that there were three major sociological theories which have been proposed for explaining the Native American suicide rate. One theory focuses on *social disorganization*. The dominance of the Anglo-American culture has forced Native American culture to change and has eroded traditional cultural systems and values. This changes the level of social regulation and social integration, important causal factors for suicide in Durkheim's (1897) theory of suicide.

A second theory focuses on *cultural conflict* itself. The pressure, especially from the educational system and mass media, on Native Americans, especially the youth, to acculturate, a pressure which is opposed by their elders, leads to great stress for the youths.

A third theory focuses on the *breakdown of the family* in Native American tribes. Parents are often unemployed, substance abusers and in trouble with the law, and divorce and desertion of the family by one or more parents is common.

Acculturation occurs when a culture encounters a dominant alternative culture. The resulting pressure from the dominant culture leads to a variety of changes in the non-dominant culture (Berry, 1990): physical changes (such as type of housing, urbanization and increasing population density), biological changes (resulting from changing diet and exposure to new diseases), political changes (such as loss of autonomy for the non-dominant culture), economic changes (such as changes in type of employment), cultural changes (in language, religion, education and the arts), social relationships (both within the culture and between the two cultures), and psychological changes at the individual level (in behavior, values, attitudes and motives).

Berry noted that four possibilities are open to the non-dominant culture: *integration* -- maintaining relations with the dominant culture while maintaining cultural identity; *assimilation* -- maintaining relations with the dominant culture but not maintaining cultural identity; *separation* -- not maintaining relations with the dominant culture but maintaining cultural identity; and *marginalization* -- not maintaining relations with the dominant culture and not maintaining cultural identity.

It would be of great interest to categorize the different Native American tribes as to which strategy appears to have been chosen and to examine the different consequences for the society and for the individuals in the society.

Does Cultural Conflict Cause Suicide?

Although the problem of acculturation has been proposed as one of the major causes of depression and suicidal behavior among Native Americans, the majority of research reports on Native American individuals who attempt or complete suicide mention precipitating causes such as grief over loss and quarrels with relatives and friends. Rarely is cultural conflict listed among the precipitating causes. Of course, it may be that the problems of acculturation raise the stress level of individuals so much that stressors, which under ordinary circumstances would not precipitate suicide, now do so.

A few brief case histories have been published which illustrate the problems of acculturation and culture conflict. For example, Berlin (1986) described the case of a bright young Native American woman who completed undergraduate school and qualified as a teacher and who was admitted to graduate school. Her clan, however, told her that she was required to teach on the reservation. Her desire to go to graduate school was seen as striving to be better than her peers, and this was unacceptable and forbidden. The young women had a psychiatric breakdown and was hospitalized. In a similar situation, the tribe and another family could not decide whether to let a young woman go to graduate school for an MBA after she obtained her undergraduate degree and, during the long wait for a decision, she attempted suicide.

In this latter case, the young woman, whom Berlin called Josie, had alcoholic parents who frequently sent her and her brothers and sisters to live with relatives while they went on drinking sprees. A teacher realized Josie's potential and received permission for Josie to live with her. With this teacher's help, her academic performance improved, and she went to college. Josie now resented that her parents who had neglected her were involved in decisions about her life. The clan leadership and tribal council were relatively enlightened about the issues and eventually gave permission for Josie to attend graduate school. While at graduate school, Josie underwent psychotherapy to deal with her depression and anger and other personal problems. After graduation, she returned to the tribe to manage their business office, marrying a young man who had fought a similar battle in order to obtain an MSW degree.

On the other hand, Westermeyer (1979) provided cases of Native Americans seen at the University of Minnesota Hospitals for whom trying to live in the mainstream American culture had presented problems. Westermeyer felt that identity problems were perhaps no more common in Native Americans than in whites, but that Native Americans did show a unique type of identity problem, namely, ambivalent or negative feelings about their ethnic identity. Westermeyer presented cases of urban Native Americans who illustrate this problem.

Five of the patients, ranging in age from 12 to 23, had identity crises -- they experienced conflict about their Native American identity and about what being "Indian" meant. All were students and economically dependent upon others. For example, one young girl, who was seen after a suicide attempt, had her Indian mother die two years earlier. She then lived with her white father and six siblings for a year. The father had trouble supporting them and sent the children to live with their Indian maternal grandmother. The patient began to use drugs and to have problems with her white teachers at school. Eventually a white welfare worker sent her to a white foster home, at which point she attempted suicide. In the hospital, she said, "I'm the only Indian here and I hate everybody like they hate me." She had a recurrent dream in which she gave birth to baby girl with blue eyes which she loved but which she also wanted to injure.

Five of the cases were judged to have a negative identity. These were older than the patients with identity crises, and all were male. They were estranged from their Indian family members, and they lived as lower class individuals on the periphery of the white society. One patient was admitted with hallucinations and paranoid delusions after a drinking binge. He had a record of multiple psychiatric admissions. Although he supported the idea of Indian activism, he felt estranged from Indians, had little respect for them and avoided them. He had joined a Jewish student activist group which he admired, and he wondered whether his Indian tribe might be a lost tribe of Israel. He identified himself as a Zionist.

Research on Acculturation

Bagley (1991) looked at the suicide rate of Canadian Indian males aged 15 to 34 on the 26 most populated reservations in Alberta, Canada, and found that the more isolated reservations had the higher suicide rates. In contrast, Garro (1988) found that the suicide rates in the more isolated communities in Manitoba were lower than in the more accessible communities. Thus, these Canadian results appear to be in conflict.

Bachman (1992) examined the correlates of the suicide rate in 120 counties in the United States which are partially or totally located on reservation land and found that economic deprivation, rather than acculturation, seemed to be the strongest correlate of Native American suicide rates.

Supportive results for the influence of acculturation on suicide in Native Americans comes from Van Winkle and May (1986) who examined suicide rates in three groups of Native Americans in New Mexico (the Apache, Navajo and Pueblo) and attempted to account for the differences in terms of the degree of acculturation. Overall, the crude suicide rates were 43.3 per 100,000 for the Apache, 27.8 for the Pueblo, and 12.0 for the Navajo.

The Jicarilla and Mescalero Apache of New Mexico were originally nomadic hunters and gatherers, organized into self-sufficient bands whose leaders held limited power. Their religion had no organized priesthood and was not a cohesive force in their lives. Individualism was a highly valued characteristic. Today they live in homes scattered about the reservation or in border towns. They raise livestock, cut timber or work in tribally-owned businesses. Formal tribal governments have been established, but religion remains unimportant. Individualism is still valued. However, the raiding parties which formerly provided a some degree of social integration have been eliminated. The Apache appear, therefore, to have few integrating forces in their culture, and Van Winkle and May saw their high suicide rate as a direct result of this lack of integration.

The Apache have been in close contact with whites. Their reservations are small and surrounded by white communities. Indeed many Apache live in mixed communities. Thus, the Apache have high acculturation in addition to their low social integration.

The Pueblo traditionally lived in compact towns and engaged in agriculture. Religion permeated their lives and was a strong integrating force. There was an organized priesthood and religious societies which took care of religious and civil matters. Individualism was discouraged and conformity valued. Thus, the Pueblo were the most integrated group, and Van Winkle and May found their intermediate suicide rate a puzzle. They tried to explain the Pueblo suicide rate using the role of acculturation. The Pueblo have had increasing contact with whites since 1959. Many of the Pueblos are near large cities such as Albuquerque and Santa Fe. Thus, they have high social integration and moderate but increasing acculturation. For the larger Pueblo tribes, Van Winkle and May compared the suicide rates of those tribes which had acculturated and those which had remained traditional and found a clear tendency for the acculturated and transitional tribes to have the higher suicide rates.

The Navajo, who have the lowest suicide rate, were nomadic hunters and gatherers who later settled down and turned to agriculture. They are organized into bands, but matrilineal clans exert a strong influence. Although religion is important in their lives, they have no organized priesthood. Individualism is valued but not as strongly as among the Apache. Thus, their social integration appears to be intermediate between that of the Apache and that of the Pueblo. However, the Navajo were the most geographically and socially isolated from whites of the three groups until the 1970s when mineral exploration increased on their reservations and some Navajo began to take wage-earning jobs.

Van Winkle and May's explanation of the suicide rates in the three groups can be summarized as follows:

	Social integration	**Acculturation**	**Suicide rate**
Apache	low	high	high
Pueblo	high	moderate	moderate
Navajo	moderate	low	low

It can be seen that acculturation performed better than social integration as an explanation of the differing suicide rates in these three tribes.

The Assumption of Cultural Invariability

Investigators often imply that a research result found in one culture will apply to other cultures. It is, therefore, important to replicate research findings in cultures other than the one in which the results were first obtained. For example, in a comparison of depression and suicide in mainland China and the United States, Chiles, et al. (1990) found that suicidal intent was predicted better by depression for Chinese psychiatric patients and better by hopelessness for American psychiatric patients. The American patients had considered suicide at an earlier age, made more prior suicide attempts, more often communicated their suicidal intent and more often viewed suicide as an effective solution to their problems.

It is important for researchers to identify which findings have cross-cultural generality (and to which cultures) and which are specific to one culture.

Suicide as a Measure of the Quality of Cultures

Naroll (1963, 1969) noted that classical Nineteenth Century ethnologists occasionally evaluated the quality of primitive cultures based on their own personal set of values. Naroll suggested instead that evaluations of cultures could be made indirectly by observing the behaviors of the cultures and that suicidal behavior might be one such yardstick. From this perspective, cultures with a high suicide rate are inferior to those with a low suicide rate.

This is a common practice today. For example, the rising rate of suicide among the youth of the world in the 1970s was seen by many as an indication that the quality of life of the youth had deteriorated (e.g., Eckersley, 1993).

However, Lester (1995) noted that his research indicated that the suicide rate was higher in modern nations with a higher quality of life (as measured objectively based on a number of social indicators), and thus suicide may instead be a measure of the psychological *health* of a society.

An Anthropological Theory of Suicide

Although many anthropologists have, of course, discussed suicide in the societies which they have studied, only one anthropologist has proposed a general theory of suicide. Naroll (1963, 1969) proposed that suicide was more likely in those who were *socially disoriented*, that is, in those who lack or lose basic social ties (such as those who are single or divorced). Since not all socially disoriented people commit suicide, there must be a psychological factor which makes suicide a more likely choice when a person is socially disoriented, and Naroll suggested was that it was the person's reaction to *thwarting disorientation contexts*. Such contexts involve a weakening of the person's social ties as a result of the actions of other people or oneself (but not as a result of impersonal, natural or cultural events). Being divorced by a spouse and murdering one's spouse are examples of such contexts, whereas storm damage to your property or losing a spouse to cancer are not such contexts. In thwarting disorientation contexts, some people commit *protest suicide*, which Naroll defined as voluntary suicide committed in such a way as to come to public notice (and, therefore, excludes unconsciously motivated suicides and culturally-motivated suicides such as suttee).

Lester (1995) noted the similarity of this theory to the classic sociological theories of suicide proposed by Durkheim and by Henry and Short (see Chapter 6), but he also noted that Naroll's theory had different implications. For example, Durkheim's theory of suicide refers more to steady state characteristics of the society as major explanatory variables, whereas Naroll's theory suggests the role of sudden, acute changes in a society. Furthermore, Naroll's theory is phrased in a way which makes it more validly applied to individuals as well as societies as a whole.

Cross-Cultural Research

As mentioned above, recent years have seen some anthropologists code samples of societies for the presence of particular behaviors and customs, enabling them to conduct quantitative research on cultures. For example, Rootman (1973) studied 55 primitive societies and used two clusters of social indicators to characterize the societies. One cluster included permanency of residence, constancy of the food supply, agriculture rather than herding as the source of food, and strong group life -- Rootman thought that this cluster measured the social integration of the society. A second cluster included elaboration of ceremony and ritual, power vested in a chief, an organized priesthood, codified laws, and authority vested in judges, a cluster which Rootman thought measured social regulation.

He classified the societies as high, moderate or low on both clusters, giving him a 3-by-3 array of societies. He found that those societies with moderate amounts of both characteristics had lower estimated suicide rates[2] than societies with high or low amounts of either or both characteristics.[3]

Psychotherapeutic Implications

All of this scholarly discourse is important at the theoretical level, but it may be asked whether there are implications of this for counseling and psychotherapy. It is sometimes argued that only 'like' can counsel 'like', that is, that only homosexuals can counsel homosexuals, women counsel women, ex-addicts counsel addicts, and so on. Is the same true also for different cultures? The majority of counselors and psychotherapists deny this, claiming that a good counselor or psychotherapist can counsel any kind of patient. However, to counsel someone very different in background from oneself may require that the counselor learn about the background and culture from which the individual comes. Sue and Sue (1990) have addressed the issues that psychotherapists of one culture must confront when counseling clients from different cultures, such as racism and cultural differences in verbal and nonverbal communication styles.

Zimmerman and Zayas (1995) have illustrated this point in their discussion of treating the suicidal adolescent Hispanic female. They noted that, in New York City, the values of the adolescent latina often clash with those of her more traditional mother. Both mother and daughter experience problems in communication and a rupture in their relationship. Thus, the problem of acculturation exacerbates the normal adolescent turmoil. The latina's mother wants her daughter to succeed in this new culture, yet she also wants her daughter to maintain traditional cultural attitudes and roles. The adolescent latina feels overwhelmed by this conflict and, in extreme cases, makes a suicide attempt in an effort to reduce the tension felt in this conflict. After a suicide attempt, the psychotherapist must explain the conflict to the mother and daughter and help them find ways to re-establish mutual understanding and empathy.

It is possible, of course, that psychotherapists could identify the nature of the problems confronting suicidal people and their families each time they encounter such a family, but the psychotherapeutic process is facilitated if psychotherapists have some notion of the cultural issues which they are likely to encounter.

Sue and Sue (1990) presented the case of Janet, a Chinese-American female college senior majoring in sociology, who came to the college counseling center complaining of

---

[2] The suicide rates could not measured accurately, but had to be estimated from the reports of the anthropologists who had described the societies.

[3] This study is one of the rare studies which tests Durkheim's theory of suicide (see Chapter 6) in a methodologically sound way.

depression, feelings of worthlessness and suicidal thoughts. She had difficulty identifying the causes of her depression, but she seemed quite hostile to the psychotherapist who was also Chinese-American.

Discussion of this revealed that Janet resented being seen by a Chinese psychotherapist, feeling that she had been assigned to one because of her own race. Janet disliked everything Chinese, including Chinese men whom she found sexually unattractive. She dated only white men, which had upset her parents. However, her last romance had broken up partly because her boyfriend's parents objected to him dating a Chinese woman.

Janet clearly had difficulties in her continuing denial of her Chinese heritage. She was being forced to realize that she was Chinese for she was not fully accepted by white America. Initially she blamed the Chinese for her dilemma, but then she turned her hostility toward herself. Feeling alienated from her own culture and rejected by the white culture, she was experiencing an identity crisis with a resulting depression.

The psychotherapist in such a case must deal with cultural racism and its effects on minorities. Positive acculturation must be distinguished from rejection of one's own cultural values, as well as typical adolescent rebellion from one's parents. Psychotherapists can work with such a client more effectively if they are conversant with the cultural history and experiences of Asian-Americans.

References

Bachman, R. *Death and violence on the reservation.* New York: Auburn House, 1992..

Bagley, C. Poverty and suicide among Native Canadians. *Psychological Reports*, 1991, 69, 149-150.

Berlin, I. N. Psychopathology and its antecedents among American Indian adolescents. *Advances in Clinical Child Psychology*, 1986, 9, 125-152.

Berry, J. W. Acculturation and adaptation. *Arctic Medical Research*, 1990, 49, 142-150.

Burvill, P., McCall, M., Woodings, T., & Stenhouse, N. Comparison of suicide rates and methods in English, Scots and Irish immigrants in Australia. *Social Science & Medicine*, 1983, 17, 705-708.

Canetto, S. S. Gender roles, suicide attempts, and substance abuse. *Journal of Psychology*, 1991, 125, 605-620.

Chiles, J. A., Ping, Z. Y., & Strosahl, D. A Chinese/American cross-cultural study of depression, hopelessness, and suicidal behavior. In G. Ferrari, M. Bellini & P. Crepet (Eds.) *Suicidal behavior and risk factors*, pp. 609-614. Bologna, Italy: Monduzzi-Editore, 1990.

Conklin, G. H., & Simpson, M. E. The family, socioeconomic development and suicide. *Journal of Comparative Family Studies*, 1987, 18, 99-111.

Counts, D. A. Fighting back is not the way: Suicide and the women on Kaliai. *American Ethnologist*, 1980, 7, 332-351.

Counts, D. A. Ambiguity in the interpretation of suicide. In D. Lester (Ed.) *Why women kill themselves*, pp. 87-109. Springfield, IL: Charles Thomas, 1988.

D'Azevedo, W. L., Freed, S. A., Freed, R. S., Leis, P. E., Scotch, N. A., Scotch, F. L., Price, J. A., & Downs, J. F. *The Washo Indians of California and Nevada.* Salt Lake City, UT: University of Utah, 1963.

DeCatanzaro, D. *Suicide and self-damaging behavior*. New York: Academic Press, 1981.

Devereux, G. *Mohave ethnopsychiatry: The psychic disturbances of an Indian tribe*. Washington, DC: Smithsonian Institution, 1961.

Douglas, J. D. *The social meanings of suicide*. Princeton, NJ: Princeton University Press, 1967.

Durkheim, E. *Le suicide*. Paris: Felix Alcan, 1897.

Eckersley, R. Failing a generation. *Journal of Pediatric & Child Health*, 1993, 29, supplement 1, 16-19.

Firth, R. Suicide and risk taking in Tikopia. *Psychiatry*, 1961, 24, 1-17.

Garro, L. C. Suicides by status Indians in Manitoba. *Arctic Medical Research*, 1988, 47, supplement 1, 590-592.

Gastil, R. Homicide and a regional culture of violence. *American Sociological Review*, 1971, 36, 412-427.

Haviland, W. A. *Cultural anthropology*. Fort Worth, TX: Harcourt Brace Jovanovich, 1993.

Hendin, H. *Suicide and Scandinavia*. New York: Grune & Stratton, 1964.

Hlady, W. G., & Middaugh, J. P. The underrecording of suicide in state and national records, Alaska, 1983-1984. *Suicide & Life-Threatening Behavior*, 1988, 18, 237-244.

Honigmann, J. J. *Culture and ethos of Kaska society*. New Haven, CT: Yale University, 1949.

Lester, D. Migration and suicide. *Medical Journal of Australia*, 1972, 1, 941-942.

_____ . Ectomorphy and suicide. *Journal of Social Psychology*, 1981, 113, 135-136.

_____ . Variation in suicide and homicide rates by latitude and longitude in the US, Canada and Australia. *American Journal of Psychiatry*, 1985, 142, 523-524.

_____ . National distribution of blood groups, personal violence (suicide and homicide), and national character. *Personality & Individual Differences*, 1987a, 8, 575-576.

_____ . *Suicide as a learned behavior*. Springfield, IL: Charles Thomas, 1987b.

_____ . Suicide rates around the world. *Crisis*, 1990, 11, 82-84.

_____ . Differences in the epidemiology of suicide in Asian Americans by nation of origin. *Omega*, 1994a, 29, 89-93.

_____ . The epidemiology of suicide in Chinese populations in six regions of the world. *Chinese Journal of Mental Health*, 1994b, 7, 25-36.

_____ . Suicide by jumping in Singapore as a function of high-rise apartment availability. *Perceptual & Motor Skills*, 1994c, 79, 74.

_____ . Thwarting disorientation and suicide. *Cross-cultural Research*, 1995, 29, 14-26.

_____ . *Patterns of suicide and homicide in the world*. Commack, NY: Nova Science, 1996.

Linehan, M. Suicide and attempted suicide. *Perceptual & Motor Skills*, 1973, 37, 31-34.

Malla, A., & Hoenig, J. Differences in suicide rates. *Canadian Journal of Psychiatry*, 1983, 28, 291-293.

May, P. A., & Dizmang, L. H. Suicide and the American Indian. *Psychiatric Annals*, 1974, 4(11), 22-28.

Menninger, K. *Man against himself*. New York: Harcourt, Brace & World, 1938.

Naroll, R. *Thwarting disorientation and suicide*. Unpublished, Northwestern University, 1963.

Naroll, R. Cultural determinants and the concept of the sick society. In S. C. Plog & R. B. Edgerton (Eds.) *Changing perspectives in mental illness*, pp. 128-155. New York: Holt, Rinehart & Winston, 1969.

Ramon, S. Attitudes of doctors and nurses to self-poisoning patients. *Social Science & Medicine*, 1980, 14A, 317-324.

Rootman, I. A cross-cultural note on Durkheim's theory of suicide. *Life-Threatening Behavior*, 1973, 3, 83-94.

Sainsbury, P., & Barraclough, B. M. Differences in suicide rates. *Nature*, 1968, 220, 1252.

Sue, D. W., & Sue, D. *Counseling the culturally different*. New York: Wiley. 1990.

Van Winkle, N. W., & May, P. A. Native American suicide in New Mexico, 1959-1979. *Human Organization*, 1986, 45, 296-309.

Westermeyer, J. Ethnic identity problems among ten Indian psychiatric patients. *International Journal of Social Psychiatry*, 1979, 25, 188-197.

Wolfgang, M. E., & Ferracuti, F. *The subculture of violence*. New York: Tavistock, 1969.

Zimmerman, J. K., & Zayas, L. Suicidal adolescent latinas. In S. Canetto & D. Lester (Ed.) *Women and suicidal behavior*, pp. 120-132. New York: Springer, 1995.

Chapter 8

CRIMINOLOGY AND SUICIDE[1]

In most nations of the world, suicide is not a crime. However, criminal behavior is a deviant act, as is suicide, and the theories which have been proposed to explain criminal behavior might have application as explanations of suicide. Thus, this chapter is concerned with how our understanding of suicide would be furthered if we viewed suicide from a criminological perspective.

Crime and delinquency has attracted a great deal of attention from sociologists so that it has become a major field with its own associations and journals. Furthermore, it has been truly an interdisciplinary field. As we shall see, it is possible to identify at least seven major theories of crime and delinquency. Some of these have parallels in the study of suicide, but others do not. These latter theories, therefore, suggest areas of theorizing that suicidologists might profitably consider.

CLASSICAL THEORIES

The principles of the Classical School of criminology were stated most clearly by Cesare Beccaria (1738-1794) in Italy and Jeremy Bentham (1758-1832) in England. For example, Jeremy Bentham (1967), a philosopher who also studied law, wanted to maximize the good in the society -- the greatest good for the greatest number of people. Like others in the Eighteenth Century, Bentham believed that people were rational and would choose to maximize pleasure and minimize pain.

Bentham proposed that specific punishments assigned to each crime would increase the pain and, thereby, decrease the incidence of crime. The potential pain of the criminal act when the offender is caught must outweigh the potential pleasure obtained. If this is so, then the rational person will refrain from committing the criminal act. Bentham rejected severe punishment, and he urged that only crimes which damage the society should be punished. Acts which are an offense only to morals and which do not interfere with the rights of others should not be considered criminal.

The classical position had a major impact on the criminal justice system for over a hundred years, but eventually it was replaced in the Twentieth Century by the view that

---

[1] For a more detailed presentation of these ideas, see Lester (1990a).

criminals should be *treated* rather than *punished*. However, in recent years, the classical position has grown in strength again as efforts at rehabilitating criminals appear to have had little success (von Hirsch, 1976; Newman, 1983).

Modern classical theorists argue for swift and certain punishments which do not necessarily have to be severe, punishments which are uniform and which fit the crime, and incapacitation of known chronic offenders so that they cannot commit additional crimes. Today we see many jurisdictions imposing fixed minimum terms for certain crimes (such as dealing drugs or crimes committed with a gun) and increasing incarceration rates (which is leading at the present time to overcrowded prisons).

The Law and Suicide

Suicide has been declared criminal in the past by three great legal traditions: Roman Law, Church Law and English Law. In England in 1809, Blackstone in his *Commentaries* argued that suicide should be punished because it is against God and King. He suggested mangling the body of the suicide and exposing it to public view as a way of preventing suicide. John Wesley, the methodist reformer, suggested in 1790 dragging the naked bodies of female suicides through the street. Desecration of the body of the suicide was meant to show how heinous the crime was (Hillman, 1964). However, the deterrent against suicide was usually confiscation of the property of the suicide, which was forfeited to the crown. Penalties against the estate of the suicide could still be levied up until 1961 in England, and life insurance was often denied to the survivors of a suicide.

Victoroff (1983) reviewed the (then) current laws on suicide in the states of America. No state assigned criminal penalties for completed suicide, but Oklahoma and Texas assigned criminal penalties for attempted suicide. Lester (1988) suggested that state laws on suicide might reflect the attitudes of the people in each state on suicide. States with more punitive laws might have residents more opposed to suicide. He correlated the presence or absence of these provisions with the state suicide rates in 1980 but found no associations. A multiple regression analysis of the eight state law provisions accounted for only 19 percent of the variance in the suicide rates.

Is Suicide a Rational Choice?

The classical position argues that people choose behaviors based on rational decisions, and we have discussed the issues involved in deciding whether suicide is a rational decision in Chapter 5.

Implications for Prevention Suicide

It is not feasible to introduce punishment for suicide in the modern age. However, there are various moral philosophies which are opposed to suicide, and it would perhaps not be unreasonable to emphasize the position taken by these philosophies. The Roman Catholic Church, for example, has taken a very strong moral stand on abortion in the 1980s. A similar stand could be taken against suicide.

Lester (1989a) has argued that public education about suicide differs, for example, from public education about medical diseases. In educating the public about smoking, for example, public health information has focussed on the dangers of smoking. The fact that smoking causes lung cancer and may damage the babies of pregnant women is stressed. A recent television advertisement featured Yul Bryner, who had died from lung cancer, in a videotape made before he died in which he urged people, "Don't smoke!" Those who are vehemently opposed to smoking have in the past published shocking photographs of diseased lung tissue and heart-rending stories about persons who have suffered from lung cancer. Public education about AIDS and drug abuse are similarly strong and blunt.

In contrast public education programs about suicide have had a very different focus. Entertaining dramas involving suicidal teenagers have appeared on television. The public has been informed on the warning clues to suicide in others. Local suicide prevention services are also advertised. Suicide education could be re-focused in order to stress the negative consequences of suicidal behavior, for example, by focusing on the physical damage incurred when attempting suicide, the suffering caused to relatives and friends, and the moral objections to suicide embodied in the religions.

Positivist Individualistic Theories

The classical theory of crime reviewed in the previous section is one of the major *individualistic* theories of crime because it focuses on the individual criminal and how he might be deterred from engaging in criminal acts. Within a hundred years of the formulation of the classical theory of crime, people began to look at the physiological and psychological characteristics of criminals and the circumstances of their social milieu for an explanation of why people turn to criminal behavior. This *positivist* school rejected the emphasis on free will of the classical school in favor of determinism. They sought to identify the *causes* of criminal behavior using value-free scientific methods.

There are three major thrusts in the search for an explanation of criminal behavior: physiological, psychological and psychiatric. Physiological theories of crime focus on the role of the inheritance of criminal tendencies and on the role of biochemical processes (such as neurological dysfunction). Psychological approaches focus on the personality of criminals and the role of childhood experiences in the development of criminal tendencies. Psychiatric approaches classify criminality as a psychiatric disorder (for example, antisocial personality disorder) or as the product of a psychiatric disorder.

Positivist Individualistic Theories of Suicide

As we will see in Chapter 11, the major psychological theories of suicide are positivist individualistic theories, and there is no need to review these theories again here. Furthermore, the positivist individualistic approach to understanding suicide has dominated the prevention scene for several decades now.

Social Structure Theories

There are several positivist theories of crime which focus on the social structure or organization of society as causative factors. Some of these theories focus on the destructive social forces which arise from the prevailing cultural norms and values existing in lower class culture and may be called *culture deviance theories*, while another set focuses upon the frustration felt by lower class youths when they are prevented from obtaining rewards in the legitimate sphere and may be called *strain theories*.

Culture Deviance Theories

If the cultural values of the people in the area you grow up in do not conform to those of the main society, then conformity to these deviant rules, values and norms will lead to deviant behavior. For example, Shaw and McKay (1972), studying Chicago in the 1920s, noted that the city had greatly differing neighborhoods. Some were marked by wealth and luxury while others were slums. Shaw and McKay argued that delinquency was caused by the conditions in these slum areas. Often teenage gangs developed in these neighborhoods, and these gangs assisted the youths in surviving and provided economic gain and friendship. The gangs then served as cultural agents, transmitting the new norms and values to the younger kids as they grew up and joined the gangs.

Miller (1958) also explained crime and delinquency as the result of lower classs culture. He stressed the role of female-headed households and the absence of good male role models for the adolescents, and he felt that the absence of men facilitated the establishment of male gangs as a substitute. He also noted the importance of several focal concerns in this culture which become goals: getting into and staying out of trouble, recognition of physical and mental toughness, establishing an image of street-wise smartness, the search for excitement, a belief in fate and luck as determinants of outcomes in life, and a concern with personal freedom and autonomy. Youths who become delinquents and criminals do so by conforming to these cultural demands.

Wolfgang and Ferracuti (1967) proposed a subcultural theory of crime which suggested that there was a subculture which had its own norms separate from those of the dominant culture. In particular, Wolfgang and Ferracuti suggested that a common subculture was one of violence especially among some groups of the population (such as younger men) and in some regions, such as the southern states of America.

Some subcultural theories have focussed on whole regions of the United States, such as the theory that there is a southern subculture (Gastil, 1971), while others have focussed on a whole social group such as the lower social class. However, subcultural theories of delinquency often focus on smaller groups, such as the gang (Cohen, 1955). To apply subcultural theory to suicidal behavior may further reduce the size of the group involved. Groups of depressed and suicidal teenagers, for example, are often quite small. However, such groups do share values and attitudes that are common to other teenagers, and the subculture can be seen as quite large if we focus on those who hold similar attitudes and values, even if they are not in contact (as in a gang). For example, Lester (1987a) described a group of five teenagers of whom three killed themselves. He detailed their dependence upon their leader, heavy drug involvement, preference for heavy metal music, difficult relations with their parents characterized by intense resentment or apparent indifference, poor self-image (feelings of worthlessness and ugliness combined with shyness), and suicidal preoccupation.

Platt (1985) has looked at the stable yet differing rates of attempted suicide in city wards and formulated a subcultural hypothesis to account for them. Kreitman, et al. (1970) suggested that many attempted suicides come from a group who view self-aggression as an acceptable means of conveying certain kinds of information to others. Attempted suicide is viewed as understandable and appropriate in some circumstances, if not formally condoned. Platt suggested a more formal hypotheses: there is a subculture in contemporary society in which the communicational functions of attempted suicide are particularly well-defined (Platt, 1985, p. 258).

Strain Theory

Strain theories focus on the feelings of the those in different groups or subcultures in the society. If you are unable to achieve success, prestige or status through legitimate means, then it is likely that you will feel anger and frustration. Strain theories propose that we all share similar goals and values (a very different assumption from the cultural deviance theories), but that we differ in our ability to achieve these goals, especially if we come from the lower social classes.

For example, Merton (1957) argued that social structures establish goals for the members of the society and label some methods for obtaining these goals as approved. Nonconforming behavior results when people reject either the goals or the means for obtaining the goals. Merton suggested that modern America emphasizes goals rather than means and that the most sought after goal is wealth and material goods.

Cohen (1955) argued that the criminal behavior in slum districts is really a protest against the norms and values of middle class culture. The social conditions of the slums make it difficult, if not impossible, for the youths to obtain the approved goals by the approved methods. These youths experience frustration which results in nonutilitarian, malicious and negativistic behavior. Parents in these districts fail to teach their children the proper skills for entering into the middle class culture, and so their children lack educational and communication skills and are unable to delay gratification. They fail to measure up to the *middle class measuring rods*.

Cloward and Ohlin (1960) added to these analyses by noting that not even illegitimate means for achieving goals are evenly distributed in the society. Some lower class neighborhoods provide more opportunities for getting into a criminal career. Youths who know adults already engaged in crime can enter the criminal subculture as apprentices. If the peer groups and the adults do not provide this criminal learning experience, then the youth may retreat into drug use or simply seek catharsis through violence.

A strain theory approach to suicide has less previous research and theorizing to build upon than the culture deviance theories proposed above. Strain theory must focus upon the emotional experiences (such as anger and frustration) of the suicidal individual resulting from the difficulties in working toward culturally approved goals by socially acceptable means.

A common theme in suicides is the notion that the person has failed in some way. For example, Livermore (1985) found that 30 percent of the suicide notes of those who killed themselves said "You'll be better off without me", while five percent of the notes from those who killed themselves and 30 percent of the notes from those who attempted suicide said "I'm a failure." In addition, Livermore noted that about half of the notes from completed suicides mentioned financial problems as one of the precipitating causes of their suicide as did a quarter of the notes from suicide attempters, suggesting that the conventional American goal of wealth was of concern to these suicidal individuals.

Stephens (1988), in her discussion of the suicidal behavior of women she had studied, concluded that the women "had interpersonal histories of relentlessly negative relationships (with others).....Their social and psychological experiences have prepared them to be victims, victims of parents, of men, of relationship in which the self is continually mortified...(p. 84)." These women often said that they were "bad", and they were convinced that they were different from others. Yet they desired to be normal. As one women expressed it, "All my life I've felt like nothing, nothing, just nothing." Again, these lives suggest that the women have struggled and consider themselves to have failed, and the suicidal behavior appears to be an escapist strategy.

These ideas suggest that it would be fruitful to explore the degree to which suicidal people had and still have the conventional goals of people in their society, which methods they have tried to achieve these goals, and whether they have in fact given up trying to achieve them.

LEARNING THEORIES

The theories discussed in the previous section proposed that the structure of the society was a primary cause of crime and delinquency. In contrast, the theories described in this and the following section focus on *social processes*, the relationships between the individual and people in the society, such as parents, teachers, friends, and so on. Thus, these theories have a socio-psychological orientation, stressing such factors as the learning of criminal attitudes, feelings of alienation from society, and a poor self-concept.

There are two major types of social process theory. *Learning theories* hold that crime is learned from one's associates and friends. *Social control theory* holds that delinquency and crime are the result of disrupted ties between the individual and the major institutions of the society -- family, peers and school.

Differential Association Theory

Sutherland (1947) proposed that criminal behavior was learned in interaction with other persons. People do not become criminals simply by living in a particular type of society. Criminal, and other deviant patterns of behavior, are actively learned by people from others who serve as teachers and guides. This learning occurs primarily within intimate personal groups. It is family members, friends, and peers who have the most influence.

The learning covers the techniques of committing the crime as well as the specific motives, drives, rationalizations and attitudes. (Thus, criminals come to hold different values and attitudes from those held by law-abiding people.) People have to be coached on how to pick a lock or shoplift, as well as learning how to react to their crimes and their victims. If more of the person's friends and family are violating the law rather than following the law, the balance is tipped in favor of the person becoming a law violator. Furthermore, the quality and intensity of the person's relationships with the potential teachers and guides is critical. The more durable relationships have more influence on the person, as do those that occur at a young age, and the prestige of the potential teacher increases the likelihood of learning.

Although a learning theory of suicide had been tentatively suggested before (Frederick and Resnick, 1971; Diekstra, 1974), Lester (1987b) presented the strongest case possible for a learning theory of suicide. Lester's thesis is discussed in full in Chapter 11 and need not be presented again here.

Neutralization Theory

Sykes and Matza (1957) proposed a theory which has come to be known as *neutralization theory* or *drift theory*. They proposed that delinquents hold values and attitudes similar to those of law-abiding people, but they learn techniques which enable them to neutralize these values and attitudes temporarily when committing crimes. The potential criminal learns through his interactions with others to disregard the controlling influences of the society's social rules.

On a continuum from total freedom to total constraint, most people lie somewhere in the middle, but we can move toward one end or the other depending upon our state of mind or the social situation we are in. This movement is called drift. The delinquent subculture encourages drift toward the freedom end of the continuum, and it provides a set of justifications for the violations of law and order.

The techniques of neutralization include:

(1) Denial of responsibility -- the act was not their fault or was due to forces beyond their control. "It wasn't my fault"
(2) Denial of criminal intent -- they were not stealing, they were borrowing -- or they did not mean to damage the property, they were simply playing. "I didn't mean to do it."
(3) Denigration of the victim -- the crime may be justified by disparaging the victim -- he was an offensive authority figure or a member of an outgroup (such as a homosexual) -- the owner of the property was absent. "He had it coming to him."
(4) Condemning the moral authorities -- police are seen as brutal oppressors and judges as corrupt -- teachers and parents are unfair. "Why pick on me? Politicians get away with it."
(5) Appealing to higher loyalties -- seeing loyalty to their peer group as more important than following the rules of the larger society. "I had to help my buddy."

There is much less evidence currently available for a neutralization theory of suicide. For example, do suicides show denial of the sort that would facilitate them committing a suicidal act? Only two studies appear to be relevant to this.

First, Spiegel and Neuringer (1963) compared genuine suicide notes with notes written by nonsuicidal individuals pretending that they were about to kill themselves (simulated notes). They found that the genuine notes mentioned the word "suicide" or suicide synonyms less often than the simulated notes, and they interpreted this to mean that the suicidal people were trying to deceive themselves about their imminent suicide and to concentrate on things other than suicide.

Jacobs (1982) focussed upon the moral justification for suicide. Jacobs introduced the notion of trust violation, the individual's violation of the sacred trust of life. As a result of this trust violation, the individual who is going to kill himself must reconcile the image of himself as a to-be-trusted person with the fact that he is about to break that trust through his act of suicide. Jacobs examined suicide notes to document this process.

Jacobs proposed the following sequence for the suicidal process: the person (a) is faced with extremely distressing problems, (b) views this state of affairs as part of a long history of such distressing crises, (c) believes that death is the only solution to these problems, (d) has become increasingly socially isolated so that he cannot share his distress with others, (e) has overcome his internalized moral constraints that categorize suicide as irrational or immoral, (f) has succeeded in this since his social isolation makes him feel less constrained by societal rules, (g) constructs some verbal rationalization than enables him to view himself as a to-be-trusted person in spite of his trust violation by defining the problem as not of his own making or as open to no other solution, and (h) makes some provision that his problems will not occur after death.

The authors of the most common form of notes characteristically beg forgiveness or request indulgence, show that the problem is not of their making, note the history of the problem, communicate that the problems have grown beyond endurance, note the necessity of death, and communicate that they are fully aware of what they are doing but know that the reader will not understand their reasons.

In order to take precautions that the life-after-death will be free from problems, Jacobs noted that there are several courses open to the suicidal person. He sometimes stops attending church and becomes an atheist, thereby disposing of heaven and hell. Occasionally he tries to find consensual evidence from others that God forgives everything (including suicide) and so becomes very religious, or he can merely suppress the knowledge that God will not forgive. Another alternative is to persuade oneself that even hell will be better than the present life on earth. Often the suicidal person will ask God for forgiveness in the suicide note and request others to pray for his soul. Finally, the individual may come to believe in reincarnation, thereby forcing out of awareness conventional religious beliefs.

Social Control Theories

The second major type of social process theory of criminal behavior focuses on the ties between the individual on the one hand and conventional groups in the society, other law-abiding individuals, and the organizations and institutions of the society on the other. Those who have close relationships with parents, friends, and teachers are more likely to have a positive self-image and to be able to resist the temptation of crime. Those who feel detached from conventional society are unaffected by its social control functions. These theories are usually called *social control theories*.

The social controls may be internal or external. Internal controls involve such personality traits as a positive self-image and a strong internalized conscience. External controls involve positive close relationships with parents and with teachers who are conventional and law-abiding.

Social Bond Theory

Hirschi (1969) assumed that all of us are potential criminals and that social controls (not moral values) prevent us from behaving in a criminal manner. Hirschi noted four elements in the social bond between the individual and society.

(1) *Attachment* refers to the individual's interest in, sensitivity to, and caring for others, as well as concern for the wishes and expectations of others. The norms and values of the society are shared by the members and, if one cares about the reactions of others, then there is good reason to follow the norms.
Attachment to parents is the most important tie. If parents divorce or if one or both parents behave in such a way (abusively, for example) that the child's tie to them is weakened, then attachment will not take place. Without attachment to these first important people in our life, our parents, it is unlikely that the person will develop feelings of respect for others.

(2) *Commitment* refers to the time, energy and effort in pursuing conventional pursuits in our society. If the individual has a stake in the society, then behaving deviantly endangers this. For example, if the person pursues an education, obtains a good job, seeks prestige and status, and becomes a property owner, then he will be less likely to engage in criminal behavior because that would jeopardize his position in the society.

(3) A person who is *involved* in conventional activities in the society not only has less desire to engage in criminal behavior, but he also has less time.

(4) Finally the social bond involves *belief* in the moral validity of the norms established by the society for himself. Those norms must be seen as both good and correct for the society and as relevant to our own actions.

Containment Theory

Reckless (1967) focussed on internal controls as well as external controls. He noted that there were both pressures toward delinquency and away from it.

(1) *Inner containments* consisted of those forces in the personality resisting criminal involvement. People with a positive self-image, a strong ego, high frustration tolerance, goal orientation, and the ability to reduce tension in socially acceptable ways are less likely to engage in criminal behavior.

(2) *Outer containments* are those normative rules and values that society possesses which restrain antisocial and criminal behavior. People with a sense of belonging, who are effectively supervised and disciplined, and who have a meaningful social role are less likely to commit criminal acts.

(3) *Internal pushes* are those forces within the individual which propel him toward criminal behavior, such as restlessness, hostility, rebellion, internal conflicts, and the need for immediate gratification.

(4) *External pulls* are those forces in the society which pull the individual toward criminal acts such as deviant companions and the mass media.

(5) *External pressures* are those adverse social conditions which increase the likelihood of deviant behavior, such as poverty, unemployment, minority status, and limited opportunities.

Reckless proposed that the internal containments were more important than the external containments since we spend most of our time away from our family and the other groups supportive of the social order. We have to rely most of the time, then, on our internal strengths to control our criminal impulses.

A Social Control Theory of Suicide

Durkheim's (1897) theory of suicide, discussed in Chapter 6, focuses upon the social bond between the individual and the society and so fits into social control theory. As a sociologist, Durkheim was not interested in the factors affecting the development of social integration and social regulation. However, he did point to a number of social processes that affected the strength of these two social forces, such as marriage versus divorce and religious affiliation.

As we also have seen in Chapter 6, Henry and Short (1954) developed a theory of suicide which focussed primarily upon the concept of social regulation, exploring which social and psychological factors legitimized other-oriented aggression (murder) versus self-oriented aggression (suicide). Henry and Short saw the strength of external restraints as the primary basis for legitimizing other-oriented aggression. When behavior is required to conform rigidly to the demands and expectations of others, the share of others in the responsibility for the consequences of the behavior increases, thereby legitimizing other-oriented aggression. When external restraints are weak, the self must bear the responsibility for the frustration generated, and other-oriented aggression fails to be legitimized.

Several possible factors operate at the individual level of analysis.

The Social Bond

It has long been known that suicide rates are highest among the divorced and the widowed and lowest for those who are married (Dublin, 1963). Completed suicide may also be less common among people who have children (Breed, 1966). Lester's (1983) review of the literature found consistent evidence that suicidal individuals came from more disorganized homes and felt less close to their parents than non-suicidal individuals. Ganzler (1967) found that attempted suicides were experiencing greater social isolation than psychiatrically disturbed but nonsuicidal patients. Furthermore, both Lester (1969) and Ganzler (1967) found that suicidal individuals rated their significant others more negatively than did nonsuicidal individuals.

Ego Strength

Several studies have reported low self-esteem in suicidal individuals. For example, Neuringer (1974) found that attempted suicides rated themselves as more negatively and others as more positively than did psychosomatic patients. Kaplan and Pokorny (1976) found that low self-esteem predicted subsequent suicidal ideation and suicidal attempts in seventh-grade children. These reports of low self-esteem in suicidal individuals are consistent with reports of the high levels of depression and feelings of hopelessness in suicidal individuals (Beck, et al., 1975).

Many authors have commented on impulsiveness in suicidal individuals. For example, Corder, et al. (1974) found that adolescent suicide attempters were generally more impulsive than nonsuicidal adolescents. Lester (1990b) found that college students who had threatened suicide scored higher on a test of general impulsivity than equally depressed but nonsuicidal college students. Epstein, et al. (1973) found that medical students who subsequently committed suicide later in their lives were rated as more impulsive while in medical school.

It can be seen that a strong case can be made for a social control theory of suicide. Most of the sociological theorizing about suicide is really based on social controls, and a good deal of psychological research has pointed to the influence of poor relationships with parents, conflicts with lovers and friends, and social isolation on the development and appearance of suicidal behavior. Suicidal people also appear to be deficient in internal controls. They have poor self-images and are seriously depressed, tend to be impulsive, and prone to blame others for their misfortunes.

Social Reaction Theories

Social reaction theory is more commonly known as *labeling theory* (Lemert, 1967). It focuses upon how other people in the society react toward the delinquent. Most kids break the rules of the society at one time or another, and many break the laws. A few of these kids get labeled. Some may be labeled by their parents, relatives, friends and teachers -- "You're going to grow up and come to no good," "You are evil," and similar statements. Others will get formally processed by the criminal justice system and officially called juvenile delinquents. Social reaction theory focuses upon this informal and formal labeling process.

A person may be called many things as they grow up. For social reaction theory, there is sometimes a point at which the adolescent decides that a particular label is appropriate and accepts it. Once the label is accepted, then the person has truly entered on a 'career.'

The social reaction perspective draws our attention to the audience, to those who label others. It immediately makes it clear that labeling is culturally determined. What is unlawful in one society or in one group within a society may be acceptable in another. For example, bribery of public officials is punishable in some societies while considered the norm in others. Sexually promiscuous behavior is considered a delinquent behavior in American girls but not in American boys.

Social reaction theory, therefore, focuses on discrimination in the criminal justice system. Middle-class offenders are less likely to be labeled and less likely to be severely punished than lower-class offenders. Blacks and Hispanics may be treated differently than whites, and females treated differently than males.

Social reaction theory also inquires into the stigma of labels. The labels are usually quite long-lasting and involve a loss of status. The labeled person becomes a social outcast. This in turn leads to alienation from the mainstream of the society and makes continuation of a criminal career even more likely. If you are an "X," then it is more pleasant to seek the company of others who are also labeled "Xs." Thus, labeling leads to the development of a new deviant identity and deviant subcultures. Individuals become what the society says they are.

A Social Reaction Theory of Suicide

It is interesting that no social reaction theory of suicide has yet appeared. Despite the prominence of the perspective in criminology and its application to psychiatric disturbance over twenty-five years ago, it has had no impact in suicidology. This suggests that it might be provocative, and perhaps fruitful, to try to formulate a social reaction theory of suicide.

The first question to consider is whether people do indeed become labeled as "suicidal" and by whom. Some situations may be infrequent but likely situations for labeling. In those cases where a parent has committed suicide, people may worry that the spouse or the children of the suicide will likewise commit suicide. Today, there are many survivor groups specifically to help survivors work through their feelings about the suicide and to prevent them turning to suicide (Lukas and Seiden, 1987).

Let us imagine that the friends and relatives of these survivors, especially if they are children, are anxious about them becoming suicidal and are constantly on the look-out for suicidal cues. The children are very likely to pick up this anxiety and constant observation and to draw the obvious inference -- they are worried that I will kill myself like Daddy did.

Relatives, parents and friends may even put this concern in words and, indeed, even label the child as a potential suicide. "If you don't watch it, you'll kill yourself just like your father." Peers at school can be particularly cruel. In a school in which three students committed suicide, many students in the school became suicidal in the following weeks. One student who attempted suicide found a bottle of Tylenol in her locker with a note saying, "Do it right next time" (Lester, 1987b). Thus, it is possible that informal labeling of individuals occurs in these situations.

Formal labeling can also occur. I remember working as a crisis counselor at a suicide prevention center and receiving a call from an individual who asked me, "Do I have to be suicidal to talk to you?" I was reminded of the situation in the United States before abortion was, to some extent, legalized. In some states, in order to have a legal abortion, a psychiatrist had to certify that the women would be seriously disturbed if an abortion was not permitted. In those states, informed pregnant women knew to threaten suicide if they wanted to have an abortion, whereupon the cooperating psychiatrist would have the required conditions to sign the appropriate forms. Perhaps one has to appear and be labeled as suicidal in order to obtain certain things in a society and, after so appearing, perhaps the role becomes appealing?

The existence of suicide prevention centers, suicide prevention programs and suicide awareness programs all raise the possibility that you may be suicidal. An advertisement for a suicide prevention center informs people that suicide is an option. If you call or visit a suicide prevention center, are you now a "suicidal person?" When you watch a suicide prevention or awareness program in the media or at school, you learn the cues for recognizing suicidal preoccupation in others. These programs provide the direct learning of how to play the role of a suicidal individual.

If you are in a psychiatric hospital or a jail or prison, the staff may become concerned about whether you might kill yourself and put you on "suicide alert." This means that potential methods for committing suicide will be taken from you and you will be monitored continuously. Might not being put on suicide alert actually increase the risk of your subsequent death by suicide at some point in your life? Labeling theory would argue so.

Thus, it would appear that there are opportunities for learning the suicidal role in life and for being labeled, both informally and formally, as a potential suicide. Since there are such opportunities, it would seem important in future to research to explore whether there is any evidence that such labeling occurs and leads to changes in the suicidal potential of the individuals so labeled.

Social Conflict Theories

Social conflict theories of crime focus on the ways that governments make and enforce laws both informally and formally. Might these laws simply be a way in which those in power maintain their power and control the oppressed in a society?

In this perspective, laws and the criminal justice serve the interests of those in power. The criminal justice system oppresses those without power and status in the society and serves the interests only of those in power. The powerful seek to impose their conceptions of morality and their standards of behavior on the society and to protect their property and power. To do this, they are usually able to draw the middle classes into this pattern of control since maintenance of the control seems to serve middle-class interests as well.

According to this perspective, the poor, the lower classes and the oppressed do not commit more crimes than the oppressors. They are simply caught more often and punished more severely. Let us take a simple example which illustrates this.

Let us consider a poor lower-class citizen who takes a gun and robs a store owner of one thousand dollars. If caught he will be convicted of a felony and serve a long term in prison. Let us consider one of the firms that provides armaments for the Pentagon. We have read in recent years of the government being charged thousands of dollars for parts which can be bought in stores for a few dollars. We have read of companies found guilty of defrauding the government on contracts for millions of dollars. What happens to the owners of these companies? Nothing. The company may be fined, but that simply comes out of profits. The dividend to shareholders might be reduced by a few cents. Has the chief executive officer of any of those companies paid a fine out of his own pocket, let alone gone to prison? Of course not.

In 1990, Michael Milken pleaded guilty to just six counts of the 98 against him, including conspiracy and mail fraud. His fine was $600 million, though his personal fortune was estimated to be over $1 billion. Speculation was that $400 million of the fine was tax deductible (Greenwald, 1990). Milken was sentenced to prison, but federal prisons are often called "Club Feds" to indicate that they are more like holidays than comparable time spent at a state prison. If I were poor and unemployed and serving ten years in state prison for a robbery netting a few thousand dollars, I would be angry.

Most social conflict theorists of crime are Westerners, so they often attack the capitalist system in their theories. A social conflict theory of crime could be applied just as easily to communist dictatorships. Stalin and Brezhnev in the Soviet Union or Mao Zedong in the People's Republic of China were very skilled in using the criminal justice system to maintain the status of the elite in power, despite supposedly having a Marxist ideology at the basis of their system of government which is opposed to oppression.

Sykes (1974) has argued that the rules imposed by the ruling classes have little relationship to the cultural norms of the poor. In a society where affluence is well-publicized and becomes a major goal for people, frustration is bound to be generated in those who cannot attain and share in this affluence. The have-nots, therefore, develop a deep-rooted hostility toward the social order.

Schwendinger and Schwendinger (1979) argued that the legal system in the United States serves to secure an economic system that is centered around capitalism and guards the position of the owners at the expense of the workers. Many of the support systems, such as the education system, are designed to secure the labor force. Because of the antagonism built into the capitalist system, the legal system can never achieve its stated purpose of producing justice.

There is an important distinction between Marxist conflict theories and other conflict theories (Vold, 1979). In the Marxist perspective, criminal behavior may be still be seen as pathological, but it is attributed to the pathological nature of capitalist society. Since the workers are denied a productive role in society, they become demoralized and act in criminal ways. If society was more socialist, the workers would less oppressed and criminal behavior would become less frequent. Other conflict criminologists, however, consider criminal behavior to be the normal actions of normal people who have insufficient power to control the criminalization process.

In the social conflict view, criminals are really "political criminals," and the solution to the crime problem is to reform the society. The oppression of one segment by another segment must be stopped and, unlike what has happened in previous attempts to do this, not simply replaced by alternative types of oppression. Social conflict theorists, therefore, would urge the elimination of racism, sexism, and other forms of oppression through a social revolution.

A Social Conflict Theory of Suicide

As we will see in Chapter 10, suicide can be a political act. People have killed themselves in order to publicize some cause and to attempt to bring about some change. Suicide can also be seen more broadly as a political act in the sense that it may seek to shift a balance of power between the suicidal person and significant others, and this will be discussed in more detail in Chapter 10.

A social conflict theory of suicide would predict that suicide should be more common in modern (capitalist) societies. It appears that there is a large variation in the suicide rates of primitive societies, ranging from a rate of 23 per 100,000 per year in Kandrian (New Guinea) (Hoskin, et al., 1969) to zero among the Zuni in America (Lester, 1987b). However, anthropologists studying primitive societies are studying them in the Twentieth Century, long after the colonial powers had influenced these societies. Thus, primitive societies may have had low suicide rates before the colonial powers arrived and interfered.

Lester (1997) examined the effect of modernization on suicide rates in twelve nations of the world (all of which were capitalist) from 1901 to 1988. He found that modernization was associated with increased suicide rates in eight of the nations. In a sample of fourteen nations, Lester found that the suicide rates rose from an average of 7.8 per 100,000 per year in 1875 to 15.0 in 1975.

In nations with white oppressors and black oppressed, it has been documented that suicide rates are higher for the whites while homicide rates are higher for the blacks (Lester, 1989b). However, Hendin (1982) documented high rates of suicide among urban young black males in the United States. Hendin found that they had been exposed to family and peer violence, but that they also lived in disastrous social conditions, experiencing the bitterness and disappointments of ghetto life. Hendin felt that the culture's overt rejection of black people in the ghetto reinforced their feelings of anger and worthlessness already present as a result of their upbringing. Hendin suggested, in addition, that the cultural rejection of blacks is one of the reasons why black adults are such poor parents to their children, for their own rage and feelings of worthlessness prevent them from being effective parents. Hendin noted that the young blacks he studied felt trapped in an unalterable life situation by their lack of education and lack of job opportunities and by the destructive effect of the ghetto on their own personalities.

A standard component of the economic situation of capitalist nations is that there is unemployment. Reasonable rates of unemployment keep wages down and so reduce the costs of manufacturing goods, and there are economic dangers to having too low rates of unemployment. The evidence is overwhelming that unemployment is associated with high rates of suicide. Platt (1984) in a review of the research literature found that suicides more often had a history of job loss and job instability than nonsuicides and, in addition, the unemployed have a higher risk of subsequent suicide.

A Victimology Perspective[2]

The word *victimology* has come to mean the scientific study of victims of criminal acts. If we try to apply the concepts and theories in victimology to suicidal behavior, we have to ask who is the offender and who is the victim. It seems most reasonably to cast the suicide as the "offender" and the survivor as the "victim."

Although survivors have played a large role in suicidology organizations, such as the American Association of Suicidology, and although there is some research on the grieving and mourning process of survivors, applying the concepts and theories of victimology to survivors points to several topics which suicidologists have ignored.

The Consequences for the Victim

The consequences for crime victims include financial loss and expenses, physical injuries and psychological damage, including post-traumatic stress reactions. The survivors of suicides often incur financial loss and expenses, although these have not been studied; nor have tentative estimates of them been made. Most of the research conducted so far on survivors has focused on the psychological damage -- in particular, whether the psychological reactions of the survivors of suicides differ from those who experience a significant other die from other causes of death.

2 This section is based on the discussion by Karmen (1984).

Victimization Surveys

Victimologists have conducted several surveys of citizens in order to estimate the prevalence of victimization from crime. Beginning in 1972, there was a nationwide victimization survey carried out called the National Crime Survey, originally funded by the Law Enforcement Assistance Administration, but taken over by the Bureau of Justice Statistics. This survey enables the prevalence of different types of crimes to be estimated, estimates which differ quite considerably from official crime statistics based on crimes reported to law enforcement agencies. Secondly, the surveys provide data about who becomes a victim, when and where the incidents occur and the extent of injuries and losses suffered by the victims.

In suicidology, we have no idea of the prevalence of survivors and no indication of who they are. We know that there are roughly 32,000 suicides in America each year, but how many people would consider themselves survivors is unknown. It would be easy in a survey to ask respondents whether they know of a suicide, when it occurred, what relationship the suicide had to them, etc.

We also have little idea of the characteristics of survivors (which, of course, would vary with the relationship of the survivor to the suicide), even such characteristics as age, gender, race, income level, education, occupation, place of residence, etc. If we had this information, we could then see whether survivor groups are attracting a general sample of all survivors or whether they appeal only to some types of survivors.

Victim-Offender Interactions

In criminology, the victim-offender is not characterized by equality or mutual benefit. The relationship is unequal, parasitical, exploitive and oppressive The victim-offender interaction can be described in terms of roles, roles which are complementary. For example, Luckenbill (1977) has described the roles of murderer and murdered and how the interactions typically develop as the murder takes place.

What roles, then, do survivors and suicide play? Although there have been clinical descriptions of the roles played by survivors and suicides by psychotherapists (e.g., Richman, 1986), there has been no systematic research on these interactions. There are several related issues here.

Victim Proneness

In criminal behavior, some people appear to become victims of crime more often than others, leading to the suggestion that "crime-proneness" may exist in the same way that "accident-proneness" may exist. Might some people be "prone" to be survivors, that is, are some people survivors of suicide more often than others and does this proneness imply that the survivors have a role in determining their proneness? For example, Sylvia Plath, the American poet, committed suicide within a year after her husband left her for an affair with another woman. Several years later, this woman also committed suicide. Ted Hughes appears, therefore, to have been more "survivor-prone" than a person who loses only one significant other to suicide.

Victim-Facilitation and Precipitation

The notion that a victim may play a role in facilitating, precipitating and provoking the crime of which they are victim was first brought to prominence by Wolfgang's (1958) research on murder, in which he found that about a quarter of the murder victims in his study were judged to have played some role in precipitating their own murder.

The same question may be asked of survivors of suicide, namely, what role did they play in facilitating and precipitating the suicide of their significant other, a question rather more pointed that merely asking about the general role that they played.[3]

The notion of victim-precipitator implies that the suicide might not have occurred were it not for the actions of the survivor. For example, Richman and Rosenbaum (1970) documented interactions between attempted suicides and their significant others such as the following. A mother visiting her son in the hospital after had suicide attempt told him to pick a higher bridge next time. Another mother said to her daughter in front of the therapist that she would do anything to show her love for the daughter -- she'd even open the window so she could jump. A father said to his adolescent daughter, "Why don't you kill yourself; at least we'd know where you are (Richman, 1986, p. 80). Such hostility, accompanied by overt wishes for the other's suicide, may play a role in precipitating suicide.

Conclusions

This chapter has shown quite convincingly that theories of crime can be tailored so that they provide theories of suicide. In some cases, the theories of crime suggest theoretical approaches which have already been explored for suicide. In other cases, however, they suggest new and provocative approaches, particularly, the social processs, reaction and conflict theories and a victimology perspective.

References

Beck, A. T., Kovacs, M., & Weissman, A. Hopelessness and suicidal behavior. *Journal of the American Medical Association*, 1975, 234, 1146-1149.

Bentham, J. *A fragment on government and an introduction to the principles of morals and legislation*. Edited by W. Harrison. Oxford: Basil Blackwell, 1967.

Breed, W. Suicide, migration, and race. *Journal of Social Issues*, 1966, 22, 30-43.

Cloward, R., & Ohlin, L. *Delinquency and opportunity*. New York: Free Press, 1960.

Cohen, A. *Delinquent boys*. New York: Free Press, 1955.

Corder, B., Shorr, W., & Corder, R. A study of social and psychological characteristics of adolescent suicide attempters in an urban disadvantaged area. *Adolescence*, 1974, 9, 1-6.

[3] The general role may include variants such as "care-giver" or someone who responds to "cries for help."

Diekstra, R. A social learning theory approach to the prediction of suicidal behavior. *Proceedings of the 7th International Congress for Suicide Prevention*, pp. 55-66. Amsterdam: Swets & Zeitlinger BV, 1974.

Dublin, L. *Suicide*. New York: Ronald, 1963.

Durkheim, E. *Le suicide*. Paris: Felix Alcan, 1897.

Epstein, L., Thomas, C., Schaffer, J., & Perlin, S. Clinical predictors of physician suicide based on medical student data. *Journal of Nervous & Mental Disease*, 1973, 156, 19-29.

Frederick, C., & Resnick, H. How suicidal behaviors are learned. *American Journal of Psychotherapy*, 1971, 25, 37-55.

Ganzler, S. Some interpersonal and social dimensions of suicidal behavior. *Dissertation Abstracts*, 1967, 28B, 1192-1193.

Gastil, R. Homicide and a regional culture of violence. *American Sociological Review*, 1971, 36, 412-427.

Greenwald, J. Baby, you're a rich man still. *Time*, 1990, 135(20), 72.

Hendin, H. *Suicide in America*. New York: Norton, 1982.

Henry, A. F., & Short, J. F. *Suicide and homicide*. New York: Free Press, 1954.

Hillman, J. *Suicide and the soul*. New York: Harper & Row, 1964.

Hirschi, T. *Causes of delinquency*. Berkeley, CA: University of California, 1969.

Hoskin, J., Friedman, M., & Cawte, J. A high incidence of suicide in a pre-literate primitive society. *Psychiatry*, 1969, 32, 200-210.

Jacobs, J. *The moral justification of suicide*. Springfield, IL: Charles Thomas, 1982.

Kaplan, H., & Pokorny, A. D. Self-derogation and suicide. *Social Science & Medicine*, 1976, 10, 113-121.

Karmen, A. *Crime victims*. Monterey, CA: Brooks/Cole, 1984.

Kreitman, N., Smith, P., & Eng-Seong, T. Attempted suicide as language. *British Journal of Psychiatry*, 1970, 116, 465-473.

Lemert, E. *Human deviance, social problems, and social control*. Englewood Cliffs, NJ: Prentice-Hall, 1967.

Lester, D. Resentment and dependency in the suicidal individual. *Journal of General Psychology*, 1969, 81, 137-145.

_____ . *Why people kill themselves*. Springfield, IL: Charles Thomas, 1983.

_____ . A subcultural theory of teenage suicide. *Adolescence*, 1987a, 22, 317-320.

_____ . *Suicide as a learned behavior*. Springfield, IL: Charles Thomas, 1987b.

_____ . State laws on suicide and suicide rates. *Psychological Reports*, 1988, 62, 134.

_____ . Public health education against suicide. *Crisis*, 1989a, 10, 181-183.

_____ . Personal violence (suicide and homicide) in South Africa. *Acta Psychiatrica Scandinavica*, 1989b, 79, 235-237.

_____ . *Understanding and preventing suicide*. Springfield, IL: Charles Thomas, 1990a.

_____ . Impulsivity and threatened suicide. *Personality & 7 Individual Differences*, 1990b, 11, 1097-1098.

_____ . An empirical examination of Thomas Masaryk's theory of suicide. *Archives of Suicide Research*, 1997, 3, 125-131.

Livermore, A. Forty suicide notes. *Proceedings of the 18th Annual Meeting*, pp. 47-49. Denver: American Association of Suicidology, 1985.

Luckenbill, D. Criminal homicide as a situated transaction. *Social Problems*, 1977, 25, 176-186.

Lukas, C., & Seiden, H. M. *Silent grief.* New York: Scribners, 1987.

Merton, R. *Social theory and social structure*. Glencoe, IL: Free Press, 1957.

Miller, W. Lower class culture as a generating milieu of gang delinquency. *Journal of Social Issues*, 1958, 14, 5-19.

Neuringer, C. Self and other-appraisals by suicidal, psychosomatic and normal hospital patients. *Journal of Consulting & Clinical Psychology*, 1974, 42, 306.

Newman, G. *Just and painful*. New York: Macmillan, 1983.

Platt, S. Unemployment and suicidal behavior. *Social Science & Medicine*, 1984, 19, 93-115.

_____ . A subculture of parasuicide? *Human Relations* 1985, 38, 257-297.

Reckless, W. *The crime problem*. New York: Appleton-Century-Crofts, 1967.

Richman, J. *Family therapy for suicidal people*. New York: Springer, 1986.

Richman, J., & Rosenbaum, M. A. A clinical study of the role of hostility and death wishes by the family and society in suicidal attempts. *Israel Annals of Psychiatry & Related Disciplines*, 1970, 8, 213-231.

Schwendinger, H., & Schwendinger, J. Delinquency and social reform. In L. Empey (Ed.) *Juvenile justice*, pp. 246-290. Charlottesville, VA: University of Virginia Press, 1979.

Shaw, C. R., & McKay, H. D. *Juvenile delinquency and urban areas*. Revised edition. Chicago: University of Chicago Press, 1972.

Spiegel, D., & Neuringer, C. Role of dread in suicidal behavior. *Journal of Abnormal & Social Psychology*, 1963, 66, 507-511.

Stephens, B. J. The social relationships of women. In D. Lester (Ed.) *Why women kill themselves*. pp. 73-85. Springfield, IL: Charles Thomas, 1988.

Sutherland, E. H. *Principles of criminology*. Philadelphia: Lippincott, 1947.

Sykes, G. The rise of critical criminology. *Journal of Criminal Law & Criminology*, 1974, 22, 335-347.

Sykes, G., & Matza, D. Techniques of neutralization. *American Sociological Review*, 1957, 22, 664-670.

Victoroff, V. M. *The suicidal patient*. Oradell, NJ: Medical Economics Books, 1983.

Vold, G. B. *Theoretical criminology*. New York: Oxford University Press, 1979.

von Hirsch, A. *Doing justice*. New York: Hill and Wang, 1976.

Wolfgang, M. E. *Patterns in criminal homicide*. Philadelphia: University of Pennsylvania, 1958.

Wolfgang, M. E., & Ferracuti, F. *The subculture of violence*. London: Tavistock, 1967.

Chapter 9

ECONOMICS AND SUICIDE[1]

INTRODUCTION

Economics is "a social science concerned chiefly with the way society employs its limited resources, which have alternative uses, to produce goods and services for present and future consumption" (Spencer, 1986, p. 2). As such, suicidal behavior would not seem to be relevant to economics, and indeed you will not find suicidal behavior mentioned in economics textbooks. However, economic issues are relevant to suicidal in three ways.

First, what is the economic cost to society of suicidal behavior? Second, do the economic conditions in the society have an impact on the suicidal behavior of its members? After all, tradition has it that large numbers of stockbrokers jumped out of their office windows to their death after the stock exchange crash in the 1920s.[2]

Third, economists have realized that the models which they have proposed to explain economic phenomenon can be applied to other behaviors, such as deciding to have to children and the deterrent effect of the death penalty to name a couple (Yang and Lester, 1995). In recent years, several economists have applied economic models and ideas in order to explain suicidal behavior, and these applications will be reviewed here.

THE ECONOMIC COST OF SUICIDE

Epidemiological studies suggest that major depressive illness affects about two percent of the population of the United States, and there are about 30,000 suicides each year. What economic cost do these behaviors involve for the nation? Stoudemire, et al. (1986) made an effort to estimate this cost.

For those suffering from a major depressive illness, there are both direct costs and indirect costs. The direct costs include the cost of treatment (such as physician visits, hospitalization, pharmaceuticals and travel costs when seeking care), while the indirect costs accrue from the loss of productivity of those who have a major depression. For those who commit suicide, the costs are mainly indirect.

---

1 This chapter was co-authored by Bijou Yang.
2 A myth, however (Lester and Yang, 1997).

Depressive Illness

Using data from studies conducted under the auspices of the National Institute of Mental Health, Stoudemire estimated that the number of cases of major depressive illness in a six month period in 1980 was 4.8 million. From other epidemiological studies, Stoudemire estimated that affective disorders accounted for about half a million hospital admissions in 1980, 7.4 million hospital days, and 13.3 million physician visits.

For inpatient care, the total cost came to 1.3 billion dollars. For outpatient care, the cost was 0.6 billion dollars. Other costs (including medication) came to 0.2 billion dollars, giving a grand total of 2.1 billion dollars.

The indirect costs of major depressive illnesses were based on an estimate of 5.7 million treated cases and 2.8 million untreated cases in 1980. Stoudemire estimated that these cases led to 127 million days lost involving treatment and 92 million days lost over and above the treatment days. Using data on the proportion of men and women in the labor force, Stoudemire estimated a loss of 10.0 billion dollars in earnings.

Many persons with depressive illness commit suicide. Stoudemire estimated that about 60 percent of all suicides have a major depressive illness. In 1980, there were 26,869 suicides, and Stoudemire estimated that the suicides of those with major depressive illness (using sex-specific estimates of discounted lifetime earnings) involved an indirect cost of 4.2 billion dollars.

Thus the total cost of major depressive illness in 1980 was estimated to be 2.1 billion dollars for direct costs, 10.0 billion dollars due to lost productivity, and 4.2 billion dollars due to mortality from suicide. These costs add up to 16.3 billion dollars.

More recent estimates of the cost to the society for depressive disorders are four times the amount estimated by Stoudemire (Miller, 1993).

Suicide

Stoudemire's estimate for the indirect cost as a result of the suicide of those with a major depressive illness was 4.2 billion dollars. This was based on an estimate of 60 percent of suicides having a major depressive illness. From this, we can estimate that the indirect costs of all of the suicides through lost lifetime earnings would be 7 billion dollars.

In addition, suicides also involve medical and legal costs in the efforts to revive suicides and to certify the deaths, but these costs are probably dwarfed by the indirect costs. For example, Weinstein and Saturno (1989) estimated the economic effects of a single youth suicide (among those aged 15 to 24 years of age) as $431,000 from lost life-time earnings (roughly $10,400 per year) and $1,067 in medicolegal expenses.

In addition to the behavior of suicide in which the person dies, there are many attempts at suicide each year where the individual survives. It is difficult to count the number of attempts at suicide each year because many attempters do not require medical attention and so do not come to the attention of the authorities. However, it has been estimated by Farberow and Shneidman (1961) that there at least eight suicide attempts for every completed suicide (the technical term for those who die). Thus, if there are 30,000 completed suicides in one year, there may be upwards of 240,000 attempted suicides.

Many attempted suicides require medical care, and a good proportion of them receive psychological and psychiatric treatment. These attempters will be lost to the labor force during this period, incurring additional economic costs. Rodger and Scott (1995) estimated that the medical costs of treating an attempted suicide for merely the subsequent suicidal behavior was thirty-four thousand British Pounds in 1986-1987 prices over a six year period.

Comment

It can be seen that the economic costs of suicide may be considerable, and in addition there is the psychological pain and suffering of both the people who commit suicide and those who survive the suicide of a loved one. Understanding and preventing suicidal behavior is clearly an important economic task for our society.

However, Lester (1995) has suggested that these estimates may be gross exaggerations of the true cost of suicide. Applying the work of Viscuso (1994) on the economic impact of diseases caused by smoking, Lester noted that (a) suicides avoid the cost of treating the underlying psychiatric disorder had the person continued living, (b) estimates of the life-time earnings do not take into account the fact that many suicides are marginal people who do not function productively in the workplace, and (c) premature death reduces the eventual costs of later medical treatments, nursing home care, and pension and social security payments. Viscuso concluded that each package of cigarettes sold *saves* the society some money, and the same might be true of suicides. We must beware of selectively choosing economic data to fit our perspective.

THE IMPACT OF THE ECONOMY ON SUICIDAL BEHAVIOR

One of the clearest phenomenon in the study of suicidal behavior is that the suicide rates of nations vary considerably and that the wealthiest nations have the highest suicide rates (Lester, 1996). Thus, it is very likely that the economy may have an impact on suicidal behavior.

Lester and Yang (1997) reviewed three theories of suicide which proposed that the economy has an impact on suicide and found three different predictions. Durkheim (1897) predicted that suicide rates should rise during times of both economic booms and economic depressions; Ginsberg (1966) predicted that suicide rates should rise only during economic booms; Henry and Short (1954) predicted that suicide rates should rise only during economic depressions. The results are not completely clear-cut, but the preponderance of evidence seems to favor Henry and Short.

Let us look here just at the impact of unemployment. In general, unemployment has been found to lead to reduced levels of psychological well-being (Ezzy, 1993). In particular, unemployment is clearly associated with increased rates of completed and attempted suicide (Platt, 1984, 1986), and these associations have been confirmed both at the societal level and at the individual level. These results, therefore, support Henry and Short's theory.

However, the explanation for this association is not altogether clear at the present time. For example, it could well be that unemployment is a stressor which increases the risk of suicidal behavior in people. Alternatively, it could be that those who are psychiatrically disturbed are more likely to be become unemployed and less likely to find new employment; in addition, those who are psychiatrically disturbed are much more likely to be suicidal and actually attempt and complete suicide. So far, no research has appeared which examines the validity of these two alternative explanations.

Economic Models of Suicide

In most economic models for suicide, committing suicide is considered to be a rational act. Individuals are acting "rationally" if, given a choice between various alternatives, they select what seems to be the most desirable or least undesirable alternative. Economists are not concerned with whether suicide is wrong, immoral or a deviant act.

Costs and Benefits

Yeh and Lester (1987) suggested that the decision to commit suicide depends upon the benefits and costs associated with suicide and with alternative actions. An individual will be less likely to commit suicide if the benefits from suicide decrease, the costs of suicide increase, the costs of alternative actions decrease or the benefits from alternative activities increase.

The benefits from suicide include escape from physical or psychological pain (as in the suicide of someone dying from terminal cancer), the anticipation of the impact of the suicide's death on other people (as in someone who hopes to make the survivors feel guilt), or restoring one's public image (as in the suicide of Antigone in Sophocles's play of the same name). In addition, the act itself may be enjoyable. Those who self-injure themselves by cutting their wrists sometimes report that the act of cutting relieves built-up tension and that they feel no pain.

There are several costs in committing suicide. These include the money and effort spent in obtaining the information and equipment needed for the act of suicide, the pain involved in preparing to kill oneself and in the process of committing suicide, the expected loss as a result of committing suicide such as the expected punishment predicted by most of the major religions of the world, and the opportunity costs (that is, the net gain to be expected if other alternative activities were chosen and life continued).

From this perspective, an individual will engage in suicidal only if its benefits are greater than all of the costs mentioned above. Therefore, a cost-benefit economic model would suggest that suicide could be prevented by increasing its costs or by decreasing its benefits.

A Demand and Supply Analysis of Suicide

Let us assume that suicide is a commodity or service that we purchase. It is obvious that suicide is very different from the typical objects that we purchase. For example, when we buy an object, we pay a specific price to obtain it and then we enjoy it. Since suicide results in death, we have to conceptualize our enjoyment of it quite differently.

(Suicide is somewhat similar to the purchasing of health care services. In both, we pay a price to get rid of something, life in the case of suicide and sickness in the case of health care.

Yet there is a basic difference between suicide and health care in that suicide leads to death while health care, hopefully, leads to further life. Of course, for those who believe that there will be a "life-after-death," suicide also leads to further life, but of a different kind.)

Looking at matters from a demand side perspective, when we purchase a commodity (or a service), the price we pay for the commodity (or service) reflects the benefits we expect to receive from consuming that commodity. From a demand side perspective, beef costs more than chicken because the public desires beef more, and their stronger desire for beef reflects their expectation of greater satisfaction from eating beef than from eating chicken.

In the demand side analysis of suicide, the notion of its "price" is different from the ordinary price of a commodity. The benefit expected by a suicide is the relief of tremendous distress. Accordingly, we must use a scale of distress to measure the benefit expected by the suicidal individual. This benefit expected by the suicidal individual is reflected in the price he must pay for his suicide.

Accordingly, the demand curve is a relationship indicating the probability of committing suicide as a function of the amount of distress felt by the individual. As the amount of distress increase, the probability of committing suicide increases. The demand for suicide is, therefore, an upward sloping curve, which is quite different from the typical downward sloping demand curve found in most economic analyses.

On the supply side, the probability of committing suicide is related to the cost of committing suicide. The cost of committing suicide includes the cost of losing your life, collecting information about how to commit the act, purchasing the means for suicide, etc. While the latter two items have a clear-cut scale of measurement, the cost of losing life is much harder to measure. It includes at least three components, namely, the psychological fear of death, the loss of income in the future which otherwise would have been earned by the suicide, and the loss of any enjoyment that would be experienced during the rest of your "normal" life.

The higher the cost of committing suicide, the lower the probability that an individual would actually commit suicide. Therefore, the supply curve should be a downward sloping curve.

(It is important in such a demand-supply analysis of suicide to convert the psychological variables [level of distress and future pleasure] into measures comparable to monetary units, so that an equilibrium can be obtained through equating the demand and supply for suicide. One way to measure the level of distress is to operationalize it as the cost of the psychological services required to eliminate the distress that the suicidal person is experiencing. This is complicated by the fact that psychological services are not always effective. Some people do not benefit from treatment. This could be taken into account by incorporating the probability of success of the treatment into the calculations, as a multiplier of the cost of treatment. Converting future pleasure from life into monetary units is more difficult. One alternative could be to convert all of the components of the cost into subjective units, based on the ratings given by representative members of society.)

The demand for suicide and the supply for suicide can be diagrammed as shown below:

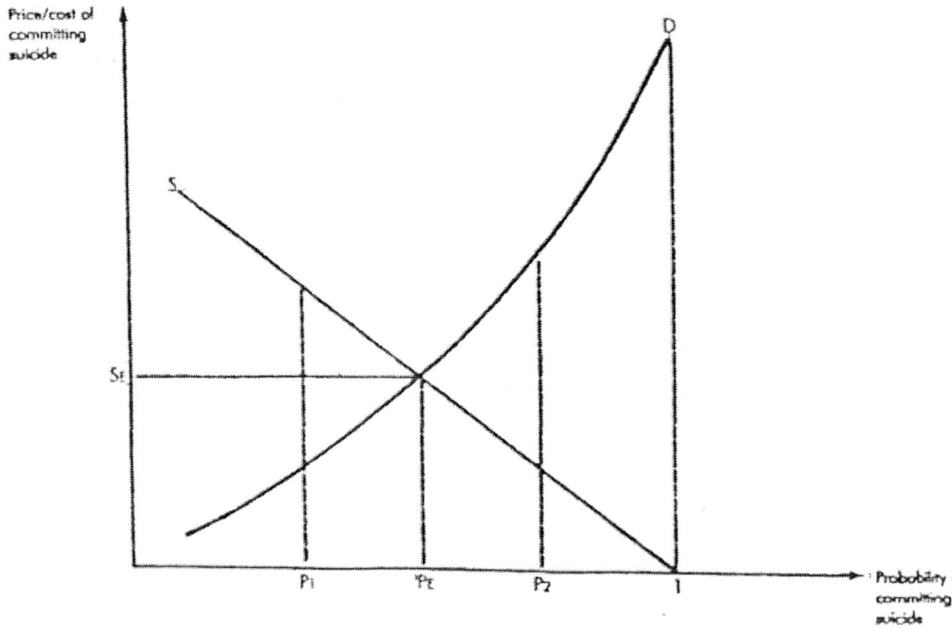

Figure. A Demand and Supply Curve for Suicide

The vertical axis indicates the price (or the cost) of committing suicide, while the horizontal axis represents the probability of committing suicide. Since the probability of committing suicide is used to indicate the quantity demanded or supplied, the upper limit for this variable is one. The demand curve is an upward sloping curve and becomes vertical when the probability of committing suicide is equal to one. The price level for committing suicide which corresponds to the point where the probability is equal to one refers to the threshold level of distress that an individual can no longer tolerate. In this situation, committing suicide becomes inevitable.

The intersection of the demand and supply curves represents an equilibrium for an individual. For that equilibrium level of distress and the corresponding costs of committing suicide there is an equilibrium probability of committing suicide. As the supply curve might intersect any section of the demand curve, the equilibrium probability of committing suicide can range anywhere from zero to one.

By definition, the equilibrium of committing suicide is determined by the intersection of the supply and demand curves. Due to the peculiar nature of the demand and supply of suicide, the equilibrium so obtained is not a stable one.

Since the demand for suicide is an upward sloping line, the higher the distress level, the higher the probability of committing suicide. Since the supply curve is downward sloping, the higher the cost of committing suicide, the lower the probability of committing suicide. Let us label the equilibrium level of distress and the cost of committing suicide S_E and the corresponding equilibrium probability P_E.

Let us examine the implications of these supply and demand curves. If the probability of committing suicide is initially at P_1 which is lower than the equilibrium probability P_E, this corresponds to a low level of distress from the demand side perspective and a high cost of committing suicide from the supply side perspective. As a result, the situation will lead to an even lower probability of committing suicide, and the individual will eventually withdraw from the suicidal situation.

On the other hand, if the probability of committing suicide initially is higher than the equilibrium probability P_E, say at P_2, this corresponds to a high level of distress from the demand side perspective and a low cost of committing suicide from a supply side perspective. Thus, this situation will lead to an even higher probability of committing suicide.

Both situations, whether the initial probability of committing suicide is higher or lower than the equilibrium, result in movement away from the equilibrium. If the initial probability of committing suicide is lower than the equilibrium, then the individual becomes less likely to commit suicide; while if the initial probability of committing suicide is higher than the equilibrium the individual becomes more likely to commit suicide. In short, this economic model of suicide implies that suicidal behavior is an unstable behavior.

Yeh and Lester (1987) examined some of the factors which contributed to the decision to commit suicide based on a review of the literature of suicide by Lester (1983). They noted that most of the factors, such as psychiatric disturbance, gender and age, and dysfunctional families of origin, are reasonably stable characteristics. Thus, once the demand curve is formed, it will remain quite stable over time. Sudden shifts in the demand curve might be caused by events such as sudden deaths of significant others, illness or work difficulties, but the extent of the shifts in the demand curve as a result of these factors may be quite limited.

Labor-Force Analogies

Huang (1997) applied economic analyses of the decision to enter and leave the labor market to suicidal behavior conceptualized as a decision to enter or leave the "life-market." The decision to leave the life-market will be based on maximizing utility. The utility, according to Huang, will encompass more than income, including as well all dimensions of the worth or value of life, such as love, health, fame, beauty, fun, adventure, prestige, respect, security, etc. This life income has to be earned, and it is a struggle to gain some of these rewards. Obtaining them requires a great deal of hard "labor" (L).

The opposite of work is leisure, rest and relaxation (R). Leisure entails letting go of pressure and responsibility. The maximum manifestation of leisure is complete and permanent rest -- death. Labor measures the extent of effort and resolve to live while leisure measures its lack. The expected market rate wage (W) is the perceived opportunity of ability to earn life income for a unit of life effort.

Two solutions are possible. Most people will choose an interior solution, choosing to live with a varying amount of effort. Some will be unable to find an interior solution, and they may choose to drop out of the life market, that is, commit suicide, analogous to discouraged workers dropping out of the labor market.

People will decide to drop out of the life market if the perceived obtainable wage in the life market falls short of some minimally acceptable level, perhaps as a result of a terminal disease, recurring depressions, business fiascoes, public humiliation, etc. Less likely, the decision to commit suicide can also be caused by an increase in the reservation wage. An individual, wealthy in the sense of life, may need more to keep life interesting and challenging. Having so much of everything, his utility from life diminishes and he may become tired of life. Given a much higher reservation wage than the average person, and without a matched increase in perceived wage, the individual may find the corner solution desirable and choose to commit suicide.

Huang noted that, in this perspective, suicide is not irrational. However, suicide may not be the correct solution, especially because of the uncertainty of the future. Life market information is always incomplete and imperfect. In the model W was the *perceived* expected wage from living, and the individual's perception may be erroneous.

Becker on Irrationality

Economists define rational behavior as maximizing some variable such as utility or profit. Becker (1962) defined two types of irrational behavior: (1) random, erratic and whimsical choices and (2) perseverative choices in which the person chooses what he or she has always chosen in the past. Lester and Yang (1991) argued that these two types of irrational behavior paralleled the major typology of suicidal behavior in which suicidal behavior is seen as a time-limited impulsive crisis or as a chronic maladaptive pattern.

Becker and Murphy (1988) have recently proposed a rational model for addictive behaviors in which they view addicts as rational optimizers, exhibiting consistent, forward-looking and individually optimal behavior. They have accurate perceptions of the trade-off between present benefits and future costs, and they are capable of making rational decisions based on these perceptions. A model for suicide might be based on such principles.

More recently, Fehr and Zych (1994) have proposed a theory of addictive behavior which they have called irrationally myopic, in which people are assumed to base their decisions on the benefits which accrue immediately rather than on the costs which accrue over a longer period of time. This model may be applicable to suicidal behavior.

Suicide Attempts and Signalling Games

Rosenthal (1993) focused on suicide attempts which have chances of either success or failure, that is, suicide attempts of moderate to severe severity, where the individual is "gambling" with the outcome. He suggested that the suicide attempt can be seen as a signal intended to manipulate the receiver's behavior in a way favorable to the sender. As such, it resembles a game.

In this perspective, the sender may be either depressed or normal, and it is assumed that the players know the respective probabilities of these two possibilities. The sender knows his type while the receiver does not. The sender chooses an attempt (signal) strength (which determines whether he or she survives). The receiver then chooses a sympathetic or unsympathetic response. The receiver would prefer to respond sympathetically to a depressed sender and unsympathetically to a normal sender. Both types of sender would prefer a sympathetic response, but the preference is stronger in the depressed sender.

Rosenthal's analysis suggested two hypotheses. First, gambling-type suicidal behavior would be less common if the suicidal individual strongly demanded a sympathetic response. Second, if the receiver is very likely to give a sympathetic response, then depressed senders are less likely to engage in gambling-type suicidal behavior.

Suicide as Investment under Uncertainty

Dixit and Pindyck (1994) examined the nature of investment under conditions of uncertainty. Although their book focused on the investment decisions of firms, they noted that other decisions are made with the same conditions as investments: the decision is irreversible, there is uncertainty over the future rewards of the decision, and there is some leeway over the timing of the decision.

Dixit and Pindyck suggested that suicide fits these criteria. They noted that Hamermesh and Soss (1974) had proposed that an individual will commit suicide when the expected value of the utility of the rest of his or her life falls short of some benchmark (or down to zero). Dixit and Pindyck argued that Hamermesh and Soss failed to consider the option of staying alive. Suicide is irreversible, and the future is quite uncertain. Therefore, the option of waiting to see if the situation improves should be a likely choice. Even if the expected direction of life is downward, there may still be some non-zero positive probability that it will improve.

Dixit and Pindyck speculated that suicides project the bleak present into an equally bleak future. They ignore the uncertainty of the future and the option value of life. In this respect, Dixit and Pindyck saw suicides as irrational.

They noted that religious and moral proscriptions against suicide compensate to some extent for this failure of rationality. These proscriptions raise the perceived cost of suicide and lower the threshold of the quality of life that precipitates suicide.

Discussion

Suicidal behavior clearly incurs economic costs, although these may not be as great as those estimating these costs in the past have led us to believe. Secondly, the economy has an impact on suicidal behavior, with economic downturns increasing the risk of suicidal behavior, at least in the wealthiest nations.

Finally, it is clear that economic models can be applied to suicidal behavior and, sometimes, lead to interesting conclusions about the nature of suicide. In particular, economic models have much to say about the rationality or irrationality of suicide, proposing a variety of criteria by which to make such judgments.

References

Becker, G. S. Irrational behavior and economic theory. *Journal of Political Economy*, 1962, 70, 1-13.

Becker, G. S., & Murphy, K. M. A theory of rational addiction. *Journal of Political Economy*, 1988, 96, 675-700.

Dixit, A. K., & Pindyck, R. S. *Investment under uncertainty*. Princeton: Princeton University, 1994.

Durkheim, E. *Le suicide*. Paris: Felix Alcan, 1897.

Ezzy, D. Unemployment and mental health. *Social Science & Medicine*, 1993, 37, 41-52.

Farberow, N. L., & Shneidman, E. S. (Eds.) *The cry for help*. New York: McGraw-Hill, 1961.

Fehr, E., & Zych, P. K. The power of temptation. In G. Antonides & W. F. van Raaij (Eds.) *Proceedings of the IAREP/SABE Conference*, pp. 196-215. Rotterdam: Erasmus University, 1994.

Hamermesh, D. S., & Soss, N. An economic theory of suicide. *Journal of Political Economy*, 1974, 82, 83-98.

Henry, A. F., & Short, J. F. *Suicide and homicide*. New York: Free Press, 1954.

Huang, W. C. "Life force" participation perspective of suicide. In D. Lester & B. Yang, *The economy and suicide*, pp. 81-89. Commack, NY: Nova Science, 1997.

Ginsberg, R. B. Anomie and aspirations. *Dissertation Abstracts*, 1966, 27A, 3945-3946.

Lester, D. *Why people kill themselves*. Springfield, IL: Charles Thomas, 1983.

_____ . Estimating the true economic cost of suicide. *Perceptual & Motor Skills*, 1995, 80, 746.

Lester, D. *Patterns of suicide and homicide in the world.* Commack, NY: Nova Science, 1996.

Lester, D., & Yang, B. Suicidal behavior and Becker's definition of irrationality. *Psychological Reports*, 1991, 68, 655-656.

_____ . *The economy and suicide*. Commack, NY: Nova Science, 1997.

Miller, M. W. Dark days: the staggering cost of depression. *Wall Street Journal*, 1993, December 2, B1, B8.

Platt, S.D. Unemployment and suicidal behavior. *Social Science & Medicine*, 1984, 19, 93-115.

Platt, S. D. Parasuicide and unemployment. *British Journal of Psychiatry*, 1986, 149, 401-405.

Rodger, C. R., & Scott, A. I. F. Frequent deliberate self-harm. *Scottish Medical Journal*, 1995, 40, 10-13.

Rosenthal, R. W. Suicide attempts and signalling games. *Mathematical Social Sciences*, 1993, 26, 25-33.

Spencer, M. H. *Contemporary macroeconomics*. New York: Worth, 1986.

Stoudemire, A., Frank, R., Hedemark, N., Kamlet, M., & Blazer, D. The economic burden of depression. *General Hospital Psychiatry*, 1986, 8, 387-394.

Viscuso, W. K. *Cigarette taxation and the social consequences of smoking*. Cambridge, MA: NBER, 1994.

Weinstein, M. C., & Saturno, P. J. Economic impact of youth suicide and suicide attempts. *Report of the Secretary's Task Force on Youth Suicide*, 1989, 4, 82-93. Washington, DC: United States Government Printing Office.

Yang, B., & Lester, D. New direction for economics. *Journal of Socio-Economics*, 1995, 24, 433-446.

Yeh, B. Y., & Lester, D. An economic model for suicide. In D. Lester, *Suicide as a learned behavior*, pp. 51-57. Springfield, IL: Charles Thomas, 1987.

Chapter 10

POLITICS AND SUICIDE

INTRODUCTION

Political science is "the study of the processes, principles, and structure of government and of political institutions" (Morris, 1976, p. 1015). Political science, therefore, has little relevance to suicide. Suicide can, however, be a political act. People have killed themselves in order to publicize some cause and to attempt to bring about some change. For example, the Buddhist monk Thich Quang Duc immolated himself in Saigon on June 11th, 1963, as a protest against the regime of Ngo Dinh Diem in South Vietnam, following which other people immolated themselves in Vietnam, the United States and elsewhere to protest the political situation in Vietnam (Jorgensen-Earp, 1987; Coleman, 1987).

Furthermore, suicide can be conceptualized more broadly as a political act, using the word 'politics' in the sense that Laing (1967) uses the word to describe any behavior in which one or more people exert power over others. Writers such as Haley (1969) and Laborit (1970) have argued forcefully that the desire for power and for dominating others may be one of the more powerful desires motivating human behavior, and its effects can be documented quite clearly in suicidal behavior where the suicidal act can easily change the power balance in relationships.

Attempted suicide has long been seen as a manipulative act (Sifneos, 1966; Lester, 1968). The attempted suicide is often trying to force certain responses from significant others. Perhaps the lover about to leave will stay? Perhaps he or she will pay attention to your distress? A threat of suicide can have equally powerful effects on significant others in changing their immediate response to the threatener.

Menninger (1938) described three motives in the suicidal act: to escape from pain, anger directed toward oneself, and anger directed toward others. This latter motive often manifests itself in obvious efforts to exert power over others. The person who shoots himself, for example, in front of significant others or in such a way that they discover him clearly wants to traumatize them and shape the memory they have of him. The person may be trying to leave the survivors with guilt, and the stigma that attaches to the survivors of suicides adds to their trauma (Rudestam, 1990).

The efforts of the suicide may not always be directed toward causing others pain. Antigone, in Sophocles's play of the same name, is trying to restore honor to the name of her family and glory to herself by her suicidal actions (Faber, 1970), and Japanese officials who commit suicide often do so for similar reasons of honor. By trying to shape how others will experience them, they are behaving politically in Laing's sense of the word.

Counts (1988) too has documented how suicide may be used to change one's image in the social group. In Papua New Guinea, suicide often acts as a form of social sanction. It has political consequences for the surviving kin and for those who are held responsible for the events precipitating the suicide. Counts relates a case of Agnes, a woman who tried to seduce Victor into marriage, whereupon the whole village turned against her. Victor's family rejected her as a bride, and she killed herself. Her suicide changed the feeling in the village, and now Victor and his family were seen to be at fault. Whereas Victor's family had refused to pay Agnes a bridal fee, they were now willing to pay her kin compensation. Victor's kin now faced both the disgrace of having caused Agnes's death and the financial loss. Agnes also removed her shame by killing herself. This case shows nicely the dual aspects in the suicidal act of freeing oneself while oppressing others. (Such freeing of oneself may be the underlying motive in cases of *fatalistic* suicide [Durkheim, 1897].)

In another vein, Meerloo (1962) has described *psychic homicide* in which a person commits murder by getting someone else to commit suicide. More recent cases have been described by Richman (1986) where suicide takes place in the context of a family, in which members covertly and sometimes overtly communicate their desire that the person die and may even 'force' one family member to kill himself.

Thus, in the many ways describe here, suicide may be conceptualized as a political act in which the suicidal person seeks to change the balance of power in his or her social group or more broadly in the society.

Suicide as a Manipulative Act

Suicidal behavior has often been viewed as a manipulative behavior. Adler (Ansbacher, 1961) noted that suicidal individuals often show evidence that they wish to produce reactions indicating love and attention from those close to them. Indeed, Farberow and Shneidman's (1961) classic book on attempted suicide was called *The Cry For Help*, drawing attention to the desire to manipulate the environment by means of the suicidal act. Adler noted also the intent of some suicidal people to hurt others, which in extreme cases casts suicide as an act of revenge.

Sifneos (1966) studied attempted suicides and was struck by the manipulative aspects of their behavior: two-thirds were judged to have used manipulation (that is, tried to prevent another from leaving, thereby interrupting the relationship, or tried to control another person's actions in some way). Sifneos noted that the majority of these patients were not motivated to receive psychotherapy and were usually satisfied with the results of their manipulative behavior, particularly if it had been effective. Sifneos noted that anxiety was often lacking in these patients, and they appeared to be apathetic and fatalistic. Sifneos hypothesized that manipulative suicides were characterized by being more introspective, having few but intense relationships, having difficulty in expressing emotions, having exaggerated expectations for themselves, being self-centered, and internalizing emotional problems.

The following is a case in which the suicide attempt was designed to elicit rejection from the environment.

> The attempted suicide was a male undergraduate who was disliked by most of those who met him. He displayed a "psychological sadism" toward others, finding pleasure in causing others to suffer. He attempted suicide during vacation time, when his roommate (who presumably liked him) was home and when he was living with others who knew him less well and did not like him. He took an overdose and then went down to the communal area of the dormitory to announce the fact. The others there barely listened and then went back to watching television. He went to bed and woke up 48 hours later. His roommate arrived back at the college and took him to the campus infirmary. When discussing this attempt, he said, "Those bastards let me die," yet he seemed pleased by the whole episode. When I looked at his psychological test results, his scores on the Buss and Durkee (1957) hostility inventory were high, especially on the Resentment Scale which measures a cynical and distrustful view of the world. His suicide attempt seemed designed to extort rejection from the others, carefully timed so that those who might rescue him were away. The rejection, once obtained, pleased him since it confirmed his view of the world.

The use of a suicide as a manipulative act, in order to extort particular responses from others, may lead to a sequence in which the severity of successive suicide actions has to increase in order to keep extorting the desired response from others. Lester, et al. (1978) found that attempted suicides who later completed suicide did indeed increase their suicidal intent (as measured by an objective scale based upon the circumstances of the suicidal act) in their final suicidal action from that on the earlier attempt.

Such manipulative behavior may have been learned in childhood and adolescence. A child may learn to hurt himself in order that he can manipulate others by getting a positive response from his parents to his self-injuries. For example, a parent who "suffers" because of misdeeds of his child, such as the child failing academic work, teaches the child that he can make others suffer (anxiety, grief, or rage) by doing things that admittedly are also self-injurious.

One type of manipulativeness may be loosely described Machiavellianism, and Christie and Geis (1970) have devised a scale to measure this trait. Psychiatrists (as compared to other doctors) and those who win at poker-type games (as compared to those who lose) are high scorers on this scale. Lester (1970) found that high scorers on a scale of suicidal potential had higher Machiavellian scores than low scorers. Thus there may be an association between manipulativeness and suicidal potential. It is of interest to note that the manipulativeness of the suicidal person has been one of the most often discussed character traits in writings about suicide, and yet little research has focused on this variable.

Suicide as a Hostile Act

Kelly (1955, 1957, 1965) has written about those who manipulate others. For Kelly such individuals are hostile people. By "hostile" Kelly takes pains to show that he does not mean hostile in the usual sense of the word, namely, an impulse to hurt someone or to cause pain. Such a definition stresses the experience of the other person rather than the experience of the hostile person. "We consider you to be hostile when you hurt us." Kelly felt that hostility should be investigated from the point of view of the hostile person himself. How does it feel to the hostile individual to be hostile?

Kelly removed the notion of aggression from his definition of hostility. Aggression for Kelly is one extreme of a passive-assertive dimension of behavior. Aggression is very similar to adventuresomeness. Hostility, on the other hand, lies in the reactions of the individual to information from the environment that is incongruent with his beliefs. When an individual meets such incongruent evidence he may accept it and attempt to erect a new system of beliefs from the ruins of the old system which will be consistent with the incongruent evidence. But he has an alternative. He can attempt to distort the data to fit his beliefs, or he can attempt to extract or extort new evidence from the environment that is congruent with his beliefs. Hostility then, for Kelly, is a refusal to accept, and its opposite is realistic acceptance. The hostile person can be aggressive or passive but aggression is not an essential component of hostility.

If the suicidal individual is to be considered a hostile person we must ask whether two necessary conditions are met.

I. Is he rigid in his thought and so unlikely to change or modify his beliefs? There is some evidence that this may be true. Neuringer (1964), working from a different point of view, has reported that on a variety of psychological tasks suicidal individuals are more rigid in their thinking than are nonsuicidal individuals or psychoneurotic patients.

II. To what end does the suicidal individual extort and distort evidence? The seeking of love and attention by the suicidal individual through his suicidal behavior has been noted above. The suicidal individual may expect love and attention from others and may believe that they do indeed love him. If they do not spontaneously give him evidence of this love, then his suicidal behavior may be an attempt to extort demonstrations of affection from them.

Suicidal behavior may serve to confirm other beliefs of the individual. The suicidal person frequently experiences feelings of worthlessness and depression. By risking rejection through his suicidal behavior, the suicidal individual can seek a confirmation of his worthlessness and a demonstration that he is not worth caring about (Lester, 1968).

The Sexual Politics of Double Suicide

The political aspects of suicidal behavior can be illustrated dramatically in some cases of double suicide in which one person decides to commit suicide and persuades the partner to do so also.

Couple suicide pacts are not very common. For example, according to a survey conducted in Dade County, Florida (Fishbain and Aldrich, 1985) suicide pacts constituted only 0.007 percent of the suicides. The most common pacts involved married couples, with young lovers next most common. Based on a survey of the United States from 1980 to 1987, Wickett (1990) documented 97 couples involving the suicide of one or both partners. Two-thirds of these cases involved mercy killings followed by suicide, while one-third were double suicides. In the typical case, the wife or both partners were ill, and the husband initiated the plan. The couple often left evidence indicating that they felt exhausted and hopeless, and that they feared parting or being institutionalized. In the mercy killing cases, the husband could not bear his wife's suffering or life without her.

Rosenbaum (1983) studied cases of double suicide in which one partner survived. The instigator, usually a male with a history of attempted suicide, did not survive the suicidal action. The surviving partner was typically a female who did not appear to be emotionally disturbed or to have a history of nonfatal suicidal behavior. The instigators had characteristics similar to those of murderers and murder-suicides.

For double suicides (rather than mercy killings), these studies suggest the role of a domineering and dominating husband who decides that both partners must commit suicide. Insight into double suicide may be obtained from the biographies of famous double suicides. One such case involves Arthur Koestler and his wife Cynthia (Levene, 1984).[1]

Arthur Koestler was born on September 5, 1905, in Budapest, the only child of Henrik and Adela Koestler. The first trauma for Arthur was an unexpected and unexplained tonsillectomy without anesthesia in 1910. Because of his father's poor business sense and his mother's dislike of Hungary, the family moved to Vienna in 1914 amidst much conflict between his parents.

Shy and insecure, Koestler studied science and engineering, but he became involved in a Zionist dueling fraternity at a polytechnic college in Vienna. The three years he spent in this group were very happy and began his involvement in politics. He became a follower of Vladimir Jabotinsky, burned his matriculation papers and left for Palestine in 1926. After a hard period of adjustment there, he obtained a job as Middle East correspondent for a German publishing company.

In 1929, disillusioned with Palestine, he returned to Europe where he continued to work as a newspaper correspondent. He joined the German Communist Party in 1931 and lost his job as a result. He traveled to Russia to report on events there and returned to Paris to write, although the Communist Party disapproved of many of his articles and books and greatly restricted his freedom. He married Dorothy Asher but separated a few months later. (They were divorced in 1950.)

He made three trips to Spain during the Civil War and was arrested and imprisoned for three months by Franco's Nationalists as a spy. He was sentenced to death but freed after British protests. Disillusioned now with Communism, he resigned from the Communist Party. He was detained and imprisoned in both England and France but, after the publication of *Darkness at Noon*, was released and worked for the Ministry of Information in England during the war.

After the war, the cause of Zionism again captured his attention, and he traveled to Palestine and both reported on events and wrote novels about his experiences. In 1950 he married Mamaine Paget, but she separated from him in 1951 and died in 1954 soon after their divorce. His third and final marriage was to Cynthia Jeffries in 1965, his secretary since 1950.

He settled in England in 1952 and became a British citizen, and he continued to work for and write about political issues. His writings, including both novels, essays, and biographies, always exploring the important social issues of the times, and his work has been compared to that of George Orwell's in its impact on the times.

Cynthia Jeffries was twenty-two when she started working for Koestler. She was from South Africa and had gone to Paris with the aim of working for a writer. There had been

[1] Another case involves Stefan Zweig and his wife Lotte (Lester, 1997).

stress in her life -- her father committed suicide when she was thirteen, and there was a brief, unsuccessful marriage. From the time that she joined him, her life was bound up with Koestler.

One of the causes for which Koestler worked was euthanasia. As he grew older, he developed Parkinson's disease and then leukemia. When the effects of these illnesses worsened, he decided to commit suicide, and Cynthia decided that she could not live without him.

Interestingly, all of his wives remained in some way attached and, for some, devoted to and dependent on him. Dorothy Asher helped free Koestler from prison in Spain. Mamaine Paget, who suffered from his drunken rages, wrote that she would do anything, even leave him, if it were necessary to help him fulfil his destiny. Cynthia went further. On March 3, 1983, she committed suicide with him in their London home.

There was some outcry after the double suicide of the Koestlers. Mikes (1984) noted that Arthur Koestler treated Cynthia "abominably". She had to be on duty to serve Arthur twenty-four hours a day, and she had to be perfect in everything she did. She was secretary, lover, wife, nurse, housekeeper, cook, mother, daughter and inseparable companion. Mikes gives an example of Arthur criticizing Cynthia's cooking early in their relationship and sending her to cooking school to improve. In the 1970s, Arthur became more dependent on Cynthia, first after he lost his driving license for drunk driving and later as he developed Parkinson's disease and leukemia. He became Cynthia's prisoner. Cynthia seemed more relaxed to Mikes and teased Arthur more.

Blue (1983) argued that Cynthia should not have killed herself. She was in good health, energetic and able. She had a home, many friends and financial security. But Cynthia had come to live entirely for Arthur and through him. As she added to Arthur's suicide note, "I cannot face life without Arthur."

It is common for those physically abused by others to feel that they deserve the abuse and for them to become dependent upon and attached to their abusers. Cynthia was not physically abused as far as we know, but the psychological abuse may have created a similarly strong dependency upon Arthur. As Arthur sickened, Cynthia's attachment to him became less pathological, but no less intense. His sickness, by making him more dependent upon her, gave her a little more power. But he obviously made no effort to prepare her for his death by encouraging her to have interests outside of his life or by encouraging her independence.

Canetto (1992-1993) has described the myth in our society that women die for love while men die for glory. This myth, acting as a culturally shared assumption, may influence the suicidal choices of women, and it is evident that such a culturally shaped attitude may have played a role in the decision Cynthia Koestler to commit suicide with her husband.

In fact, although the death of Cynthia Koestler was technically a suicide, her death has the quality of murder,[2] murder by a self-centered, power-seeking husband who gave little or no thought for the quality of life for his wife.

---

[2] It may be viewed as a case of "psychic homicide," described above.

Sexism in Suicidology

Sexism is an issue that has relevance for politics, and sexism in suicidology is easily demonstrated.

Terminology

Lester (1989a) examined the commonly used words *completed suicide* and *attempted suicide*. Suicidologists have typically labeled those suicidal actions in which the person dies as completed suicides and those in which the person survives as attempted suicides. Recently, suicidologists, especially in Europe, have felt that many attempted suicides were not actually trying to die since they often make very mild gestures at suicide, such as taking what they know is less than a lethal dose of medication. These suicidologists first suggested using the word *parasuicide* (Kreitman, et al., 1969) instead of attempted suicide and, more recently, have began to use the terms *self-poisoners* and *self-injurers*.

There is a strong gender difference in suicidal behavior. Men complete suicide in almost all nations of the world at a higher rate than do women, while women attempt suicide at a higher rate than men (Lester, 1984). For example, in the most comprehensive survey conducted in the United States, by Farberow and Shneidman (1961) in Los Angeles in 1957, 540 male and 228 female completed suicides were identified as compared to 828 male and 1824 female attempted suicides. This gender difference has been reported in Hong Kong (Yap, 1958), Israel (Shichor and Bergman, 1979), and the Netherlands (De Graaf and Kruyt, 1976).

Lester (1989a) noted that it was clear that women engaged in more suicidal actions than did men -- 2052 versus 1368 in Los Angeles in 1957. It can assumed that, had mild nonlethal suicidal actions also been counted (they were not counted because most did not come to the attention of authorities), the relative predominance of suicidal actions by women would have been even greater.

Linehan (1973) documented the extent to which this gender difference in suicidal outcome is well-known to members of the society. She found that college students viewed completing suicide as a "masculine" behavior and attempting suicide as a "feminine" behavior. The students in her studies predicted completed suicide as an outcome for a fictitious person more often if the person was a man or had a traditionally stereotypical "masculine" personality.

Calling those suicidal actions in which the person dies *completed* indicates that suicidologists consider the goal of the action to be death. Dying as a result of the suicidal action, a "masculine" behavior, is a successful outcome. Surviving the suicidal action, a "feminine" behavior, is a failure. From the female point of view, however, the statistically more common outcome is to survive the suicidal action. The modal outcome is continued life! Thus, completing suicide could be viewed as a failure because the individuals died.

With this transformed perspective, suicidal behavior can be viewed as a way of changing one's environment and of communicating distress to others. The goal is to survive so as to benefit from these changes in one's world and to continue the process of communication. Men fail to accomplish this as well as women do. The analogy comes to mind of depression, in which it has been argued that more women in the United States are depressed than are men,

This hostility toward the nonfatal suicide may reflect our bias toward seeing nonfatal suicide as inappropriate behavior. Nonfatal suicides are not "serious" in their intent to die and so do not deserve sympathy and good care. Such prejudice is inappropriate in the staff of mental health facilities, and supervisors should seek to change these attitudes.

A Possible Feminist Perspective on Suicide: Suicide and Oppression

It was proposed above that suicide can be conceptualized as a political act. Recently, Lester (1990b) proposed a general social conflict theory of suicide in which suicide is hypothesized to be a reaction against oppression. Social conflict theories of crime have been quite popular, and those theories stress that criminal behavior is often viewed by the have-nots in the society as a legitimate act to acquire what they lack and to express hostility toward the ruling classes (Sykes, 1974). For example, Hendin (1969) argued that suicide in African Americans could be understood only in the light of the society's overt rejection of African Americans over the years. The young African American suicidal males studied by Hendin felt trapped in unbearable life situations by their lack of education and lack of job opportunities and by the destructive effect of the ghetto on their own personalities.

Stephens (1988) has examined the role of the interpersonal relationships of modern American women in their suicidal behavior and concluded that their social and psychological experiences prepared them to be victims -- victims of parents, of men, and of relationships in which the self is continually mortified. The price of intimacy for the suicidal women studied by Stephens was very high, involving physical abuse, sexual betrayal, emotional impoverishment and self-negation. As one suicidal woman expressed it: "All my life I've felt like nothing, nothing, just nothing."

Some suicides may be seen as the a direct result of oppression rather than as a way of seeking freedom from oppression. For example, Yang (1989) argued that suttee (the self-immolation of Indian widows on their husband's funeral pyres) was the result of the social conditioning (indoctrination) of Indian women. The "choice" of suttee was made more likely by the cruel treatment accorded to widows who choose to live after their husband's death.

Discussion

It is easy to raise the issue of sexism in suicidology. It is, however, far from easy to suggest remedies. It is certainly possible to focus on suicidal behavior in women. It is easy to replicate research on suicide in men using women. But can the study of suicide be reconceptualized?

For example, it may be that psychological traits which predict future suicidal behavior in women differ from those which predict future suicidal behavior in men. This is important to know. But such research on men and on women would use the same psychological tests. Might it not be that completely different psychological traits could be proposed if researchers took a feminine perspective?

On the other hand, far more radical would be the proposal of completely new ways of conceptualizing suicidal behavior if we took a feminine viewpoint. For example, a theory of

This hostility toward the nonfatal suicide may reflect our bias toward seeing nonfatal suicide as inappropriate behavior. Nonfatal suicides are not "serious" in their intent to die and so do not deserve sympathy and good care. Such prejudice is inappropriate in the staff of mental health facilities, and supervisors should seek to change these attitudes.

A Possible Feminist Perspective on Suicide: Suicide and Oppression

It was proposed above that suicide can be conceptualized as a political act. Recently, Lester (1990b) proposed a general social conflict theory of suicide in which suicide is hypothesized to be a reaction against oppression. Social conflict theories of crime have been quite popular, and those theories stress that criminal behavior is often viewed by the have-nots in the society as a legitimate act to acquire what they lack and to express hostility toward the ruling classes (Sykes, 1974). For example, Hendin (1969) argued that suicide in African Americans could be understood only in the light of the society's overt rejection of African Americans over the years. The young African American suicidal males studied by Hendin felt trapped in unbearable life situations by their lack of education and lack of job opportunities and by the destructive effect of the ghetto on their own personalities.

Stephens (1988) has examined the role of the interpersonal relationships of modern American women in their suicidal behavior and concluded that their social and psychological experiences prepared them to be victims -- victims of parents, of men, and of relationships in which the self is continually mortified. The price of intimacy for the suicidal women studied by Stephens was very high, involving physical abuse, sexual betrayal, emotional impoverishment and self-negation. As one suicidal woman expressed it: "All my life I've felt like nothing, nothing, just nothing."

Some suicides may be seen as the a direct result of oppression rather than as a way of seeking freedom from oppression. For example, Yang (1989) argued that suttee (the self-immolation of Indian widows on their husband's funeral pyres) was the result of the social conditioning (indoctrination) of Indian women. The "choice" of suttee was made more likely by the cruel treatment accorded to widows who choose to live after their husband's death.

Discussion

It is easy to raise the issue of sexism in suicidology. It is, however, far from easy to suggest remedies. It is certainly possible to focus on suicidal behavior in women. It is easy to replicate research on suicide in men using women. But can the study of suicide be reconceptualized?

For example, it may be that psychological traits which predict future suicidal behavior in women differ from those which predict future suicidal behavior in men. This is important to know. But such research on men and on women would use the same psychological tests. Might it not be that completely different psychological traits could be proposed if researchers took a feminine perspective?

On the other hand, far more radical would be the proposal of completely new ways of conceptualizing suicidal behavior if we took a feminine viewpoint. For example, a theory of

Sexism in Suicidology

Sexism is an issue that has relevance for politics, and sexism in suicidology is easily demonstrated.

Terminology

Lester (1989a) examined the commonly used words *completed suicide* and *attempted suicide*. Suicidologists have typically labeled those suicidal actions in which the person dies as completed suicides and those in which the person survives as attempted suicides. Recently, suicidologists, especially in Europe, have felt that many attempted suicides were not actually trying to die since they often make very mild gestures at suicide, such as taking what they know is less than a lethal dose of medication. These suicidologists first suggested using the word *parasuicide* (Kreitman, et al., 1969) instead of attempted suicide and, more recently, have began to use the terms *self-poisoners* and *self-injurers*.

There is a strong gender difference in suicidal behavior. Men complete suicide in almost all nations of the world at a higher rate than do women, while women attempt suicide at a higher rate than men (Lester, 1984). For example, in the most comprehensive survey conducted in the United States, by Farberow and Shneidman (1961) in Los Angeles in 1957, 540 male and 228 female completed suicides were identified as compared to 828 male and 1824 female attempted suicides. This gender difference has been reported in Hong Kong (Yap, 1958), Israel (Shichor and Bergman, 1979), and the Netherlands (De Graaf and Kruyt, 1976).

Lester (1989a) noted that it was clear that women engaged in more suicidal actions than did men -- 2052 versus 1368 in Los Angeles in 1957. It can assumed that, had mild nonlethal suicidal actions also been counted (they were not counted because most did not come to the attention of authorities), the relative predominance of suicidal actions by women would have been even greater.

Linehan (1973) documented the extent to which this gender difference in suicidal outcome is well-known to members of the society. She found that college students viewed completing suicide as a "masculine" behavior and attempting suicide as a "feminine" behavior. The students in her studies predicted completed suicide as an outcome for a fictitious person more often if the person was a man or had a traditionally stereotypical "masculine" personality.

Calling those suicidal actions in which the person dies *completed* indicates that suicidologists consider the goal of the action to be death. Dying as a result of the suicidal action, a "masculine" behavior, is a successful outcome. Surviving the suicidal action, a "feminine" behavior, is a failure. From the female point of view, however, the statistically more common outcome is to survive the suicidal action. The modal outcome is continued life! Thus, completing suicide could be viewed as a failure because the individuals died.

With this transformed perspective, suicidal behavior can be viewed as a way of changing one's environment and of communicating distress to others. The goal is to survive so as to benefit from these changes in one's world and to continue the process of communication. Men fail to accomplish this as well as women do. The analogy comes to mind of depression, in which it has been argued that more women in the United States are depressed than are men, suicide as a response to oppression might be developed only after a female perspective is adopted.

What would be stimulating for suicidology would be the discovery of new conceptualization of suicide, completely different from those already identified.

REFERENCES

Ansbacher, H. L. Suicide: The Adlerian point of view. In N. L. Farberow & E. S. Shneidman (Eds.) *The cry for help*, pp. 204-219. New York: McGraw-Hill, 1961.

Blue, A. Who was "Mrs. Arthur Koestler" and why did she kill herself? *Ms Magazine*, 1983, 12(1), 110.

Buss, A. H., & Durkee, A. An inventory for assessing different kinds of hostility. *Journal of Consulting Psychology*, 1957, 21, 343-348.

Canetto, S. S. Gender and suicide in the elderly. *Suicide & Life-Threatening Behavior*, 1992, 22, 80-97.

_____ . She died for love and he for glory: Gender myths of suicidal behavior. *Omega*, 1992-1993, 26, 1-17.

Canetto, S. S., & Lester, D. (Eds.) *Women and suicidal behavior*. New York: Springer, 1995

Christie, R., & Geis, F. L. *Studies in Machiavellianism*. New York: Academic. 1970.

Coleman, L. *Suicide clusters*. Boston: Faber & Faber, 1987.

Counts, D. A. Ambiguity in the interpretation of suicide. In D. Lester (Ed.) *Why women kill themselves*, pp. 87-109. Springfield, IL: Charles Thomas. 1988.

Davis, J. C. Suicide with some illustrative cases. *Journal of the American Medical Association*, 1904, 43, 121-123.

De Graaf, A. C., & Kruyt, C. S. Some results of the response to a national survey of suicide and attempted suicide. In *Suicide and attempted suicide in young people*, pp. 52-58. Copenhagen: World Health Organization, 1976.

Dressler, D. M., Prussof, B., Hark, H., & Shapiro, D. Clinicians, attitudes toward the suicide attempter. *Journal of Nervous & Mental Disease*, 1975, 160, 146-155.

Durkheim, E. *Le suicide*. Paris: Felix Alcan, 1897.

Faber, M. D. *Suicide and Greek tragedy*. New York: Sphinx. 1970.

Farberow, N. L., & Shneidman, E. S. *The cry for help*. New York: McGraw-Hill, 1961.

Fishbain, D. A., & Aldrich, T. E. Suicide pacts. *Journal of Clinical Psychiatry*, 1985, 46, 11-15.

Haley, J. *The power tactics of Jesus Christ and other essays*. New York: Grossman, 1969.

Hendin, H. *Black suicide*. New York: Basic Books. 1969.

Jorgensen-Earp, C. R. "Toys of desperation:" Suicide as protest rhetoric. *Southern Speech Communication Journal*, 1987, 53(Fall), 80-96.

Kelly, G. A. *The psychology of personal constructs*. New York: Norton, 1955.

_____ . *Hostility*. Presidential address, Clinical Division, American Psychological Association, New York City, 1957.

Kelly, G. A. The threat of aggression. *Journal of Humanistic Psychology*, 1965, 5, 195-201.

Kreitman, N., Philip, A. E., Greer, S., & Bagley, C. R. Parasuicide. *British Journal of Psychiatry*, 1969, 115, 746-747.

Laborit, H. *L'homme imaginant*. Paris: Union General d'Editions, 1970.

Laing, R. D. *The politics of experience*. New York: Pantheon, 1967.

Lester, D. Attempted suicide as a hostile act. *Journal of Psychology*, 1968, 68, 243-248.

_____ . Suicide and Machiavellianism. Unpublished paper, Suicide Prevention & Crisis Service, Buffalo, 1970.

_____ . Suicide. In C. S. Widom (Ed.) *Sex roles and psychopathology*, pp. 145-156. New York: Plenum, 1984.

_____ . The study of suicide from a feminist perspective. *Crisis*, 1989a, 11, 38-43.

_____ . *Suicide from a sociological perspective*. Springfield, IL: Charles Thomas, 1989b.

_____ . Ecological correlates of adolescent attempted suicide. *Adolescence*, 1990a, 25, 483-485.

_____ . *Understanding and preventing suicide*. Springfield, IL: Charles Thomas. 1990b.

_____ . Testosterone and suicide. *Personality & Individual Differences*, 1993, 15, 347-348.

_____ . The sexual politics of double suicide. *Feminism & Psychology*, 1997, 7, 148-154.

Lester, D., Beck, A. T., & Narrett, S. Suicidal intent in successive suicidal actions. *Psychological Reports*, 1978, 43, 110.

Levene, M. *Arthur Koestler*. New York: Frederick Ungar, 1984.

Linehan, M. Suicide and attempted suicide. *Perceptual & Motor Skills*, 1973, 37, 31-34.

Meerloo, J. A. M. *Suicide and mass suicide*. New York: Grune & Stratton, 1962.

Menninger, K. *Man against himself*. New York: Harcourt, Brace & World, 1938.

Mikes, G. Remembering the Koestlers. *American Scholar*, 1984, 53, 219-224.

Morris, W. (Ed.) *The American heritage dictionary of the English language*. Boston: Houghton-Mifflin, 1976.

Neuringer, C. Methodological problems in suicide research. *Journal of Consulting Psychology*, 1962, 26, 273-278.

Neuringer, C. Rigid thinking in suicidal individuals. *Journal of Consulting Psychology*, 1964, 28, 54-58.

Neuringer, C., & Lettieri, D. J. *Suicidal women*. New York: Gardner Press, 1982.

Richman, J. *Family therapy for suicidal people*. New York: Springer, 1986.

Rosenbaum, M. Crime and punishment. *Archives of General Psychiatry*, 1983, 40, 979-982.

Rudestam, K. E. Survivors of suicide. In D. Lester (Ed.) *Currents concepts of suicide*, pp. 203-213. Philadelphia: Charles Press, 1990.

Shichor, D., & Bergman, S. Patterns of suicide among the elderly in Israel. *Gerontology*, 1979, 19, 487-495.

Shneidman, E. S., & Farberow, N. L. The logic of suicide. In E. S. Shneidman & N. L. Farberow (Eds.) *Clues to suicide*, pp. 31-40. New York: McGraw-Hill, 1957.

Sifneos, P. Manipulative suicide. *Psychiatric Quarterly*, 1966, 40, 525-537.

Silverman, C. *The epidemiology of depression*. Baltimore, MD: Johns Hopkins University, 1968.

Stephens, B. J. The social relationships of suicidal women. In D. Lester (Ed.) *Why women kill themselves*, pp. 73-85. Springfield, IL: Charles Thomas, 1988.

Sykes, G. The rise of critical criminology. *Journal of Criminal Law & Criminology*, 1974, 22, 335-347.

Taylor, S. *Durkheim and the study of suicide*. London: Macmillan, 1982.

Wickett, A. *Double exit*. Eugene, OR: Hemlock Society, 1989.

Wilkins, J. Suicidal behavior. *American Sociological Review*, 1967, 32, 286-298.

Yang, A. A. Whose sati? *Journal of Women's History*. 1989, 1(2), 8-33.

Yap, P. Suicide in Hong Kong. *Journal of Mental Science*, 1958, 104, 266-301.

Chapter 11

PSYCHOLOGY AND SUICIDE

INTRODUCTION

There are many psychological perspectives on suicide, and in this chapter I do not intend to be exhaustive, but I hope to be provocative by suggesting a variety of perspectives (or meanings) for suicide, hoping that they will stimulate thinking about suicide.

SUICIDE AS DEPRESSION

Suicide appears to be strongly linked to depression. Although only about one percent of all deaths are due to suicide, Achté (1986) found that the proportion of deaths due to completed suicide for those diagnosed with affective disorders (disorders involving severe depression and sometimes mania) was 15 percent.

A few studies have calculated suicide rates for patients with various psychiatric diagnoses. For example, Pokorny (1964) found a suicide rate of 566 per 100,000 per year for male American VA psychiatric patients as compared to a rate of only 165 for psychiatric patients in general and 18 for males in the general population. Barraclough (1972) examined one hundred cases of suicide in England and found that 64 had depressive illnesses. Of these, 44 had previous depressive episodes, and 21 of these met a strict criterion for diagnosing "recurrent affective illness."

Depression is strongly associated with attempted suicide too. Chabrol and Moron (1988) reported that depressive diagnoses were more common in attempted suicides than in other psychiatric patients, while McHugh and Goodell (1971) found that attempted suicides diagnosed as having depressive disorders made more serious attempts than those diagnosed as having personality disorders.

Beck and his associates have explored the relationship between suicidal preoccupation and depression in depth. It appears that the cognitive components of depression are most strongly associated with suicidal tendencies. Beck has called this component hopelessness and has devised a special psychological test to measure it. For example, Beck, et al. (1985, 1989) found that hopelessness scores predicted subsequent suicide in groups of psychiatric patients and patients with suicidal ideation better than did depression scores.

Biochemical theories of psychiatric disorder are very popular these days (see Chapter 4), and Lester (1988a) has reviewed the extensive research into the biochemical correlates, and perhaps causes, of suicidal behavior. He concluded that the research supported the involvement of the neurotransmitter serotonin in the etiology of suicide.

Although claims have been made for the involvement of serotonin in the etiology of assaultive aggression (Van Praag, 1986) and impulsive behavior (Brown and Goodwin, 1986), the psychiatric syndrome most likely to be associated with serotonergic processes is affective disorder. Indeed, studies of the biochemistry of suicides are conducted primarily to throw light on the biochemistry of depression since it assumed that most suicides are depressed. Thus, the involvement of the serotonergic system in suicide may simply reduce to a recognition that suicide is associated with depression.

Since depression and depressive disorder are both strong correlates of suicidal behavior, it seems reasonable to conceptualize suicide simply as an extreme manifestation of severe depression. Indeed, in the Freudian view of suicide, depression is anger, originally felt toward others, turned inward upon the self, and suicide is conceptualized in the same way. As Edwin Shneidman has eloquently stated, it: suicide is murder in the one hundred and eightieth degree!

Suicide as Aggression

Suicide can be seen as an aggressive act in two ways. Menninger's (1938) classification of the motives for suicide illustrates this clearly. In the motive Menninger called *to kill*, the person is angry at others and uses the suicidal act to aggress against them. This anger may be expressed directly through the suicidal act as when someone disfigures themselves in the process of committing suicide (for example, by shooting himself in the head) and then is discovered by a loved one. Ernest Hemingway shot himself in the head one morning downstairs in his home with his wife upstairs, bound to hear the shot and discover him.

The anger can also be experienced through the fantasies of the suicide. He may enjoy in fantasy how the survivors will feel guilt for behaving so badly that they forced him to kill himself. Or perhaps his suicide will expose some misdeed of theirs for which they will feel ashamed, such as deserting him for another lover. This anger may be expressed on occasion directly in the suicide. For example,

> Bill, I do hope you'll suffer more than I have done. I wish you'll die in a beer joint. (Wagner, 1960, p. 63)

A second motive described by Menninger was that of *to be killed*. In this motive, the anger felt toward others is turned inward upon the self. This is the typical psychoanalytic position on depression and suicide. Depression is blocked anger, felt toward another, but unable to be expressed. It is either suppressed or, eventually, repressed, resulting in depression and suicide. A suicide note which expresses this motive is,

> Mary Darling, It's all my fault. I've thought this over a million times and this seems to be the only way I can settle all the trouble I have caused you and others. This is only a sample of how sorry I am. This should cancel all. (Shneidman and Farberow, 1957, p. 206).

Interestingly, suicidal individuals do not appear to have a general tendency to block anger and direct it inwards rather than outwards. There is a good deal of evidence that suicidal individuals are among the more angry and violent psychiatric patients, and psychological tests reveal no tendency for suicidal people to block their anger (Lester, 1987a).

Thus, suicide can be viewed as an act of aggression, different from murder only in the target of the aggression.

Suicide as a Learned Behavior

The learning theory of human behavior uses the same learning paradigms that have been identified by psychologists who experiment with lower animals in laboratory research. It is assumed that these paradigms are applicable to humans, and that humans learn behaviors in the same way as these lower animals learn.

Two major learning paradigms have been identified over the years. In *classical conditioning*, previously neutral stimuli (the conditioned stimuli) become associated with other stimuli (the unconditioned stimuli) that produce responses. Eventually, after many pairings, the formerly neutral stimuli now elicit the response. For example, *punishment* functions by means of classical conditioning. The punishment (the unconditioned stimulus) produces responses such as fear and pain, which by classical conditioning become attached to the misbehavior of which the punisher disapproves.

The second major learning paradigm is *operant conditioning*. In operant conditioning, if a response is made in the presence of a stimulus and is followed by a reinforcer (or reward), then the response is more likely to be emitted in the presence of the stimulus in future. Reinforcers are of two kinds. Positive reinforcers are the onset of something nice whereas negative reinforcers are the ending of something nasty.

To take an example here, our baby is left alone in his crib, and the light turned out as his mother leaves his bedroom. He cries and, after a while, his mother returns and turns the light on to see if he is all right. The response of crying has been rewarded, both by the positive reinforcer of his mother's presence and attention, but also by the negative reinforcer of the ending of darkness and of being alone. His mother is teaching him to cry at night.

Operant conditioning can be used to *shape* a new behavior. Initially, the person is rewarded for approximations to the response that the teacher wants. As the person begins to offer these approximations to the desired behavior, the teacher enforces a stricter criterion before rewarding responses. This is the way, for example, that children acquire competent speech.

Social learning theory (Bandura, 1977) modified simple learning theory by taking into account the fact that humans have thoughts, beliefs and expectations which can affect the simple learning paradigms described above. Thoughts can provide stimuli, responses can be imagined and reinforcers can be cognitions (such as self-praise). Thus, for example, a person can engage in a trial-and-error problem-solving tasks using solely internal thoughts, so that an observer would observe no stimuli, responses, or reinforcers. Social learning theory also accepts too that humans can learn by watching others (by modeling or imitation).

There are several learning theories of depression. Depression can result from a lack of reinforcement. For example, responses that were rewarded in the past are no longer rewarded because the source of the rewards is no longer present. A spouse may have died, children may have moved away, or a job may have been lost through being laid-off or through retirement. Without these positive reinforcers, the person no longer performs the responses that were formerly rewarded. The person, therefore, becomes passive and withdrawn.

Seligman (1975) argued that depression was a manifestation of a phenomenon that he called learned helplessness. Seligman exposed dogs to inescapable electric shock. When he then permitted these dogs to escape the painful electric shocks, they did not learn to do so. In contrast, dogs not previously exposed to the inescapable electric shock soon learned to escape the electric shocks. Seligman suggested that the dogs who were forced to endure inescapable electric shock had learned to be helpless, that is, they had learned that the shock was always *inescapable*. The experience of previous failure caused them to make little effort in the future. In human depression, therefore, it has been argued that, in psychologically painful situations, the person tried to escape the pain, but failed. He then generalized from this experience and learned (or decided) that he could never escape the pain.

Frederick and Resnick (1971) noted that depression may also be rewarded by significant others. Depressed behaviors may elicit positive reinforcers from others such as care-taking behaviors, the so-called secondary gain.

As we have noted above, suicide is strongly linked to depression, and the existence of learning theories of depression suggests that suicidal behavior may also be learned. We have already discussed in earlier chapters some of the aspects of suicidal behavior which indicate the role of learning. For example, in Chapter 10 on Politics And Suicide, the manipulative aspects of suicidal behavior were highlighted, and manipulative behavior is often rewarded since the manipulator gets what he or she desires.

Societal Shaping of Suicidal Behavior

We have seen in Chapter 6 and Chapter 7 that society and culture plays a role in suicidal behavior, and in the present context this involves social learning. Societies vary in how much they condemn suicide, and they also vary in the expectations they have for people. For example, one well-known phenomenon in suicidal behavior is that males complete suicide more than females, whereas females attempt suicide more than males. This phenomenon occurs in almost all nations of the world and in almost all subgroups of the population in any nation (Lester, 1979). Linehan (1973) presented undergraduate students with case studies involving males and females in crisis and varied the characteristics of the patients so that some were portrayed as "masculine": while others were portrayed as "feminine." She found that the students predicted suicide as an outcome more often for males than for females, and also that suicide was the predicted outcome more often for masculine patients than for feminine patients. The students predicted suicide 71% of the time for the masculine males, 62% of the time for masculine females, 43% of the time for feminine males, and 22% of the time for feminine females. This suggests that sex role expectations may function as to shape sex differences in suicidal behavior.

Families also can play a role in shaping suicidal behavior. Children may imitate suicidal parents, and parents may have (possibly unconscious) murderous desires toward their children which the children introject as suicidal desires[1] and may even show these desires openly later.

[1] This is a theory proposed by Transactional Analysis (Lester, 1988c).

Richman (1986) noted many instances in which parents made clearly murderous statements to their children who had attempted suicide, in the presence of the psychologist! For example, a father of a 16 year-old girl said to her "Why don't you kill yourself. At least we'd know where you are."

In Chapter 8, we discussed how the subculture may encourage suicidal behavior. Lester (1987c) presented a case from a small town in Pennsylvania, in which three teenagers from a group of five completed suicide. Although this group was quite self-contained, their suicides generated a great deal of suicidal preoccupation and acting-out in their peers. This suggests that the subcultural values were quite widespread. Interestingly, hostility was also aroused. One girl overdosed on Tylenol and, on her return to school, found a full bottle of Tylenol in her locker with a note saying, "Do it right next time."

We discussed in Chapter 6 Henry and Short's theory of suicide which predicts that love-oriented punishment and punishment by the same person who nurtures the child may increase the risk of suicide. In Chapter 4 we mentioned that experiences of physical and sexual abuse in childhood can increase the risk of later suicide.

There is also good evidence that the society plays a role in influencing the methods chosen for committing suicide. Hirsh (1960) reported on fads for methods of suicide. Gas was very popular in the early 1900s, and "to take the pipe" became a common phrase. Plastic bags were used more often following reports of accidental deaths by suffocation soon after their invention. There are many famous suicide venues around the world. Two popular ones in the United States are Niagara Falls (Lester and Brockopp, 1971) and the Golden Gate Bridge in San Francisco.

Burvill, et al. (1973) reported on the methods for suicide used by suicides in England and Wales and compared these with the methods used by immigrants from those countries when they arrive in Australia. They found that the immigrants switched from the British pattern to the Australian pattern.

Newspaper Publicity

Phillips (1974) found that front page newspaper stories on suicide increased the number of suicides in the following month. The rise was found only in the region served by the newspaper. There was no subsequent dip in the number of suicides each month, and so Phillips concluded that newspaper publicity creates additional suicides rather than speeding up suicide in those who would have killed themselves anyway. A similar phenomenon has been noted after television news and movies on suicide.

Imitation also appears to play a role in "epidemics" of suicidal behavior. Coleman (1987) has reported many cases of suicide clusters that appear to show imitation, including many recent clusters of teenage suicides.

The evidence that suicide is, at least in part, a learned behavior is, therefore, strong.

Suicide as Deviance

In most cultures suicide is frowned upon. Indeed, in some it is a sin. Furthermore, in any culture, suicide is rare. For example, Hungary has one of the highest suicide rates in the world. Yet its rate was only about 45 per 100,000 people per year in 1980. Suicide is always a statistically deviant act.

This suggests that suicidal individuals may be nonsocialized. Those who kill themselves have not been socialized into the traditional nonsuicidal culture. Thus, suicidal individuals should appear to be relatively unsocialized on psychological tests of socialization and conformity. Of course, Durkheim's (1897) ideas on suicide included the notion that suicide would be especially common in those who were not well socially integrated and not well socially regulated. He called these types of suicide egoistic and anomic, respectively.

The absence of adequate parenting is also an important factor here. The quality of parenting can be poor, as in disorganized families. One or both parents can be absent, physically or psychologically. Jacobs (1971) has documented in detail the extremely disorganized family life of suicidal teenagers.

Religion is also a strong factor. Membership in a religious group will act against suicidal tendencies by providing a disapproving set of values for suicide and by providing social integration for the individual. Religious participation can also substitute for, in part, inadequate parenting. Finally, religious membership is a sign that the person has been adequately socialized.

This factor (of being poorly socialized into the traditional nonsuicidal culture) is a necessary, but not sufficient factor. For the nonsocialized person, peers and role models provide a crucial input. Those who are nonsocialized will often associate with other similarly nonsocialized people. Thus, this nonsocialized group forms its own small subculture. This subculture may share the information necessary for suicide. What methods to use? How many pills to take?

Role models, whether familiar friends or mythic heroes, provide models for nonconformity. When a Marilyn Monroe or Freddie Prinze completes suicide, they act as role models for the ordinary person. And when one teenager in a school completes suicide, it occasionally leads to further suicides among the peer group.

Lester (1983) reviewed research on the person who makes repeated attempts at suicide. He concluded that the research shows them to be more often diagnosed as psychopathic (that is, with an antisocial personality disorder) or with another type of personality disorder (such as borderline personality disorder), to be more often unemployed, to more often have a criminal record and to be more likely to be alcohol abusers. They seem to have a chronic maladaptive life-style and to be socially deviant in general.

Regional studies of attempted suicide also have found that rates are higher where indices of social disorganization are higher including overcrowding and poverty (Lester, 1983). Thus, it seems that the chronic attempter is a social deviant who comes from locales where social deviance is common. Families in these areas often fail to discipline their children and teach them the values of the larger society. They also fail to encourage them in interests and activities which would serve as deterrents to deviant behavior.

Such a child typically grows up without acquiring the attitudes and skills necessary for achieving long-term goals. The person then turns to short-term tactics for achieving goals, such as drugs, delinquent behavior, and suicide attempts. There may also be a gender difference here, with males choosing behaviors such as drugs and crime more often while females choose suicide attempts. (Females in these locales also have a high rate of illegitimate births.) A suicide attempt for such a person is a cathartic act and one which often brings about an immediate response from others.

An interesting question is why people in these locales turn to suicide rather than drugs or criminal behavior, given the predisposing factors. It may be that the choice is gender-linked as mentioned above. It may also be related to such factors as the availability of drugs in the area, the presence of a support group (or gang), and parental models.

Suicide, then, no matter how much stress a person is under, is always a rare and, thus, a deviant act. It may, therefore, be heuristic to view the suicidal person as a nonsocialized individual, one who has failed to learn the normal cultural values, especially toward life and death.

Suicide as Gambling

Suicide has often been considered to be a gamble. The suicidal individual sometimes does not know whether or not he will die when he makes his suicide attempt. This can be because the factors affecting survival are not known fully. For example, the suicidal person may not be able to predict which potential rescuers will come by and intervene. Alternatively, the suicidal individual may not have sufficient information to know how to kill himself. What is a lethal dose of a particular medication, for example?

Lester and Lester (1971) noted that the seriously suicidal person does not know what death is like. He risks disappointment, but hopes for triumph or contentment. The mildly suicidal person may hope that his act will change his life, but he risks dying instead of awakening to an improved life. In addition to winning happiness or escaping from misery, the person may try suicide with the hope of preserving his threatened self-image. If he foresees severe illness, poverty, or mental disorder, he may use suicide to preserve the memory of himself as he was at his peak. This, again, is a gamble, especially since the disapproved act of suicide is likely to tarnish his image.

In Tikopia, Firth (1961) has described how people commit suicide by swimming out to sea. The suicidal individual can affect the chances of rescue and survival by choosing when to start swimming (late at night or early morning), how fast to swim, whether to swim directly out to sea or at an angle, and so on. Furthermore, the suicidal individual faces unpredictable factors such as when his absence will be discovered and whether the rescuers will make directly for where he is swimming. Thus, the suicidal attempt is a gamble, and the suicidal individual can affect the odds of survival by his choices.

Suicide as an Addiction

There are many definitions of the term "addiction" and so those proposed here are not meant to be definitive. They are presented so that we may consider the possibility that suicidal behavior, at least in some forms, may resemble an addiction.

The use of the word addiction came into prominence, of course, from its use in drug addiction. Drug addiction is characterized by two characteristics. First over time, more and more of the drug must be taken in order to achieve the same effects -- a characteristic called *tolerance*. Second, when the drug is not used, the body has a deleterious physiological response which may, in some cases, lead to death -- a characteristic called *withdrawal*.

Over the years, the notion of addiction has been broadened (Walker, 1988). For example, the term has been extended to include any substance ingested, including food in general, and certain types of food such as sugar and salt. Since food is necessary for physiological survival, addiction here means excessive use as compared to normal use, whereas in drug addiction there is no normal use since the chemicals are not necessary for physiological survival.

Since drug addiction involves behavioral responses (acquiring and administering the drug), the term addiction has been extended to behaviors. Thus, the term has also been applied to such activities as gambling, jogging and excessive working (the "workaholic"). In these applications, the distinction between addiction and psychological dependence becomes blurred, and the terms are sometimes used interchangeably. Addictions become similar to habits which are difficult to give up.

Jacobs (1986) views addiction as encompassing "persistent out-of-control behavioral patterns involving substances such as food, alcohol, other licit and illicit drugs, as well as activities such as gambling" (p. 18). Generalizing from such ideas, Walker (1988, p. 53) defines a psychological addiction as involving:

(1) a desire or need to continue the activity which is not under the individual's voluntary control,
(2) a tendency to increase the frequency or amount of the activity over time,
(3) a psychological dependence on the pleasurable effects of the activity, and
(4) a detrimental effect on the individual and society.

For suicidal behavior to be addictive, it must be repeated. Thus, the addiction model, if applicable, must pertain to nonfatal suicidal behavior that is repeated. This seems valid for self-mutilating behaviors, such as delicate wrist-cutting, in which the behavior is repetitive and tension releasing, often occurring in a trance-like state (Lester, 1972).

An early study by Callender (1968) found that people underwent experiences of less suicidal preoccupation before undergoing more seriously suicidal experiences. Callender felt that the lesser preoccupations constituted a necessary and integral part of the suicidal career. Thus, the successive suicidal experiences, in Callender's subjects, showed the pattern to be expected if tolerance were operating.

Research on the lethality of successive suicidal attempts is relevant to the model of suicidal behavior as addiction. Cutter, et al. (1969) found that the lethality of earlier suicide attempts were less lethal than the final fatal acts in a sample of completed suicides, a result later replicated by Lester, et al. (1978). More recently, Eyman and Smith (1986) found that the lethality of successive nonfatal suicidal acts increased monotonically, as did Pierce (1981, 1984) who found, in addition, that the people whose suicidal acts did increase in lethality were more likely to subsequently complete suicide.

Of course, *withdrawal* would not seem to apply to suicidal behavior -- distress caused in the suicidal individual if he or she were no longer able to behave suicidally. There is no research relevant to this issue. However, some scholars have suggested that suicidal behavior is but one alternative to a variety of symptoms that individuals may choose when in distress (Canetto, 1991; Lester, 1988b). Thus, if people are prevented in some way from behaving suicidally, they may well choose other behaviors (such as drug abuse or assaultive behavior) which may be more severe symptoms of psychological disturbance than suicidal behavior.

Let us now consider Jacobs's four components of addictive behavior mentioned above. The desire to continue suicidal activity seems to be under the individual's voluntary control. We have mentioned the tendency to increase the amount of the behavior over time above. The possibility that the suicidal individual becomes dependent on the pleasurable effects of suicidal behavior raises the question of whether suicidal behavior can be pleasurable. It has been suggested that suicidal behavior can be cathartic, and this has been documented (van Praag and Plutchik, 1985). Since nonfatal suicidal behavior can be motivated by desires to manipulate others in the environment, if the manipulation is successful, then the results may be pleasurable and this tactic may become a habit for the individual.

Finally, does suicidal behavior have a detrimental effect on the individual and the society? Even without severe psychiatric disturbance being present in the suicidal individual, at the very least a personality disorder is usually present -- a chronic maladaptive life-style, which may be presumed to be detrimental to the individual. Furthermore, it is hard to see how nonfatal suicidal behavior is other than detrimental to the society.

It can be seen that, rather than providing a good model for nonfatal suicidal behavior as we currently understand it, the addictive model of suicidal behavior suggests areas for investigation for the future to see in which ways suicidal behavior resembles other addictive behaviors and in which ways it differs. It would be nice to have answers within the next decade for some of the issues raised in this essay.

Discussion

In this essay, I have suggested a number of ways in which suicide can be conceptualized. These conceptualizations are very different types, and I would like to conclude by suggesting categories for them.

Many of the conceptualizations dealt with the purpose of the suicidal act (suicide as a gamble and an aggressive act). Two focussed on the development of suicide as a learned behavior (suicide as a learned behavior and as an addiction). One focussed on the psychological state of the suicidal individual (suicide as depression), while one viewed suicide as a sociopsychological state (suicide as deviance).

Not only may further conceptualizations of suicide be possible, but these new conceptualizations may suggest additional categories. We may also be able to add further conceptualizations to the categories suggested above with the aim, as mentioned at the beginning of this essay, of provoking new insights into suicidal behavior.

References

Achté, K. Depression and suicide. *Psychopathology*, 1986, 19, supplement 2, 210-214.
Bandura, A. *Social learning theory*. Englewood Cliffs: Prentice-Hall, 1977.

Barraclough, B. M. Suicide prevention, recurrent affective disorder and lithium. *British Journal of Psychiatry*, 1972, 121, 391-392.

Beck, A. T., Beck, R., & Kovacs, M. Classification of suicidal behaviors. *American Journal of Psychiatry*, 1975, 132, 285-287.

Beck, A. T., Steer, R., Kovacs, M., & Garrison, B. Hopelessness and eventual suicide. *American Journal of Psychiatry*, 1985, 142, 559-563.

Beck, A. T., Brown, G., & Steer, R. Prediction of eventual suicide in psychiatric inpatients by clinical ratings of hopelessness. *Journal of Consulting & Clinical Psychology*, 1989, 57, 309-310.

Brown, G., & Goodwin, F. Human aggression and suicide. *Suicide & Life-Threatening Behavior*, 1986, 16, 223-243.

Burvill, P., McCall, M., Reid, T., & Stenhouse, N. Methods of suicide in English and Welsh immigrants in Australia. *British Journal of Psychiatry*, 1973, 123, 285-294.

Callender, W. D. A socio-psychological study of suicide-related behavior in a student population. *Dissertation Abstracts*, 1968, 28A, 3765.

Canetto, S. Gender roles, suicide attempts, and substance abuse. *Journal of Psychology*, 1991, 125, 605-620.

Chabrol, H., & Moron, P. Depressive disorders in 100 adolescents who attempted suicide. *American Journal of Psychiatry*, 1988, 145, 379.

Coleman, L. *Suicide clusters*. Boston: Faber & Faber, 1987.

Cutter, F., Jorgensen, M., Farberow, N. L., & Ganzler, S. Ratings of intention in suicidal behavior. Unpublished, Los Angeles Suicide Prevention Center, 1969.

Durkheim, E. *Le suicide*. Paris: Felix Alcan, 1897.

Eyman, J, R., & Smith, E. K. Lethality trends in multiple suicide attempts. In R. Cohen-Sandler (Ed.) *Proceedings of the 19th Annual Meeting*, pp. 75-77. Denver, CO: American Association of Suicidology, 1986.

Firth. R. Suicide and risk-taking in Tikopia. *Psychiatry*, 1961, 24, 1-17.

Frederick, C., & Resnick, H. How suicidal behaviors are learned. *American Journal of Psychotherapy*, 1971, 25 37-55.

Hirsh, J. Methods and fashions of suicide. *Mental Hygiene*, 1960, 44, 3-11.

Jacobs, D. A general theory of addictions. *Journal of Gambling Behavior*, 1986, 2, 15-31.

Jacobs, J. *Adolescent suicide*. New York: Wiley, 1971.

Lester, D. Self-mutilating behavior. *Psychological Bulletin*, 1972, 78, 119-128.

______ . Sex differences in suicidal behavior. In E. Gomberg & V. Franks (Eds.) *Gender and disordered behavior*, pp. 287-300. New York: Brunner/Mazel, 1979.

Lester, D. *Why people kill themselves*. Springfield, IL: Charles Thomas, 1983.

______ . Murders and suicide: are they polar opposites? *Behavioral Sciences & the Law*, 1987a, 5, 49-60.

______ . *Suicide as a learned behavior*. Springfield, IL: Charles Thomas, 1987b.

______ . A subcultural theory of teenage suicide. *Adolescence*, 1987c, 22, 317-320.

______ . *The biochemical basis of suicide*. Springfield, IL: Charles Thomas, 1988a.

______ . Rational choice theory and suicide. *Activitas Nervosa Superior*, 1988b, 30, 309-312.

______ . *Suicide from a psychological perspective*. Springfield, IL: Charles Thomas, 1988c.

Lester, D., Beck, A. T., & Narrett, S. Suicidal intent in successive suicidal actions. *Psychological Reports*, 1978, 43, 110.

Lester. D., & Brockopp, G. Niagara Falls suicide. *Journal of the American Medical Association*, 1971, 215, 797-798.

Lester, G., & Lester, D. *Suicide: the gamble with death*. Englewood Cliffs, NJ: Prentice-Hall, 1971.

Linehan, M. Suicide and attempted suicide. *Perceptual & Motor Skills*, 1973, 37, 31-34.

McHugh, P., & Goodell, H. Suicidal behavior. *Archives of General Psychiatry*, 1971, 25, 456-464.

Menninger, K. *Man against himself*. New York: Harcourt, Brace & World, 1938.

Phillips, D. The influences of suggestion on suicide. *American Sociological Review*, 1974, 39: 340-354.

Pierce, D. The predictive validation of a suicide intent scale. *British Journal of Psychiatry*, 1981, 139, 391-396.

Pierce, D. Suicidal intent and repeated self-harm. *Psychological Medicine*, 1984, 14, 655-659.

Pokorny, A. D. Suicide rates in various psychiatric disorders. *Journal of Nervous & Mental Disease*, 1964, 139, 499-506.

Richman, J. *Family therapy for suicidal people*. New York: Springer, 1986.

Seligman, M. *Helplessness*. San Francisco: W. H. Freeman, 1975.

Shneidman, E. S., & Farberow, N. L. *Clues to suicide*. New York: McGraw-Hill, 1957.

Van Praag, H. Affective disorders and aggression disorders. *Suicide & Life-Threatening Behavior*, 1986, 16, 102-132.

Van Praag, H., & Plutchik, R. An empirical study of the cathartic effect of attempted suicide. *Psychiatry Research*, 1985, 16, 123-130.

Wagner, F. F. Suicide notes. *Danish Medical Bulletin*, 1960, 7, 62-64.

Walker, M. B. Should theories of addiction be generalized to include excessive gambling? W. R. Eadington (Ed.) *Gambling research: Proceedings of the Seventh International Conference on Gambling and Risk Taking*, volume 5, pp. 49-62. Reno: University of Nevada, 1988.

Chapter 12

A Developmental Perspective on Suicide

Introduction

In an effort to understand suicide, a first step is to identify the ways in which all suicidal individuals are alike and how they differ from comparison groups of people (such as depressed nonsuicidal patients or assaultive persons). For example, if we compare the suicides of Yukio Mishima (committing ritual seppuku), Sylvia Plath (a young poet putting her head in the gas stove after her marriage has broken up) and Ernest Hemingway (killing himself after release from the Mayo Clinic where he had been treated for a major depressive disorder), can we find common features in their lives?

A perusal of research on suicide reveals that there has been no variable or combination of variables which has been found to be either necessary or sufficient in the etiology of suicidal behavior (Lester, 1992a). Furthermore, of course, even when a significant difference between suicidal and nonsuicidal individuals is identified, such as depression or a history of sexual and physical abuse, the difference, though statistically significant, cannot differentiate *all* the suicidal individuals from *all* the nonsuicidal individuals.

The next step in a research program is to propose and validate a useful taxonomy of suicides. Once such a taxonomy is derived, then scholars no longer search for a variable which characterizes all suicides, but rather for one which characterizes this group of suicides. Gender, the precipitating events and the methods used for suicide have all been proposed as bases for a taxonomy of suicidal individuals, but the most useful basis so far has been psychiatric diagnosis. This has led to research on suicide in patients with particular diagnoses, such as schizophrenia, depressive disorders, borderline personality disorder, etc.

The present chapter uses the variable of age as a basis for the taxonomy of suicidal individuals. This approach has been the subject of recent interest, with three books appearing from this perspective (Blumenthal and Kupfer, 1990; Leenaars, 1991; Stillion, et al., 1989), and research clearly shows that suicidal behavior differs in people of different ages, as we shall see below.

What Is a Developmental Perspective?

Maris (1991) suggested several research designs which might be included in a developmental perspective on suicide. First, we can study *suicidal careers*, that is, what is the sequence of life events a person goes through before committing suicide. Such longitudinal studies can be done retrospectively, after the suicides have been identified (Maris, 1981), but are better done prospectively, following a group of people until a number of them kill themselves, though this method is more effortful and time-consuming since suicide is a rare behavior and occurs relatively late in life. Investigators have begun to study Terman's sample of gifted children which was initiated in the 1920s, some of whom have now killed themselves (e.g., Lester, 1991b). The time period for study can be a lifetime, but it can also be the weeks, days, and even hours leading up the suicidal act. Studies of cohorts can also be done at the societal level of analysis, examining, for example, the suicide rates of cohorts as they age (Murphy, et al., 1986)

A second strategy focuses on cross-sectional studies, comparing suicidal people of different ages for example, for differences in psychological and psychiatric factors. Thirdly, normal developmental changes, such as puberty and menopause, and states which change with age, such as psychiatric disorder, can be studied for their impact on suicide.

How Shall We Classify on the Basis of Age?

The question of how we should classify suicidal people on the basis of age seems rather silly at first consideration. Why not use age? But which age categories? Government agencies typically divide people into 5-year or 10-year groups, such as 15-24, 25-34, etc., and epidemiologists are usually restricted to using these age categories whether they like them or not, unless they obtain access to the primary data (such as death certificates). However, these age groupings may not make psychological sense.

Developmental psychologists prefer to describe stages of development which do not conform to these simple age groups. For example, Levinson (1978) described the following stages: early adult transition, entering the adult world, the age 30 transition, and settling down. Lester (1991a), laying out the framework for an edited volume on suicide over the life-span, used infancy, pre-school years, middle childhood, adolescence, young adulthood, middle adulthood and late adulthood. Other stage sequences have been proposed both by scholars (Erikson, 1959) and popular writers (Sheehy, 1976).

If we choose to use these stages, then we have the problem of defining the ages to which they correspond *or* psychologically investigating our subjects to see at which stage they have arrived. The former is difficult, the latter virtually impossible, especially since few of those who have proposed stages devise psychological tests with which we can classify people.

Are There Really Differences between Suicidal Behavior by Age?

This question must be addressed because some scholars stresss the commonalities of suicide. Shneidman (1985), for example, has listed the ten commonalities of suicide which he feels apply to every suicidal person: the purpose of seeking a solution, the goal of cessation of consciousness, the stimulus of intolerable psychological pain, the stressor of frustrated psychological needs, the emotion of hopelessness-helplessness, the cognitive state of ambivalence, the perceptual state of constriction, the action of egression, the interpersonal act of communicating intent, and the consistency of lifelong coping patterns.

Other scholars, however, have identified differences in suicidal behavior by age. Before reviewing these studies, it must be noted that most suicidologists have not studied suicidal behavior across the life span, but rather they have studied suicidal behavior in people of a particular age group, be it adolescence, adulthood or old-age. Only a few researchers have included suicidal persons of all ages, and this section reviews briefly some of these studies.

The Circumstances of the Suicidal Act

It has long been argued that the elderly use more lethal methods for suicide and, therefore, are more likely to have a fatal outcome than younger suicides (Templer and Cappelletty, 1986). In the United States, elderly male completed suicides do use guns and hanging more than younger completed suicides (McIntosh and Santos, 1985-1986), but there is little information available on the methods chosen by those attempting suicide.

Although the elderly do appear to engage less often than younger people in attempting suicide ("suicide attempts"), Osgood, et al. (1991) have documented a high incidence of indirect self-destructive behavior in the elderly, behavior which includes self-mutilation, refusing to eat or drink, and refusing to follow prescribed medical treatment.

Physiological Differences

Research on physiological factors in suicidal behavior is still in its infancy. It has been difficult to identify reliable differences between suicidal and nonsuicidal individuals (Lester, 1988). Though some reviewers of the literature attempt to address the role of age, they can produce no research data on the issue (Motto and Reus, 1991). However, using meta-analytic techniques in a recent review of the relevance of the dexamethasone suppression test in predicting suicide, Lester (1992b) found that the mean age of the sample was associated with the success of the test in predicting prior suicide attempts (the test was more effective in the younger samples) but not in predicting subsequent completed suicide. Thus, age may play a role in determining which physiological factors play a role in suicidal behavior, but a great deal more research is required before we can document this.

Psychological Differences

Stillion, et al. (1989, pp. 244-245) reviewed the literature on suicide in those of different ages and summarized their conclusions, identifying differences in biological, psychological, cognitive and environmental risk factors, warning signs, triggering events and the type of suicidal behavior. Kaplan and Worth (1993) have proposed a similar summary. However, both tables are based more on opinion than on research studies comparing younger and older suicidal individuals.

Leenaars (1989) rated suicide notes from completed suicides for various psychological characteristics and found differences by age. Statements reflective of problems in interpersonal relations, an inability to adjust to life's difficulties, indirect expressions (such as ambivalence, redirected aggression and unconscious implications), attachment to another who does not meet the person's need and maladaptive personal tendencies were all more common in young adulthood (aged 18-25) than in middle adulthood (25-55) and late adulthood (55+). The problem with Leenaars' results, however, is that he failed to identify characteristics which were more common in the notes of older adults. An older study by Farberow and Shneidman (1957) found that suicide notes of the elderly more often documented a wish to escape from suffering and less often a wish to punish themselves or to make others suffer.

The most common psychiatric illness in suicides differs with age. Rich, et al. (1986) found that elderly suicides were more often diagnosed as having an affective disorder or organic brain syndrome while younger suicides were more often diagnosed as having a substance abuse disorder or an antisocial personality disorder.

With regard to stress, Rich, et al. (1988) found that younger completed suicides had experienced more recent stressful life events (especially in the week prior to the completed suicide) and different kinds of stressors. For example, the younger suicides had experienced more interpersonal loss or conflict but less illness than the older suicides. The younger suicides also had more recent legal problems and were more often unemployed. Eisele, et al. (1987) found that psychiatric illness and medical illness were more common precipitants of elderly suicides whereas interpersonal and school/work problems were more common precipitants of young suicides.

These results are in accord with the general proposition long held that the suicides of younger people are more often interpersonally motivated while the suicides of older persons are more often intrapsychically motivated. Stillion, et al. (1989) drew attention to the experience of *cumulative* recent losses in the elderly, in which the person loses many people in rapid succession, often including the spouse, without adequate time to resolve the grief over any of the losses. There is loss of physical and mental capabilities, retirement, inadequate income, and social isolation and loneliness. Investigators, however, differ in whether they find medical illnesses more common or not in elderly versus younger suicides (Barraclough and Hughes, 1987; Cattell, 1988).

In a study of the effects of media publicity of suicides on suicidal behavior, Stack (1991) found that younger and elderly suicides, but not middle-aged suicides, showed an imitation response to media publicity in the week after a publicized suicide.

Lester (1991b) studied Terman's study of gifted children begun in the 1920s. By 1987, 34 of the 1528 children were known to have killed themselves, and Lester found that those who did so at a younger age were born after longer pregnancies, were breast-fed for a shorter period of time and were more likely to have experienced the loss of a father by death.

There is clinical opinion, not yet substantiated by research, that the suicidal behavior of younger people is more impulsive and, especially in children and adolescents, caused in part by the unconscious hostile desires of their parents. There is also the belief among some that suicide by the elderly can be more rational, but this may be a reflection of the ageist biases of our society. We appear to "approve" of suicide in the elderly, yet view the suicide of a youth as a "tragic waste."

Predicting Suicide

Lettieri (1974) noted long ago that a single suicide risk prediction scale would not necessarily be the most effective instrument. He presented prediction scales for younger (less than 40 years of age) and older men and for younger and older women. For example, the predictive scale for older men contained the following items: divorce status, somatic aspects of depression, irritation/rage/violence, accepting help now, recent loss through divorce, repetition of attempts and role failure. For the younger men the items were: marital status, Caucasian, confused and disorganized thinking, omnipresent suicidal feelings and a homicidal component.

Lettieri's idea has not been pursued as, in recent years, suicidologists have lost interest in predicting subsequent suicide.

Studies of Social Suicide Rates

Lester (1991c) examined the social correlates of suicide over the states of America in 1980. He identified seven broad clusters of social variables, and he found that a cluster measuring social integration was associated with the suicide rate of all age groups. Where social integration was stronger, the suicide rates of all age groups were lower. States with a younger population had higher suicide rates for many age groups, and the variable of southernness was associated with the suicide rates of both those aged 15 to 24 and 75 to 84. Lester concluded that the social correlates of elderly suicide rates in America were similar to those of adult and youth suicide rates.

Others, however, have found differences by age. For example, Pescosolido and Wright (1990) studied county suicide rates in America and found that, for men, age-specific divorce rates had a beneficial effect on the suicide rates of young men (18 to 24) an aggravating effect on the suicide rates of middle-aged men (45 to 64) and a negligible effect on the suicide rates of those aged 25 to 44 and over 65.

In time series studies of America from 1940 to 1984, Yang (1990) found that economic prosperity had a detrimental effect on the suicide rates of those aged 15 to 44 but a beneficial effect on the suicide rates of those 45 and older. The unemployment rate had an impact on the suicide rate only for those under the age of 45. She summarized her findings by noting that social variables had less of an impact on the suicide rates of older Americans than did economic variables, whereas the reverse was true for younger Americans.

In addition, Holinger (1987) observed that, as the proportion of young adults in the population gets larger, the suicide rate of that group increases, whereas for the elderly, the larger their proportion in the population, the lower their suicide rate.

In reviewing these studies, Lester and Yang (1992) noted that much more research is needed in order to identify reliable *unique* correlates of social suicide rates in the young versus the old.

Do Theories of Suicide Apply to All Ages?

Some theories of suicide may apply better to some groups than to others. As we have seen, investigators have noted that the precipitants of suicide appear to differ for the young and the elderly, with the younger suicides responding more to interpersonal crises. Younger individuals also make many more nonfatal attempts at suicide than do the elderly. Thus, it seems likely that not all theories of suicide apply equally well to both the young and the elderly.

To explore this, Lester (1993) took ten theories of suicide each of which Leenaars (1988) had summarized in ten propositions: Alfred Adler, Ludwig Binswanger, Sigmund Freud, Carl Jung, George Kelly, Karl Menninger, Henry Murray, Edwin Shneidman, Harry Sullivan and Gregory Zilboorg. Lester applied these statements to the lives of thirty famous suicides for whom a biography was available and found that some theories were more successful in describing the suicidal lives than others.

Looking at the success of the theories based on the age of the suicides, in general, the lives of the teenagers in the sample were not well described by the theories. Lester found that the theory of Binswanger was more appropriate for the older suicides than the younger suicides, while the theories of Jung, Murray, and Sullivan were less appropriate. Five of the suicides were over the age of sixty. For Binswanger's theory, four of these (80 percent) received a score of 6 or more (out of ten) as compared to only 16 percent of the younger suicides.

Looking at the items which correlated with age, the indications are that suicide for the elderly was more often a liberation from the effects of trauma, while for the younger suicides it was a response to interpersonal problems and intrapsychic problems.

The Relevance of a Developmental Perspective to Prevention

An important question to ask is whether a developmental perspective has implications for preventing suicide. If the suicidal act occurs in different circumstances, is predicted by different variables, and has a different meaning in the elderly as compared to the young, then efforts to prevent suicide might well differ depending upon the age of the target group.

The major strategies utilized in efforts to prevent suicide are: (1) suicide prevention centers, (2) psychiatric treatment, including medication and psychotherapy, and (3) educational programs, supplemented in recent years by (4) restricting availability to lethal methods for suicide. Let us examine each of these in turn.

Suicide Prevention Centers

Suicide prevention centers typically consist of 24-hour telephone counseling services which provide crisis counseling, supplemented in some centers by walk-in clinics which also provide crisis counseling. Who uses these centers?

A study at the suicide prevention center in Buffalo (Lester and Brockopp, 1973) showed that the modal caller was aged 20 to 29 (27%), female (70%), and single (38%). The modal person dying from suicide was, however, elderly and male. Thus, it is clear that telephone services attract a younger (and female) clientele and, therefore, are going to be more effective in preventing suicide in those groups. Suicide prevention centers are aware of this fact, and some do make extra efforts to advertise their services to those groups at high risk for suicide.

Psychiatric Treatment

Psychiatric treatment for suicidal people involves treatment for the underlying psychiatric disorder and the personal and interpersonal problems contributing to the suicidal crisis. This treatment can be given only to those who seek help, and medications, of course, can be prescribed only to patients of physicians and psychiatrists. Thus, it is of interest to ask which types of patients seek help from such resources.

In addition, it was noted above that depressive disorders are more common in older suicides than in younger suicides, suggesting that detection and treatment of depressive disorders might be more effective for preventing suicide in the elderly. Rutz, et al. (1989) found that a program to educate physicians in Gotland, Sweden, in the detection, evaluation and appropriate treatment of depression and suicide led to a reduction in the suicide rate in that region. It would of interest to see whether this reduction was obtained in all age groups.

Education Programs

Efforts to educate people about suicide and how to respond to those who are suicidal are primarily focused on school-age children (Leenaars and Wenckstern, 1991). There are several reasons for this. The rise in youth suicide rates in many nations in the 1970s galvanized mental health professionals into action, and education is a major public health strategy in prevention. Furthermore, every person goes to school, and school children are a captive audience. Thus, education directed at school children will be the most efficient in covering the population in the long-run.

There are skeptics, however, who dispute the value of these programs in preventing suicide (Shaffer, et al., 1988). Programs to improve the self-esteem and general coping skills in adolescents are open to less criticism, though obviously such programs aim for broader changes than simply preventing suicide (Stivers, 1991).

Suicidologists might give some thought as to how education programs about suicide could be designed to focus on other groups, such as working adults and the retired.

Restricting Access to Lethal Methods for Suicide

In institutions such as hospitals and prisons, inmates thought to be at risk for suicide are placed in "suicide-proof" rooms and monitored continually to minimize their opportunities for self-harm. Easy access to lethal methods for killing is often found to characterize the homes of children who engage in fatal and nonfatal suicidal behavior, especially through overdosing or use of the parents' firearms. The same strategy has been explored at the societal level.

In recent years, much research has documented that restricting access to lethal methods for suicide reduces the use of those methods for suicide and may, in some cases, reduce the total suicide rate. The switch in the United Kingdom from toxic coal gas to less toxic natural gas led to a reduction in the total suicide rate by about thirty percent (Clarke and Lester, 1989).

These changes are usually introduced for reasons other than preventing suicide. Natural gas became cheaper than coal gas in the United Kingdom; emission controls for car exhaust (which reduces the carbon monoxide content) are introduced to reduce pollution; gun control laws are tightened to prevent their use in crime. However, controls over the number and size of prescriptions of medications, medications which are intended for treatment of psychiatric disorders, but which can also be used for suicide, are specifically intended to reduce the risk of suicide.

The question in the present context is whether these methods work better for the young or for the elderly. Again, there is little research on this particular issue. Lester (1984) found that stricter state handgun control laws had similar beneficial effects on the suicide rates of the young and the old. However, Clarke and Lester (1989) noted that the detoxification of domestic gas in England and Wales had the greatest impact on the total suicide rate of men over the age of 45 and least impact on the total suicide rate of those younger than 24. Furthermore, for men over the age of 45, there was no evidence for switching to alternative methods for suicide. For younger males, there appeared to be some switching to alternative methods for suicide. Thus, perhaps restricting access to lethal methods for suicide may be a more effective strategy for the elderly than for the young, but more research needs to be conducted to examine the role of age in such associations.

Summary

It can be seen from this review that there is a paucity of research and theorizing on the *unique* features of suicide in those of different ages. All too often, the variables thought to be important in determining the appearance of suicidal behavior in those in one age group (such as depression or alcoholism) are demonstrated to be important for explaining the suicidal behavior of those in other age groups. Though such research findings are useful, we also need to ascertain what etiological factors apply specifically to each age group. The lack of information of this kind prevents us from devising and directing suicide prevention efforts specifically directed toward those of different ages.

Thus, although it might seem that we have a wide variety of strategies for preventing suicide, each strategy in fact focuses on a different age group, and so we are less well equipped to prevent suicide than it might appear.

REFERENCES

Barraclough, B. M., & Hughes, J. *Suicide*. London: Croom Helm, 1987.

Blumenthal, S. J., & Kupfer, D. J. (Eds.) *Suicide over the life cycle*. Washington, DC: American Psychiatric Press, 1990.

Cattell, H. R. Elderly suicide in London. *International Journal of Geriatric Psychiatry*, 1988, 3, 252-261.

Clarke, R. V., & Lester, D. *Suicide: closing the exits*. New York: Springer-Verlag, 1989.

Eisele, J. W., Frisino, J., Haglund, W., & Reay, D. T. Teenage suicide in King County, Washington. *American Journal of Forensic Medicine & Pathology*, 1987, 8, 208-216.

Erikson, E. *Identity and the life cycle*. New York: International Universities Press, 1959.

Farberow, N. L., & Shneidman, E. S. Suicide and age. In E. S. Shneidman & N. L. Farberow (Eds.) *Clues to suicide*, pp. 41-49. New York: McGraw-Hill, 1957.

Holinger, P. C. *Violent deaths in the United States*. New York: Guilford, 1987.

Kaplan, K. J., & Worth, S. A. Individuation-attachment and suicide trajectory. *Omega*, 1993, 27, 207-237.

Leenaars, A. A. *Suicide notes*. New York: Human Sciences, 1988.

_____ . Suicide across the adult life-span. *Crisis*, 1989, 10, 132-151.

_____ . (Ed.) *Life span perspectives of suicide*. New York: Plenum, 1991.

Leenaars, A. A., & Wenckstern, S. (Eds.) *Suicide prevention in schools*. New York: Hemisphere, 1991.

Lester, D. *Gun control*. Springfield, IL: Charles Thomas, 1984.

_____ . *The biochemical basis of suicide*. Springfield, IL: Charles Thomas, 1988.

_____ . A brief introduction to the stages of development. In A. A. Leenaars (Ed.) *Life span perspectives of suicide*, pp. 17-24. New York: Plenum, 1991a.

_____ . Childhood predictors of later suicide. *Stress Medicine*, 1991b, 7, 129-131.

_____ . Social correlates of youth suicide rates in the United States. *Adolescence*, 1991c, 26, 55-58.

_____ . *Why people kill themselves*. Springfield, IL: Charles Thomas, 1992a.

_____ . The dexamethasone suppression test as an indicator of suicide. *Pharmacopsychiatry*, 1992b, 25, 265-270.

Lester, D., & Brockopp, G. W. *Crisis intervention and counseling by telephone*. Springfield, IL: Charles Thomas, 1973.

Lester, D., & Yang, B. Social and economic correlates of the elderly suicide rate. *Suicide & Life-Threatening Behavior*, 1992, 22, 36-47.

Lettieri, D. J. Suicide death prediction scales. In A. T. Beck, H. L. P. Resnik, & D. J. Lettieri (Eds.) *The prediction of suicide*, pp. 163-192. Bowie, MD: Charles Press, 1974.

Levinson, D. *The seasons of a man's life*. New York: Knopf, 1978.

Maris, R. W. *Pathways to suicide*. Baltimore: Johns Hopkins University, 1981.

_____ . The developmental perspective of suicide. In A. A. Leenaars (Ed.) *Life span perspectives of suicide*, pp. 25-38. New York: Plenum. 1991.

McIntosh, J. L., & Santos, J. F. Methods of suicide by age. *International Journal of Aging & Human Development*, 1985-1986, 22, 123-139.

Motto, J. A., & Reus, V. I. Biological correlates of suicide across the life span. In A. A. Leenaars (Ed.) *Life span perspectives of suicide*, pp. 171-196. New York: Plenum, 1991.

Murphy, E., Lindesay, J., & Grundy, E. Sixty years of suicide in England and Wales. *Archives of General Psychiatry*, 1986, 43, 969-976.

Osgood, N. J., Brant, B. A., & Lipman, A. *Suicide among the elderly in long-term care facilities*. New York: Greenwood, 1991.

Pescosolido, B. A., & Wright, E. R. Suicide and the role of the family over the life course. *Family Perspective*, 1990, 24, 41-58.

Rich, C. L., Young, D., & Fowler, R. C. San Diego suicide study. *Archives of General Psychiatry*, 1986, 43, 577-582.

Rich, C. L., Fowler, R. C., Fogarty, L. A., & Young, D. San Diego suicide study. *Archives of General Psychiatry*, 1988, 45, 589-592.

Rutz, W., van Knorring, L., & Walinder, J. Frequency of suicide in Gotland after systematic postgraduate education of general practitioners. *Acta Psychiatrica Scandinavica*, 1989, 80, 151-154.

Shaffer, D., Garland, A., Gould, M., Fisher, P., & Trautman, P. Preventing teenage suicide. *Journal of the American Academy of Child & Adolescent Psychiatry*, 1988, 27, 675-687.

Sheehy, G. *Passages*. New York: Dutton, 1976.

Shneidman, E. S. *Definition of suicide*. New York: Wiley, 1985.

Stack, S. Social correlates of suicide by age. In A. A. Leenaars (Ed.) *Life span perspectives of suicide*, pp. 187-213. New York: Plenum, 1991.

Stillion, J. M., McDowell, E. E., & May, J. H. *Suicide across the life span*. New York: Hemisphere, 1989.

Stivers, C. Promotion of self-esteem in the prevention of suicide. In A. A. Leenaars & S. Wenckstern (Eds.) *Suicide prevention in schools*, pp. 51-69. New York: Hemisphere, 1991.

Templer, D. I., & Cappelletty, G. G. Suicide in the elderly. *Clinical Gerontologist*, 1986, 5, 475-487.

Yang, B. The impact of the economy in different social and demographic groups. Eastern Economic Association, Cincinnati, OH, March 1990.

Chapter 13

COMMUNICATION THEORY AND SUICIDE

INTRODUCTION

The classic work on nonfatal suicidal behavior is Farberow and Shneidman's (1961) *The Cry for Help,* a book which by its title focused on the communicative aspects of nonfatal suicidal behavior. Despite this focus, very little has been written on the communicative function of suicidal behavior and, in particular, suicidologists have rarely addressed the place of suicidal behavior in formal theories of communication.

The communicative aspects of suicidal behavior have certainly been implied in suicide research. The intent to manipulate others by the suicidal individual has been noted by Sifneos (1966). The intent is usually to force a significant other to express love and affection toward the suicidal individual, though occasionally a suicidal individual may be seeking rejection (Lester, 1968). Seeking to influence others by means of a nonfatal suicidal act is more common among the young than among the elderly (Lester, 1994).

Menninger (1938) classified the three major motives for fatal suicide as the desires to escape, to aggress against the self, and to aggress against others (to die, to be killed and to kill, respectively). The desire to aggress against others by means of one's suicidal death certainly involves communicative aspects. Suicide notes such as the following indicate a desire to communicate to a significant other.

> Mary, I hope you're satisfied, Bill (Jacobs, 1967, p. 69)
> Bill, I do hope you'll suffer more than I have done. I wish you'll die in a beer joint (Wagner, 1960, p. 63)

Indeed, the existence of suicide notes, both from fatal and nonfatal suicides, indicates a desire to communicate, even though only about 35 percent of completed suicides and two percent of attempted suicides leave suicide notes which are found (Shneidman and Farberow, 1961).

Research has also shown that the vast majority of suicidal individuals communicate their intent to significant others prior to their suicidal actions, either by making direct allusions to suicide and death or by indirect actions, such as cleaning out their rooms and giving possessions away. Again, this has been found to be true for both completed suicides (Robins, et al., 1959) and attempted suicides (Delong and Robins, 1961). Some suicidal actions are interrupted by others (Steer, et al. 1987) or committed in view of the public, as in those who threaten to jump off buildings

Clearly, completed and attempted suicidal behavior often has a communicative function. It is of interest to inquire, therefore, how this nonverbal behavior can be conceptualized in formal theories of nonverbal communication. To do this, this paper draws upon on the presentation of theories of human communication by Littlejohn (1983).

THEORIES OF NONVERBAL COMMUNICATION

Nonverbal communication raises four major conceptual issues (Burgoon, 1980). (1) What is the role of intention in judging a nonverbal action to be a communication? (2) Must the source or receiver be aware that the act is a communication? (3) Do the meanings of the acts have to be shared by the source and the receiver for the acts to be considered communications. (4) What constitutes a meaningful unit for analysis?

According to the first issue, nonfatal suicidal behavior is typically intended by the suicidal person to be a communication to significant others, and so intent is present. Also, both the source and the receiver are usually aware of the suicidal act (second issue). However, the source and the communicator may not see the same meaning in the communication (third issue), and we will examine below whether the major theories of nonverbal communication would consider a suicidal act to be a meaningful unit of analysis.

STRUCTURAL THEORIES

Kinesics

Birdwhistell (1970) focused on body language, *kinesics*. According to Birdwhistell, body movements are patterned and have meaning. Body movements are a function of the cultural group to which the communicators belong, and they influence the behavior of other members of the culture who perceive them. Out of the large number of body movements in which a person engages, some have a communication functions, and these are called *kines*. For example, at least twenty-three eye lid movements can be described (kines), and they are grouped into four different communication functions (*kinemes*). Complex combinations of kinemes in different bodily parts are known as *kinemorphs*. Clearly, kinesics focuses on too small units of analysis to be applicable to suicidal behavior in general. It may, however, have relevance to an analysis of the different style or manner of attempting suicide in the presence of others, if ever we were to proceed to such a microscopic analysis.

Proxemics

Proxemics studies the use of space in communication (Hall, 1966) and can refer to the space that people place between one another in ordinary interaction all the way to the space that people place between houses and buildings. At the interpersonal level, interaction can involve different senses -- some cultures may rely on touch more than others, others may rely on smell. Hall suggested that Americans have four levels of interpersonal space: intimate (zero to eighteen inches), personal (eighteen inches to four feet), social (four to twelve feet) and public (over twelve feet).

Nonverbal communication can be affected by posture (standing, sitting or lying down), the relative position of the shoulders (facing each other, at right angles, etc.), kinesthetic factors, touching factors, and sensory contact (visual, thermal, olfactory, etc.).

Again, proxemics is focusing on more microscopic features of behavior than is implied by describing suicidal behavior as a communication. Proxemics would be more interested in the detailed way in which a person makes a suicidal act in the presence of another. For example, Freddie Prinze, a young comedian, shot himself in the presence of his financial manager (Lester, 1991). Such an act could be carried out in a variety of ways which would involve different proxemics -- in a neighboring room versus the same room, distant from the person in the room versus very close, etc.

Paralanguage

Paralanguage (Trager, 1958) analyzes the vocal signs possible in verbal communication, signs such as voice qualities (forcefulness of articulation and rhythm), vocal characterizers (laughing or belching), vocal qualifiers (speaking softly or with clipped phrases), and vocal segregates (interruptions of rhythm such as "um"). This would seem to have little relevance to suicidal behavior.

FUNCTIONAL THEORIES

Ekman and Friesen

Ekman and Friesen (1975) have concentrated on kinesic behavior from three perspectives: what is the source of the act, what is the relationship of the act to its meaning, and what is the usage (or function) of the act.

The source of an act can be innate such as eyebrow raising to register surprise, universal behavior required for survival such as territorial behavior, or variable across cultures such as shaking the head from side to side to indicate negativity. Using suicidal behavior as a communication is clearly variable across cultures.

There are several possible relationships between an act and its meaning. An act may be *arbitrary* in that a culture may arbitrarily decide on what meaning to ascribe to a gesture. An act's meaning may be *iconic*, in which the gesture resembles the message being communicated, as when we position our hands to indicate a particular height. *Intrinsic* meaning is when the meaning is encoded in the behavior as in crying. Crying is both a sign of emotion *and* the emotion itself. Suicidal behavior may be best described as having an intrinsic meaning.

The usage or function of an act describes the purpose of the act -- is it purely a communication, an interactive act designed to influence the behavior of others, or informative, a category designed to describe acts not intended to be communicative but which convey information anyway.

Ekman and Friesen described five different types of nonverbal communications. *Emblems* have a particular message, known within the culture, such as a V sign with the fingers to indicate victory. *Illustrators* illustrate the verbal content such as outlining space or drawing a picture in the air. *Adaptors* release tension, such as hand wringing or foot jiggling. (*Self-adaptors* are usually carried out in private toward one's own body and include behaviors such as stroking oneself or grooming oneself. *Alter-adaptors* focus on someone else's body, while *object-adaptors* focus on objects.) *Regulators* control or coordinate interaction as when we make eye contact with the person to whom we are speaking. *Affect displays* involve the display of emotions, and suicidal behavior might more appropriately be classified as an affect-display than as one of the four other types.

Dittman

Dittman's (1972) theory of communication has three components: the channel for communicating emotion, emotional information, and emotional signs. The channel is concerned with the sensory modality in which the communication takes place. With regard to emotional information, Dittman views emotion as a behavioral deviation from some baseline behavior. In a culture, there is an expectation of how behavior should appear, and emotional expressions deviate from this expectation. A person learns from his cultural experience what the baseline is for behavior and what are the most common deviations from this baseline.

Emotional signs have three components. The communication has a degree of specification ranging from pure communication to pure expression. At the communication end of the continuum, there is cultural agreement on the specific meaning of the nonverbal act. At the expressive end of the continuum there is more idiosyncrasy in the meaning of the communication.

The second component is concerned with the level of awareness, ranging from full awareness to repressed unconscious (in the psychoanalytic sense) or subliminal unconscious (the sign is so weak that it is not perceived). The third component of emotional signs is intention -- is the communication controlled and monitored by the source or is it full and spontaneous?

Viewing suicidal behavior as a deviant behavior, deviating from baselines, is easy to do. Suicidal behavior is rare, and so statistically deviant. It is also not a socially approved method of communicating distress in most cultures, and certainly not viewed as a healthy way by psychotherapists.

On the other hand, many research studies have found that observing and hearing about suicidal behavior in family members, relatives and peers increases the chances that a person will engage in suicidal behavior themselves. Similarly, research on the effects of celebrity suicides indicates that modeling and imitation occur. Thus, experiences which increase the social acceptability of suicidal behavior do appear to make it more acceptable as a means of communicating emotion.

Suicidal behavior can also range from having a communicative to an expressive function, and be situated at some intermediate point, although perhaps only in primitive cultures is there a specific socially-agreed upon meaning for a nonfatal suicidal act.

DISCUSSION

Suicidal behavior clearly has verbal communication aspects, for example, in the suicide notes that suicidal individuals leave and in the verbal utterances made to significant others prior to the suicidal action. However, suicidal behavior has also been viewed as a communication in itself by suicidologists, and the present paper sought to explore how suicidal behavior would be viewed from the perspective of theories of nonverbal communication.

Structural theories of nonverbal communication consider elements of the communication too microscopic to be usefully applied to suicidal behavior. However, their concepts do draw attention to the particular way in which people make suicidal actions, especially when in the presence of others, when the particular body movements, positioning and paralanguage elements become of interest. This is an area not explored as yet by suicidologists.

Suicidal behavior was more consistent with functional theories of nonverbal communication. In Ekman and Friesen's theory, suicidal behavior was seen to have a variable source and an intrinsic meaning, and to be an affect display. In Dittman's theory, suicidal behavior is a deviation from baseline, intentioned, and involving full awareness.

It can be seen from this commentary that viewing suicidal behavior from the perspective of theories of nonverbal communication provides new ways of conceptualizing suicidal behavior and suggests areas for future research.

REFERENCES

Birdwhistell, R. *Kinesics and context*. Philadelphia: University of Pennsylvania, 1970.

Burgoon, J. K. Nonverbal communication research in the 1970s. In D. Nimmo (Ed.) *Communication yearbook*, volume 4, pp. 179-197. New Brunswick, NJ: Transaction Books, 1980.

Delong, W. B., & Robins, E. The communication of suicidal intent prior to psychiatric hospitalization. *American Journal of Psychiatry*, 1961, 117, 695-705.

Dittman, A. T. *Interpersonal messages of emotion*. New York; Springer, 1972.

Ekman, P., & Friesen, W. *Unmasking the face*. Englewood Cliffs, NJ: Prentice-Hall, 1975.

Farberow, N. L., & Shneidman, E. S. (Eds.) *The cry for help*. New York: McGraw-Hill, 1961.

Hall, E. T. *The hidden dimension*. New York: Random House, 1966.

Jacobs, J. A phenomenological study of suicide notes. *Social Problems*, 1967, 15, 60-72.

Lester, D. Attempted suicide as a hostile act. *Journal of Psychology*, 1968, 68, 243-248.

Lester, D. Freddie Prinze. *Proceedings of the Pavese Society*, 1991, 3, 17-23.

Lester, D. Are there unique features of suicide in adults of different ages and developmental stages? *Omega*, 1994, 29, 337-348.

Littlejohn, S. W. *Theories of human communication*. Belmont, CA: Wadsworth, 1983.

Menninger, K. *Man against himself*. New York: Harcourt, Brace & World, 1938.

Robins, E., Gassner, S., Kayes, J., Wilkinson, R. H., & Murphy, G. E. The communication of suicidal intent. *American Journal of Psychiatry*, 1959, 115, 724-733.

Shneidman, E. S., & Farberow, N. L. Statistical comparisons between attempted and committed suicides. In N. L. Farberow & E. S. Shneidman (Eds.) *The cry for help*, pp. 19-47. New York: McGraw-Hill, 1961.

Sifneos, P. E. Manipulative suicide. *Psychiatric Quarterly*, 1943, 40, 525-537.

Steer, R. A., Beck, A. T., Garrison, B., & Lester, D. Eventual suicide in interrupted and uninterrupted attempters. *Suicide & Life-Threatening Behavior*, 1988, 18, 119-128.

Trager, G. L. Paralanguage. *Studies in Linguistics*, 1958, 13, 1-12.

Wagner, F. F. Suicide notes. *Danish Medical Bulletin*, 1960, 7, 62-64.

Chapter 14

Communitarianism and Suicide Prevention

Introduction

Communitarianism is attempting to propose a new moral, social and public order which involves several core components (Etzioni, 1993): (1) a strengthening of the family without violating the rights of women, (2) having schools provide moral education without indoctrination, (3) increasing the strength of the community in people's lives, and (4) balancing the pursuit of self-interest and individual rights with a commitment to the community and an acknowledgement of individual responsibilities.

Etzioni noted that recent years have witnessed a growth in people focusing on their rights and manufacturing new rights. He suggested that there be a moratorium on such discussions, to be replaced by a discussion of the responsibilities that individuals should assume. He noted that the focus on individual rights by radical individualists (such as the American Civil Liberties Union and laissez-faire conservatives) has blocked many programs to increase public health and public safety.

Etzioni noted that conceptions in the 1950s of how the family must function were in need of revision, but the attacks on the family in the 1960s and 1970s did not result in the development of new concepts for the family. Similarly, the realization that the schools were not adequately educating children and adolescents in all aspects of living led to attacks on the prevailing system without proposals for reforming them so that they could effectively transmit a set of core values to each successive generation. Finally, although the 1960s witnessed a growth in the notion that there should be a shared community and public interest, this notion became eroded subsequently, and there is little guidance as to how the society might accomplish this.

These ideas strike a strong resonance with theories of suicidal behavior and suggest directions which might be pursued for preventing suicide, directions quite different from those currently being tried. The purpose of this article is to explore the relevance of communitarianism for understanding and preventing suicide.

Theories of Suicide

Sociological Theories

The classic sociological theory of suicide was proposed by Durkheim (1897). Durkheim argued that the suicide rate of the society was determined by two broad social forces. First, suicide was more common when the society was either too strongly or two weakly integrated, where social integration may be defined as the extent to which the members of the society are bound together in social networks. Suicide when social integration was too weak was called *egoistic* suicide and when social integration was too strong *altruistic* suicide. Second, suicide was more common when the society was either too strongly or too weakly regulated, where social regulation may be defined as the extent to which the desires and behaviors of the members of the society are regulated by the society. Suicide when social regulation was too weak was called *anomic* suicide and when social regulation was too strong *fatalistic* suicide.

Johnson (1965) argued that altruistic and fatalistic suicide were rare in modern society, and so he proposed a more simple theory, namely that suicide was more common in societies when the levels of social integration and social regulation were too weak. Thus, according to Johnson, suicide in contemporary society is predominantly egoistic and anomic in nature.

At an abstract level, therefore, Johnson's modification of Durkheim's theory suggests that suicide could be prevented by increasing the extent to which the members of the society are socially integrated and regulated, though within bounds. Too extreme social integration and regulation might lead to the appearance of altruistic and fatalistic suicide.[1] Moderation is preferred.

Research has supported this. Suicide is more common in regions and nations where the divorce rate is higher, where internal migration and immigration is higher, where church attendance is lower, and where alcohol consumption is higher (Lester, 1994). Furthermore, in regions where, for example, the divorce rate is higher, the suicide rate is higher in all groups, the single, married, divorced and widowed. Thus, it is probably not divorce per se which is causing the high rate of suicide in these regions. Rather, divorce appears to be one possible social indicator of a broader social characteristic (perhaps social integration) which causes suicide.

Other sociological theories also focus on causes of suicide that are related to concerns raised by communitarians. For example, subcultural theories of suicide have been proposed (Lester, 1989a; Platt, 1985) which have suggested that subcultures can arise within a dominant culture, subcultures which espouse values and norms which increase the likelihood of suicidal behavior, as for example in some groups of alienated adolescents.

The social deviancy theory of suicide (Lester, 1989a) proposes that suicide will be more common in those individuals who are deviant in social characteristics from the majority of the community in which they live. For example, African Americans who live in states with few African Americans have a higher suicide rate than African Americans who live in states with large numbers of African Americans.

---

1 Altruistic suicide is that committed by people for the good of others, as when the elderly commit suicide in order to cease being a burden to others. This has been documented, for example, in some Native American tribes and among the rural poor in Japan in the last century. Fatalistic suicide was thought to characterize the suicide of slaves whose lives are too strongly regulated by the slave owners (Lester, 1998).

Naroll (1969), an anthropologist, proposed that suicide would be more common in societies with a high incidence of thwarting disorientation contexts, which are situations in which a person's social ties are broken, weakened, or threatened, particularly by the actions of others. This theory, clearly, focuses on social conditions similar to those described by Durkheim (Lester, 1995).

The implications of these theories are that changes in the society along the lines of increasing social integration and regulation and decreasing thwarting situations should reduce the rate of suicide in the society. However, these theories do not provide specific guidelines for ways in which this might be done.

Psychological Theories

Psychological theories of suicidal behavior focus on early childhood experiences, psychiatric disorder and adult stressors. Among the childhood experiences which have been suggested as increasing the likelihood of suicidal behavior are experience of the loss of one or both parents (or significant others), experience of severely dysfunctional families and experience of sexual and physical abuse. The importance of loss is illustrated by a study conducted by Lester (1989b) on thirty famous suicides such as the poets Sylvia Plath and John Berryman. Exactly half of them had experienced loss in their childhood, the majority of them between the ages of six and fourteen.

One of the best studies illustrating the relevance of dysfunctional families was a study by Jacobs (1971) which found that families with suicidal adolescents had a long-standing history of problems, including broken homes, more subsequent remarriages and divorces, and parents who nagged, yelled at and physically punished their children. The suicidal adolescents had poorer rapport with their parents and were more alienated, depressed and unhappy. They were also more likely to have had peer relationships break up in recent years and to have shown behavioral problems such as running away from home. More recently, Pfeffer, et al (1988) found that suicidal adolescents had experienced more parental violence and arguments, recent deaths in the family, suicidal behavior in siblings, problems with alcohol abuse and break-ups with boy/girl friends.

Among the stressors which appear to increase the risk of suicide are unemployment, the disruption of interpersonal relationships, and legal and financial problems (Lester, 1992a), and the impact of these stressors is greater if the individual lacks social support. Suicidal behavior is more common in those diagnosed with depressive disorders, especially if combined with feelings of hopelessness about the future, and with substance abuse disorders in youths (Lester, 1992a).

What appears to be lacking in the suicidal individual is growing up in a stable, nurturing family and developing a set of values which would assist the person to deal with the crises that occur in almost all of our lives.

Suicide Prevention: The Non-Communitarian Past

The present techniques for preventing suicide are quite limited. Suicide prevention services are primarily 24-hour telephone crisis intervention centers which provide limited counseling by volunteers (Lester and Brockopp, 1973). The services certainly help many individuals through the hours of a crisis and can refer them to appropriate community services, but they provide what might be termed "band-aid" treatment.

Suicide education programs are presented to school children as part of the curriculum. These programs provide information about suicidal behavior, particularly about the cues that indicate that a peer might be suicidal, and train the children in some crisis intervention skills. There is a debate as to whether these programs are effective in achieving their limited aims, and conflicting evidence that they prevent suicide (Shaffer, et al., 1988).

A number of public health officials have stressed limiting access to lethal means for committing suicide, such as restricting access to firearms, detoxifying domestic gas and car exhaust, and limiting and monitoring the medications given to depressed clients (Clarke and Lester, 1989). Though there is good evidence that these tactics might prevent suicide, they apply to those who have already become suicidal and are in search of a method, and they do not address the problem of preventing the individuals from becoming suicidal in the first place.

Finally, the development of effective and relatively safe anti-depressant medications and short-term psychotherapy techniques has been especially useful in helping those who are depressed, and helping those who are depressed prevents suicide since the majority of suicides are depressed at the time of their suicidal actions.

SUICIDE PREVENTION: A COMMUNITARIAN APPROACH

The Family

It is clear that improving the family environment for children and adolescents, particularly those who are disturbed, would be a good strategy for improving the well-being of youth. However, almost all treatment proposals, research and articles for suicidal individuals focus on medication, short-term psychotherapy and crisis intervention. Richman (1986), almost alone, has argued for the importance of family therapy.

In addition, since loss and abuse in childhood appears frequently in the backgrounds of suicidal individuals, it would seem useful for suicide prevention services to coordinate with services working with abused and grieving adolescents. Indeed, there may be much value in services with different problem foci cooperating in their work with adolescents (Lester, 1992b).

Research has indicated that those who have engaged in nonlethal suicidal behavior (attempted suicides) are at high risk for subsequent lethal suicidal behavior (completed suicide). There has been very little work with providing social supports for attempted suicides, though Farberow (1968) did explore group therapy for suicidal individuals. More recently, however, in Australia, attempted suicides have joined with those whose loved ones have killed themselves to form a "consumer" group involved in the study and prevention of suicide.

The Schools

Those involved with crime prevention have seen the schools as opportunities for developing programs. Schools must be made more interesting and pleasant to adolescents so that they bond to the school and to the teachers. Smaller classes with more competent teachers who can be student-oriented rather than class-oriented can facilitate this. For example, Tifft (1990) set up a school program specially for young African American boys with no father at home and, in another program, invited black male professionals to come to the schools to work with minority youth.

In suicide prevention, this approach is rare, although some writers have suggested setting programs along these lines (Lester, 1990; Patrick, 1989). Patrick urged creating a school climate in which each student has opportunities to be successful and to feel valued and affirmed and in which students feel comfortable accessing help for personal issues, setting up mentor/peer programs, using cooperative team learning to promote success, and providing positive youth development activities. Such programs would not simply prevent suicide; they would prevent all kinds of emotional and behavioral problems in youth.

The Community

Again, in crime prevention, criminologists have seen the value in organizing the local community. Deteriorating neighborhoods need to be improved, the involvement of residents encouraged, recreational programs established, and employment training and opportunities developed.

The same tactic would be consistent with suicide prevention. Building a "neighborhood" with the involvement of residents and the development of recreational and educational/career programs would go far to decrease the egoism and anomie that can characterize deteriorating neighborhoods.

On the other hand, suicidal behavior is also common in isolated rural areas, where the elderly live alone with little other than alcohol to comfort them. Programs need to be developed to contact these individuals and to provide activities and social networks for them.

Final Thoughts

Suicide prevention workers would agree that the kinds of programs suggested above for schools and communities would be excellent for improving the mental health of people and, therefore, preventing suicide. But the tactics are not focused on suicide prevention, and as a result suicide prevention workers have not been motivated to get involved in setting up such programs. It is as if each problem (delinquency, drug abuse, eating disorders, suicidal behavior) attracts professionals and volunteers with a specific interest in that particular problem. They prefer to work on their problem and to concentrate on tactics that are focused on this problem. General tactics for improving the community are of less interest to them. The ideas discussed above suggest that programs with a broader focus and coordination between the different services in a community might improve the ability of each to help those with specific problems.

Those involved in providing services need to bond together and to forge a sense of community so that they can better address the psychological and social problems of the community!

References

Clarke, R. W., & Lester, D. *Suicide: Closing the exits*. New York: Springer-Verlag, 1989.

Durkheim, E. *Le suicide*. Paris: Felix Alcan, 1897.

Etzioni, A. *The spirit of community*. New York: Crown, 1993.

Farberow, N. L. Group psychotherapy with suicidal persons. In H. L. P. Resnik (Ed.) *Suicidal behaviors*, pp. 328-340. Boston: Little Brown, 1968.

Jacobs, J. *Adolescent suicide*. New York: Wiley, 1971.

Johnson, B. D. Durkheim's one cause of suicide. *American Sociological Review*, 1965, 30, 875-886.

Lester, D. *Suicide from a sociological perspective*. Springfield, IL: Charles Thomas, 1989a.

_____ . Experience of personal loss and later suicide. *Acta Psychiatrica Scandinavica*, 1989b, 79, 450-452.

_____ . *Understanding and preventing suicide*. Springfield, IL: Charles Thomas, 1990.

_____ . *Why people kill themselves*. Springfield, IL: Charles Thomas, 1992a.

_____ . Is there a need for suicide prevention? *Crisis*, 1992b, 13, 94.

_____ . *Patterns of suicide and homicide in America*. Commack, NY: Nova Science, 1994.

_____ . Thwarting disorientation and suicide. *Cross-Cultural Research*, 1995, 29, 14-26.

_____ . *Suicide in African Americans*. Commack, NY: Nova Science, 1998.

Lester, D., & Brockopp, G. W. (Eds.) *Crisis intervention and counseling by telephone*. Springfield, IL: Charles Thomas, 1973.

Naroll, R. Cultural determinants and the concept of the sick society. In S. C. Plog & R. B. Edgerton (Eds.) *Changing Perspectives in mental illness*, pp. 128-155 New York: Holt, Rinehart & Winston, 1969.

Patrick, S. K. School focused suicide prevention. In D. Lester (Ed.) *Suicide '89*, pp. 132-135. Denver: American Association of Suicidology, 1989.

Pfeffer, C., Adams, D., Weiner, A., & Rosenberg, J. Life event stresses on parents of suicidal children. *International Journal of Family Psychiatry*, 1988, 9, 341350.

Platt, S. A subculture of parasuicide? *Human Relations*, 1985, 38, 257-297.

Richman, J. *Family therapy for suicidal people*. New York: Springer, 1986.

Shaffer, D., Garland, A., Gould, M., Fisher, P., & Trautman, P. Preventing teenage suicide. *Journal of the American Academy of Child & Adolescent Psychiatry*, 1998, 27, 675-687.

Tifft, S. Fighting the failure syndrome. *Time*, 1990, 135(21), 83-84.

Chapter 15

A PUBLIC HEALTH APPROACH TO SUICIDE PREVENTION

INTRODUCTION

Earlier in this century, Winslow (1923) proposed a definition of public health which still has merit today. As paraphrased by Hanlon and Pickett (1984, p. 4), it reads as follows:

Public Health is the science and art of (1) preventing disease, (2) prolonging life, and (3) promoting health and efficiency through organized community effort for

a. the sanitation of the environment,
b. the control of communicable infections,
c. the education of the individual in personal hygiene,
d. the organization of medical and nursing services for the early diagnosis and preventive treatment of disease, and
e. the development of the social machinery to insure everyone a standard of living adequate for the maintenance of health,

so organizing these benefits so as to enable every citizen to realize his birthright of health and longevity.

Hanlon and Pickett (1984, p. 5) offered an alternative definition of the field:

> Public health is dedicated to the common attainment of the highest level of physical, mental, and social well-being and longevity consistent with available knowledge and resources at a given time and place. It holds this goal as its contribution to the most effective total development and life of the individual and society.

Clearly, this definition is less precise in the techniques which different the field of public health from the fields of medicine and general social policy interventions. However, Hanlon and Pickett go on to list the three major areas of involvement for public health: (1) health service systems, (2) health behavior and motivation, and (3) environmental hazards. This leads to seven categories of activity:

(1) activities on a community basis, such as making the environment safer,

(2) activities to prevent illness, disability, or premature death,
(3) activities related to comprehensive health care, such as promotion and operation of emergency medical service systems,
(4) activities concerned with the collection, preservation, analysis and use of vital records,
(5) public education and motivation in personal and community health,
(6) comprehensive health planning and evaluation, and
(7) scientific, technical and administrative research.

THE ROLE OF THE GOVERNMENT

Some of the goals of a public health approach to suicide prevention involve the government. With regard to suicide prevention, the United States government has played a small role. Funding for research into suicide has come from the National Institute for Mental Health (and other institutes) and from the National Science Foundation. For a few years, NIMH had a special section for suicidology (Shneidman, 1967), which produced a journal called the *Bulletin of Suicidology*, beginning in 1967, with eight issues (and a supplement on youth suicide) until it ceased publication in 1971. A government task force on youth suicide was established with a report published in 1989, but since then there has been little interest from federal, state or local governments in suicide prevention. This is in contrast to the recent central government involvement in formulating suicide prevention policy by the United Nations and the World Health Organization, in nations such as Finland, and in local governments such as the Canadian province of Alberta. For example, the Swedish government has developed a national program to develop suicide prevention programs (National Council for Suicide Prevention, 1996) which has both guidelines and strategies for future implementation.

The United States federal government does, however, collect mortality statistics and makes them available in printed summaries and, now, on data tapes. Since 1933, data have been provided for the whole nation, and this permits studies of the epidemiology of suicide. More recently, the Centers for Disease Control has published the *Morbidity and Mortality Weekly Report* which contains articles on current trends in mortality and in physical and psychiatric illnesses, including suicide, and occasional articles on guidelines for handling suicidal situations, such as the aftermath of suicides which occur in schools and the reporting of suicides by the media. The Centers for Disease Control is presently focusing on injury prevention and sponsoring conferences, publications (such as *Injury Control Update*) and research in order to catch the attention of both professionals and the general public.

This information-dissemination approach is consistent with a public health approach to prevention, but it also can galvanize public and political support for preventive efforts. These efforts are sometimes opposed by other groups in the society. For example, although strict gun control might well reduce the use of firearms for suicide, organizations such as the National Rifle Association oppose laws which strengthen gun control laws or which ban guns. Scholarly research is not, therefore, sufficient to produce changes at the government level. Public opinion must be marshalled in order to overcome the pressures exerted by those opposed to the necessary changes.

The major professional association concerned with suicide prevention in the United States is the American Association of Suicidology, founded in 1968 (Swenson, 1968), which holds annual meetings, publishes a scholarly journal and newsletters, and brings together scholars, crisis intervention workers and survivors (those who have lost a loved one to suicide). The association also accredits suicide prevention and crisis intervention services and offers a national examination for crisis counselors.

These kinds of government and professional activities are relevant to the tasks listed above which are included in a public health approach. Interestingly, Lester (1992) found that the states in America which had developed programs to combat youth suicide had improved their youth suicide rates relative to states which had taken little or no action. Thus, concern about suicide at the government level may have a beneficial impact on the communities they serve.

Education Programs

One of the strategies of a public health approach is education. Education programs have focused on two groups: school children and physicians.

School Programs

School suicide prevention programs have focused primarily on educating students about the risk factors for identifying suicidal students, changing attitudes toward suicide so that the topic can be discussed in a more supportive manner, and encouraging appropriate responses to suicidal peers. Many of the programs, therefore, seem oriented toward turning all students into potential crisis counselors.

Ryerson (1990) has developed a more comprehensive program in which the goal is to raise the level of awareness and knowledge in all members of the school community -- students, staff and parents. Her program covers such issues as the warning signs for suicidal adolescents, the epidemiology of adolescent suicide, the different face of depression in adolescents, the causes of adolescent suicide, what educators, parents and peers can do to help those in suicidal crises, and what community resources exist.

Ryerson's program involves (1) a three-hour intensive seminar for school staff (including teachers, administrators and all support staff including the cafeteria and maintenance workers, coaches and secretaries), (2) a variety of parent programs, ranging from thirty minutes to two hours, and (3) four to six hour student workshops which can be incorporated into the teaching curriculum. It is important to provide adequate mental health care in the community to handle students who are identified as suicidal and who are referred for more sustained treatment. Ryerson's goal is to make the program an on-going one in which the school staff take over running the workshops after a couple of years.

Not all commentators in this field agree that such programs are beneficial. There has been doubts raised about whether the programs reduce the incidence of suicidal behaviors and whether the programs for students might distress and increase the risk of suicide for some students (Shaffer, et al., 1988). Ryerson stresses the importance of evaluating these programs, and several evaluation studies have appeared in recent years. For example, Kalafat and Elias

(1994) found positive impacts from a general suicide awareness program for adolescents, Eggert, et al. (1995) found that a treatment program for school children identified as at risk for suicide was beneficial for the children, and Mackesy-Amiti, et al. (1996) found that a program for educators increased their knowledge about suicide in adolescents.[1]

Educating Physicians

Rutz, et al. (1989) have shown that a program to educate physicians in the detection, evaluation and appropriate treatment of depression and suicide led to a reduction in the suicide rate on the island of Gotland (Sweden) as compared to the rest of Sweden. Eventually, without continued training, especially for physicians new to the island, the suicide rate rose again. Marshall (1971) trained community nurses in a rural area to recognize suicidal risk in their clients, but he did not evaluate the effectiveness of the program.

Whereas this intensive post-graduate education had a beneficial impact on suicidal behavior, simple warnings probably do not work. For example, Soumerai, et al. (1987) found that warning physicians about the misuse of Darvon had no impact on the death rate from Darvon.

Educating the Media

It has been clearly demonstrated that media publicity about the suicides of celebrities results in an increase in the suicide rate for the next week at least (Stack, 1990). Thus, care should be taken by the media in how they present news about suicides so that imitation is minimized. For example, publishing details of the method used and how it was obtained is dangerous. Glamorizing the suicide is likely to increase the suggestive impact of the suicide on others. Furthermore, researchers in the field have suggested that the media should always accompany suicide stories with information about suicide prevention resources in the community (Centers for Disease Control, 1988).

Improving Mental Health Service Delivery

There are several tactics which appear to have potential for preventing suicide, whose effectiveness depends in part on improving the delivery of particular services to the general public, a public health concern.

Medical Emergency Services

Diggory (undated) has argued that we are preventing suicide with our emergency medical procedures. He estimated that in 1971, for example, the suicide rate in Pittsburgh was reduced from 15.2 to 12.5 (a reduction of 18 percent) simply by saving the lives of those who had

---

1 Programs have also been developed to provide crisis intervention to schools after a student has committed suicide (Wenckstern and Leenaars, 1991).

attempted suicide. Thus, an improvement in emergency medical care would probably increase the extent to which those who might have died from their suicidal actions would survive. However, in the United States at the present time, while the medical treatment of seriously-injured people has improved, emergency room services are closing down in some rural areas as hospitals attempt to increase profits, a policy which limits the ability of some communities to save the lives of attempted suicides.

General Mental Health

Prevention of suicide might also focus on providing good general mental health services for communities and for groups with high rates of psychiatric disorder such as aboriginal groups or adolescent runaways. Many years ago Ratcliffe (1962) noted that changing a mental hospital in the United Kingdom from a locked-ward to an open-door system of patient management was accompanied by a drop in the number of suicides in the surrounding community, but a drop in the suicide rate does not always occur when community mental health centers are opened (Walk, 1967). More research is need to identify what factors may affect the success of such programs.

On the other hand, in the United States in recent years, there has been a move to privatize mental health care, to release psychiatric patients from psychiatric institutions, and to reduce the coverage from medical insurance for the treatment of psychiatric disorders. The result is that many former psychiatric patients now live on the streets and those who might benefit from psychiatric treatment and psychotherapy cannot afford it. Thus, increasing access to mental health facilities is not always a realistic goal.

Suicide Prevention Centers

Suicide prevention centers have been set up in many countries in the world, and some have extensive networks of centers so that an individual always has a center near at hand. Suicide prevention centers typically have a 24-hour telephone crisis counseling service staffed by paraprofessional volunteers. Some centers have, in addition, walk-in clinics and emergency out-reach teams which can visit distressed individuals in the community.

This type of suicide prevention has been oriented around a crisis model of the suicidal process. People who are suicidal are conceptualized as being in a time-limited crisis state. Immediate crisis counseling should help the suicidal individual through the suicidal crisis, whereupon a normal life may resume.

Most of these suicide prevention efforts by these centers are essentially passive (Lester, 1989). A suicidal person has to contact the suicide prevention center. Active methods, such as seeking out discharged psychiatric patients, elderly males living alone, and other high risk groups could be undertaken. In addition, physicians as well as community workers such as police officers, clergymen, lawyers, and perhaps groups such as bartenders, prostitutes and hair dressers who also come into contact with the public, could be sensitized to the detection of depressed, disturbed and suicidal people and encouraged to refer them to appropriate resources.

At the present time, three international organizations exist to coordinate suicide prevention centers around the world and to stimulate their development -- Befrienders International, Life Line International and IFOTES (the International Federation of Telephonic Emergency Services). A recent review of the effectiveness of suicide prevention centers in preventing suicide concluded that they do appear to have a small but significant beneficial impact (Lester, 1997).

Making the Environment Safer

The two most common methods for preventing suicide proposed in the past have been (1) the establishment of suicide prevention centers, discussed above, and (2) psychiatric/psychological treatment of depressed and psychiatrically disturbed patients with effective medications and psychotherapy. Despite the obvious usefulness of these strategies for distressed individuals, the suicide rates in most nations have not declined in the last couple of decades. It seems, therefore, that the field of suicide prevention could benefit greatly from new effective strategies for preventing suicide.

One technique for preventing suicide, which has been explored in recent years and which is consistent with the public health approach, is the restriction of easily available means for suicide. If the means for suicide were less available, then suicidal persons would be less able to make lethal impulsive suicide attempts. Many scholars have alluded to the role of choice of method in affecting suicide rates, but the notion is usually attributed to Stengel (1964) who discussed the role that the detoxification of domestic gas played in changing national suicide rates. Seiden (1977; Seiden and Spence, 1983-1984) also drew attention to this strategy, noting, for example, that the Golden Gate Bridge in San Francisco was a much more "attractive" suicide locale than the Bay Bridge.

However, the first convincing demonstration of the possible effectiveness of this strategy was by Kreitman (1976) who showed that the drop in the English suicide rate was the result of the detoxification of coal gas and the switch to natural gas. The percentage of carbon monoxide in gas declined from 13% in 1955 to 0% in 1975. The suicide rate by carbon monoxide poisoning also declined in all age groups and for both sexes. In contrast, the suicide rate by other methods rose over the same period, but not sufficiently so as to prevent a decline in the overall suicide rate. This early study illustrated the two tasks involved in good research on the strategy: (1) does the restriction of access to a method for suicide lower the suicide rate by that method, and (2) if it does, do people switch to other methods for suicide?

Clarke and Lester (1989) have produced the best documentation for the effectiveness of this approach to suicide prevention. They conducted a number of studies to show that the availability of firearms, toxic car exhaust and toxic domestic gas appears to be strongly related to the use of those methods for suicide, and that reducing the easy availability of these methods for suicide often reduced the overall suicide rate since not everyone switches methods for suicide when their preferred method becomes less easily available. Research relevant to the effectiveness of these tactics for preventing suicide has been reviewed by Lester (1993, 1998), who concluded that the evidence is that they do prevent suicide, although some studies do indicate that switching to alternative methods of suicide does occasionally occur.

Clarke and Lester urged the detoxification of domestic gas, limits on the sales and ownership of firearms, restricting the size of medication prescriptions, placing the pills in plastic blisters which are hard to open, adding vomiting-inducing chemicals to medications so that an overdose will result in expulsion of the medication, prescription of suppositories rather than orally-taken tablets, prescribing the less toxic medications, cleaning up car emissions, changing the shape of the exhaust pipe to make it difficult to attach tubing, having an automatic engine turn-off mechanism if the car idles for more than a few minutes, fencing in bridges and high buildings from which people jump, and restricting the easy availability of herbicides and insecticides in developing countries.

Related to making the environment safer, another suggestion for suicide prevention is to investigate the environments into which these serious attempters are released. Does their environment contain suicidogenic stresses, hostile significant others who increase the likelihood of self-destructive tendencies, or lethal means for suicide? One suicide prevention center in the United States used to search the homes of attempted suicides, removing all guns, large knives, poisons and lethal drugs. They were able to do this, of course, only for attempted suicides who contacted them, and they did it with the tolerance of the local police force. It is not a technique that is likely to be available to most preventers of suicide, but it does illustrate a technique for "sanitizing the environment."

Applications to Other Social Problems

The notion that restricting access to lethal methods for death might reduce the incidence of the rates of homicide and accidental deaths has also been explored, with results that support the strategy. Lester (1993) reviewed a number of studies on the impact on homicide rates of restricting the availability of firearms and concluded that the evidence for a preventive effect was present but not as strong as that found for suicide. On the other hand, there was less evidence than in the case of suicide for switching to alternative methods for murder when firearms were less available. For accidental deaths, Lester and Abe (1992) found, for example, that the detoxification of domestic gas in both Japan and the United States reduced the accidental death rate from domestic gas.

The strategy has also been extended to other social problems such as the consequences of changing the availability of alcohol (Smith, 1988) and gambling opportunities (Lester, 1994), again with results that support the usefulness of the paradigm.

Comment

Though the studies do not yet lead to a definitive conclusion as to the efficacy of this strategy for preventing suicide, the results do indicate that reducing the availability of a method for suicide reduces its use for suicide and may also reduce the overall suicide rate if the method restricted is commonly used and a lethal method. In the latter case, people who switch methods for suicide are forced to switch to a less lethal method for which survival is more likely. Studies on the likelihood of people switching methods for suicide are needed, and at the present time only preliminary studies have appeared (Lester, et al., 1989). It is likely that more research on this important topic will appear in the next few years, hopefully permitting us to evaluate this method of suicide prevention more precisely. Nonetheless, at this point in time, it is possible to suggest a variety of tactics which may be used to restrict access to lethal methods for suicide -- see Table 1.

Table 1. Ways to Limit Access to Lethal Methods for Suicide

Cars:
- emission controls (to reduce carbon monoxide content)
- change shape of tail pipe to end in a narrow slit (to make attachment of hose difficult)
- have automatic ignition turn-off once engine has idled for five minutes

Domestic Gas:
- switch to less toxic natural gas
- automatic gas turn-off if gas not lit within 30 seconds
- make oven doors hinged at base (to make it difficult to put one's head in)

Jumping:
- fence in bridges
- fence in tops of high buildings
- restrict access to the tops of buildings
- fence in parking garages

Poisons:
- put the common household poisons in child-proof containers

Firearms:
- pass and enforce strict gun control laws
- require members of gun clubs to store guns at their, club in secure rooms

Medications:
- limit size of prescriptions
- eliminate automatic refills of prescriptions
- do not prescribe without seeing and evaluating patient
- enclose pills in plastic blisters
- prescribe as suppositories rather than as oral tablets
- set up monitoring system to catch multiple prescribing of patient by several doctors/pharmacists
- prescribe less toxic medications (e.g., Mianserin or Prozac rather than Amitriptyline)
- set up systems to prevent forging/changing prescriptions by patients (e.g., by having physicians directly input prescriptions into pharmacies by computer)

Attempted Suicides:
- collect lethal agents/implements before releasing attempters to their homes

Lester (1988) has argued that a failure to make lethal methods and venues for suicide less available may render people legally liable for civil damages. For example, all house-owners in the United States must fence in swimming pools in their back yards or face civil liability should someone drown in their pool. Lester argued that the municipal government in the Bay Area in California might have been held similarly liable by those whose relatives jumped from the Gold Gate Bridge, a popular suicide venue which was not fenced in.

The research relevant to this strategy for preventing suicide has implications for a theory of suicide. It is common to think of suicide as a desperate measure, chosen by seriously dysfunctional people who are at their wits' end. It seems unlikely that such people would be deterred by the effort needed to overcome the restrictions placed upon obtaining a lethal amount of their preferred method for suicide.

However, the present viewpoint suggests that suicide may be a logical decision made by people based upon rational issues such as the availability of different methods for suicide (Clarke and Lester, 1989; Yeh and Lester, 1987). Many people when asked say that they would consider one and only one method for suicide. If access to this method was restricted, then suicide may well be averted in these people. The necessity of switching to a less preferred method may introduce costs that were not originally present. For example, those who fear the pain of a bullet and the disfigurement of the wound would in all probably *not* switch to firearms were medication no longer available.

Furthermore, these results suggest that it may be heuristic to consider suicide by different methods as distinctly different acts, perhaps with different motivations and determinants (Lester, 1996). Lester (1995) has shown, for example, that the social correlates of suicide rates by different methods over the American states are quite different from one another.

Will people switch methods for suicide if their preferred method is made less easily available? Although this is the critical question for this method of preventing suicide, very few studies have appeared on this issue. It remains a matter of opinion. However, for those who would switch methods for suicide, if the new method is less lethal than the former method, then there is a greater likelihood that they will survive and, therefore, that some completed suicides will have been prevented.

Discussion

The public health model for prevention is presently growing in popularity because one key element in introducing change in the provision of mental health services is public support, which in turn galvanizes legislators to pass laws to facilitate the improvement of services. The Centers for Disease Control have sought, for example, to publicize, through reports of funded research, the extent of gun-related injuries and deaths, hoping to convince the public that this is a problem which must be addressed.

On the other hand, while educational programs about suicide and suicide prevention continue to be popular in schools, little effort has been made to replicate and extend Rutz's study of educating physicians in the detection and treatment of serious depression in their patients. In addition, government, at least in the United States, has not stepped forward to make suicide prevention an issue which merits a national strategy, although suicide prevention groups, such as the American Association of Suicidology, the American Foundation for Suicide Prevention and the Suicide Prevention Awareness Network, are making an effort to prod the government into doing so.[2]

[2] As of 2004, the United States now has a national strategy supported by the governement.

References

Centers for Disease Control. CDC recommendations for a community plan for the prevention and containment of suicide clusters. *Morbidity & Mortality Weekly Report*, 1988, 37, (supplement # 5-6), 1-12.

Clarke, R. V., & Lester, D. *Suicide: closing the exits*. New York: Springer-Verlag, 1989.

Diggory, J. Empirical evidence for the improved prediction and prevention of suicide. Pittsburgh: Chatham College, undated.

Eggert, L. L., Thompson, E. A., Herting, J. R., & Nicholas, L. J. Reducing suicide potential among high-risk youth. *Suicide & Life-Threatening Behavior*, 1995, 25, 276-296.

Hanlon, J. J., & Pickett, G. E. *Public health*. St. Louis: Times Mirror/Mosby, 1984.

Kalafat, J., & Elias, M. An evaluation of a school-based suicide awareness intervention. *Suicide & Life-Threatening Behavior*, 1994, 24, 224-233.

Kreitman, N. The coal gas story. *British Journal of Preventive & Social Medicine*, 1976, 30, 86-93.

Lester, D. The AAS and political activism. *AAS Newslink*, 1988, 14(2), 8.

______ . *Can we prevent suicide*? New York: AMS, 1989.

______ . State initiatives in addressing youth suicide. *Social Psychiatry & Psychiatric Epidemiology*, 1992, 27, 75-77.

______ . Controlling crime facilitators. *Crime Prevention Studies*, 1993, 1, 35-54.

______ . Access to gambling opportunities and compulsive gambling. *International Journal of the Addictions*, 1994, 29, 1611-1616.

______ . Explaining the regional variation of suicide and homicide. *Archives of Suicide Research*, 1995, 1, 159-174.

______ . Are murders and suicides committed by different methods intrinsically different? *Medicine, Science & the Law*, 1996, 36, 28-30.

______ . Evaluating the effectiveness of suicide prevention centers. *Suicide & Life-Threatening Behavior*, 1997, 27, 304-310.

______ . Preventing suicide by restricting access to methods for suicide. *Archives of Suicide Research*, 1998, 4, 7-24.

Lester, D., & Abe, K. The effects of the switch from coal gas to natural gas on the accidental death rate. *Accident Analysis & Prevention*, 1992, 24, 157-160.

Lester, D., Fong, C. A., & D'Angelo, A. A. Chronic suicide attempters who switch methods and those who do not. *Perceptual & Motor Skills*, 1989, 69, 1390.

Mackesy-Amiti, M. E., Fendrich, M., Libby, S., Goldenberg, D., & Grossman, J. Assessment of knowledge gains in proactive training for postvention. *Suicide & Life-Threatening Behavior*, 19966, 26, 161-180.

Marshall, M. C. D. The indigenous nurse. *Seminars in Psychiatry*, 1971, 3, 264-270.

National Council for Suicide Prevention. *Support in suicidal crises: The Swedish national programme to develop suicide prevention*. Stockholm, Sweden: National Board of Health and Welfare, 1996.

Ratcliffe, R. W. The open door. *Lancet*, 1962, ii, 188-190.

Rutz, W., van Knorring, L., & Walinder, J. Frequency of suicide on Gotland after systematic postgraduate education of general practitioners. *Acta Psychiatrica Scandinavica*, 1989, 80, 151-154.

Ryerson, D. Suicide awareness education in schools. *Death Studies*, 1990, 14, 371-390.

Seiden, R. H. Suicide prevention. *Omega*, 1977, 8, 267-276.

Seiden, R. H., & Spence, M. A tale of two bridges. *Omega*, 1983-1984, 14, 201-209.

Shaffer, D., Garland, A., Gould, M., Fisher, P., & Trautman, P. Preventing teenage suicide. *Journal of the American Academy of Child & Adolescent Psychiatry*, 1988, 27, 675-687.

Shneidman, E. S. Description of the NIMH Center for Studies of Suicide Prevention. *Bulletin of Suicidology*, 1967, July, 2-7

Smith, D. I. Effectiveness of restrictions on availability as a means of reducing alcohol-related problems. *Contemporary Drug Problems*, 1988, 15, 627-684.

Soumerai, S. B., Avorn, J., Gortmaker, S., & Hawley, S. Effect of government and commercial warnings on reducing prescription misuse. *American Journal of Public Health*, 1987, 77, 1518.

Stack, S. Media impacts on suicide. In D. Lester (Ed.) *Current concepts of suicide*, pp. 107-120. Philadelphia: Charles Press, 1990.

Stengel, E. *Suicide and attempted suicide*. Baltimore: Penguin, 1964.

Swenson, D. D. First annual conference on suicidology. *Bulletin of Suicidology*, 1968, December, 46-48.

Walk, D. Suicide and community care. *British Journal of Psychiatry*, 1967, 113, 1381-1391.

Wenckstern, S., & Leenaars, A. A. Suicide postvention. In A. A. Leenaars & S. Wenckstern (Eds.) *Suicide prevention in schools*, pp. 181-195. New York: Hemisphere, 1991.

Winslow, C. E. A. *The evolution and significance of the modern public health campaign*. New Haven, CT: Yale University Press, 1923.

Yeh, B. Y., & Lester, D. An economic model for suicide. In D. Lester. *Suicide as a learned behavior*, pp. 51-57. Springfield, IL: Charles Thomas, 1987.

Chapter 16

Psychotherapy for Suicidal Clients

Introduction

In many discussions of counseling for suicidal clients, the level of analysis does not proceed much beyond the training given to nonprofessional crisis counselors working at suicide prevention centers, training that focuses on active listening (person-centered therapy), assessment of resources, and formulation of a plan for action. Rudestam (1985-1986) observed that a crisis-oriented approach is rarely useful for chronically suicidal clients, whose level of functioning has been quite poor throughout most of their life. Such clients need long-term psychotherapy.

Textbooks on systems of psychotherapy, based on well-established theories of human behavior that provide a rationale for therapeutic techniques, typically ignore the problem of suicide, however. Lester (1991) reviewed the scholarly literature on the major systems of psychotherapy, searching for cases in which they had been applied to suicidal clients. Whereas some psychotherapists, such as psychoanalysts and cognitive therapists, have occasionally reported applications of their systems to suicidal clients, others, such as Gestalt therapists, have rarely provided such examples.

Psychotherapists who work with suicidal clients need to consider several issues. The first is whether all of the systems of psychotherapy may be used safely with suicidal clients. Some, such as person-centered therapy, seem safe enough to use with any client, including the suicidal individual. But what about the more confrontive and emotional therapies, such as Gestalt therapy and primal therapy?

A second important question is whether the major therapeutic focus should be the client's suicidal preoccupation or the problems (e.g, depression and social isolation) underlying it, a question that relates to whether the suicidal preoccupation is acute or chronic. If the suicidality is chronic, it makes sense for the psychotherapist to focus on the client's underlying psychological problems. There has been a great deal of research on suicidal behavior in the last 40 years, and some of this research has implications for therapeutic strategies that may be used specifically with suicidal clients. In addition, individual therapists have formulated their own conceptualizations of the genesis of suicidal preoccupation, some of which are empirically based (e.g., Leenaars, 1991) and some of which are clinically based (e.g., Richman and Eyman, 1990) and have suggested goals and techniques for psychotherapy based on these conceptualizations.

The third issue psychotherapists should consider is whether particular systems of psychotherapy are suitable for particular types of clients. This leads to the problem of devising a taxonomy of suicidal clients that has relevance for psychotherapy (rather than, say, research). For example, Fremouw, de Perczel, and Ellis (1990) listed six types of suicidal clients (those who are depressed and hopeless, those with communication and control problems, psychotic clients, alcoholic clients, individuals with organic brain dysfunction, and rational clients), but they failed to explore whether this classification of suicidal clients was useful for choosing a system for counseling and psychotherapy.

Psychoanalysis

Freud's View of Suicidal Behavior

Brief mentions of suicidal behavior can be found throughout Freud's writings, and Litman (1967) documented and synthesized these dispersed thoughts. From an analytic perspective, the clinical features of suicidal behavior include guilt over death wishes toward others, identification with a suicidal parent, refusal to accept loss of gratification, suicide as a communication, and the connection between death and sexuality.

The essential feature of suicidal behavior is that the person loses a love-object and energy is withdrawn form this lost love-object, relocated in the ego, and used to re-create the loved-one as a permanent feature of the self in an identification of the ego with the lost object. Litman (1967) called this process *ego-splitting*. Even before becoming suicidal, the person has probably already introjected some of the desires of the loved-one. Children introject desires of their parents, and adults introject the desires of their lovers. In this way, it is as if part of our mind is symbolic of our loved-one. If this person is lost to us, for example, by death or divorce, we still possess those introjected desires, and thus the symbolization of the lost loved-one remains as part of our mind. This process can lead to suicide if we also harbor hostile wishes toward the lost object, for now we can turn this anger toward the part of our mind that symbolizes the lost object.

More generally, however, one major influence of psychoanalytic theory on the analysis of suicide is the asking of the question, "What is the real reason for this suicide?" Although researchers often cite the obvious precipitating event for suicidal preoccupation, such as the breakup of a close relationship, financial problems, or legal problems, the vast majority of people who experience such traumas do not kill themselves. These precipitating events are neither necessary nor sufficient to account for suicide. This had led psychoanalysts to probe for the unconscious motives behind the suicidal act.

For example, the suicide of Sylvia Plath, an American poet, in 1963 was ostensibly precipitated by her husband's adulterous affair. However, Oedipal conflicts appear to have been involved in the suicidal act. In her poem Daddy (Plath, 1966), Plath casts her father as a Nazi guard for the concentration camp in which a Jewish Sylvia is interned and as a devil who bit her heart in two. She expresses both affection and anger toward her deceased father, describes her marriage as an attempt to find a father substitute, and casts her suicide as a reunion with Daddy.

The Goals of Psychoanalysis

There are many possible goals in psychoanalysis with the suicidal client, but one possible goal is to make conscious to the client what is unconscious. If clients can become conscious of their unconscious desires, then they will not necessarily satisfy them directly, but at least they will be able to make more appropriate choices in the future. Psychoanalysis does not attempt to change the client's choice, but rather to make it an informed choice.

To make a client conscious of unconscious desires is not easy. The process may make the client anxious, perhaps to the point of panic. Thus, increasing the client's awareness must be done slowly and carefully. Psychoanalysis proceeds cautiously, with three to five meetings a week for three to seven years or longer.

The techniques of psychoanalysis include free association, in which the client permits his or her mind to wander freely from memory to memory and informs the psychoanalyst of the chain of associations. The psychoanalyst listens to what the client says and observes how the client behaves toward the psychoanalyst. In particular, the psychoanalyst behaves with total neutrality toward the client, so that when the client attributes thoughts and desires to the psychoanalyst that he does not possess, the psychoanalyst can observe this transference. Some psychoanalysts say that the psychoanalysis is finished when the client fully understands and has resolved this transference and can relate to people as they really are. Finally, the psychoanalyst interprets the client's behavior to the client. The psychoanalyst tries to get the client slowly to become aware of the unconscious desires behind his or her behavior.

Because most of the client's unconscious desires derive from childhood wishes, and most of the client's superego wishes (primarily involving the conscience and the ego ideal) derive from demands that the client's parents made on him or her, psychoanalysts place much importance on the client's childhood. In psychoanalysis, much time is spent discussing the early years and the client's parents and siblings. The slow tempo and historical orientation of psychoanalysis make it unsuitable for crisis intervention with acutely suicidal clients.

Comment

The psychoanalytic perspective on suicide has generated a good deal of research, much of which is supportive of the theory. For example, in a review of the research on the experience of loss in suicidal people and the relationships between suicide and depression and between suicide and anger, Lester (1988) found that the psychoanalytic perspective had been useful in furthering our understanding of suicidal behavior.

Because psychoanalysis is a slow process, it is difficult to document the use of its techniques for dealing with suicidal people. The goal of psychoanalysis is a thorough exploration of the contents of the conscious and unconscious mind, and this has to proceed slowly for both suicidal and nonsuicidal clients. The usefulness of the perspective for suicidal clients can be illustrated in the analysis of particular cases of suicide, such as that of Sylvia Plath, mentioned earlier in which a psychoanalytic perspective reveals the real motives underlying the superficial precipitating causes for the suicide.

Cognitive Therapy

The cognitive therapies are based on the notion that negative emotions and disturbing behaviors are a consequence of irrational thinking. The symptoms result not from the unpleasant events that we experience, but from our thoughts about those events. It is not the fact that we were fired from our job or that our spouse divorced us that makes us anxious or plunges us into despair. Rather, it is what we say to ourselves after these traumatic events that leads us to anxiety and despair.

The first systematic statement of these views was outlined by Ellis (1962, 1973) in his rational-emotive therapy. As an example, let us say that the client experiences rejection by a woman. This is the *activating experience*. In the unhealthy sequence, *irrational beliefs* are activated by this experience. "Isn't it awful that she rejected me? I am worthless. No desirable woman will ever accept me. I should have done a better job of getting her to accept me. I deserve to be punished for my ineptness." Particular emotional states result from these irrational beliefs. The client may feel anxiety, depression, worthlessness, or hostility. This emotional state is the *consequence*.

In the healthy sequence, the activating experience is followed by a *rational belief*. "Isn't it unfortunate (or annoying or a pity) that she rejected me?" The consequence of the rational belief is an emotional state of regret, disappointment, or annoyance.

Cognitive psychotherapy involves teaching the client that his or her emotional states result not from the activating experiences, but from the irrational, absolutistic, and demanding beliefs they activate. The client must be taught to dispute his or her irrational beliefs. "Why is it awful? How am I worthless? Where is the evidence that no one will ever love me? Why should I have done a better job? By what law do I deserve to be punished?" Once clients can substitute rational for irrational beliefs, they will be much happier and make appropriate choices.

Beck's (1976) cognitive-behavioral therapy is a more recent version of cognitive therapy. The goal of cognitive-behavioral therapy is to modify faulty patterns of thinking both directly and indirectly. It focuses on the client's cognitions (thoughts and attitudes) and the assumptions and premises that underlie them.

Clients are taught to recognize their idiosyncratic cognitions. The term *idiosyncratic* is used because the cognitions reflect a faulty appraisal of some aspect of the world. A person may have a distorted perception or may misinterpret what he or she perceives. Despite the fact that the cognitions are faulty, they seem to the client to be plausible, and they occur involuntarily and automatically. Often, they lead to unpleasant emotions.

Clients are taught first to distance themselves from the cognitions. They then learn to examine their cognitions objectively, evaluate them critically, and distinguish between their evaluations and reality. Finally, clients are taught to correct their cognitive distortions. To do this, it helps if clients can specify the particular kind of fallacious thinking they practice. For example, the client who tends to overgeneralize makes unjustified generalizations on the basis of one incident, as when a single experience of failure leads the client to believe that he will never succeed at anything.

Therapy provides a safe situation in which to test cognitions. The client is helped to confront them and examine them. The client transfers this learning process to real-life situations by directly modifying the thoughts and by rehearsing the reality-oriented thoughts.

Thought Patterns in Suicidal Individuals

Research has appeared in recent years that has identified specific patterns of thought commonly found in suicidal individuals. Awareness of these patterns can help the cognitive therapist who is working with suicidal clients.

For example, Neuringer (1988) has shown that suicidal people are prone to dichotomous thinking and tend to have rigid patterns of thought that work against their identifying solutions to the problems they face. Hughes and Neimeyer (1990) have elaborated on Neuringer's work, noting that suicidal people have polarized and extreme views of themselves, life, and death and have closed themselves off to examining alternative solutions to suicide. In addition, a growing body of research indicates that suicidal people are extremely pessimistic and hopeless about the future (Beck, 1970; Lester, 1992). Even when compared with depressed clients in general, suicidal people have a higher level of hopelessness, which may be caused in part by irrational thinking, as proposed in Ellis's theory (Revere, 1985).

Trexler (1973) has noted that therapists may find it useful to focus cognitive therapy on these distortions. However, the decision to commit suicide is often an impulsive decision. It is important to point out to clients that impulsive decisions are often bad decisions. It may be helpful to tell suicidal clients that individuals who survive a suicide attempt are almost invariably grateful, as well as to point out that a rash decision made at a time of emotional upheaval would be an error they could not correct. Thus, they should give the decision careful and prolonged consideration.

Several cases of cognitive therapy with suicidal clients have been published. Cautela (1970), Ellis (1989), Burns and Persons (1982), and Emery, Hollon, and Bedrosian (1981) reported cases in which they helped suicidal clients using cognitive therapy techniques. In addition, some researchers who are exploring suicidal individuals" cognitive distortions and deficiencies have devised therapeutic strategies to remedy them (Clum and Lerner, 1990; Linehan, et al., 1991).

Therapist Anxiety

Therapists who work with suicidal clients often feel great anxiety over the possibility that the client might commit suicide. If a client does commit suicide, the therapist may blame him or herself and feel guilt for failing to help the client. Trexler (1973) pointed out that these feelings are often the result of irrational thinking that needs to be challenged. Although therapists are responsible for their words and actions with clients, clients are ultimately responsible for their decisions and actions. Furthermore, the therapist's input into the client's life is but one small part of the total picture, and the therapist obviously has no control over the other inputs.

Comment

Cognitive therapy is one of the few therapies for which current research on suicide is providing new insights and guidelines. Researchers are actively exploring the thinking patterns of the suicidal individual, and their discoveries will suggest possible dysfunctional and thinking patterns for cognitive therapists to look for in their suicidal clients (Hughes and Neimeyer, 1990; Neuringer, 1988). This area promises to develop considerably in the next few years.

Transactional Analysis

Transactional analysis is a simplified, holistic conception of psychoanalysis, and transactional analysts have frequently written about suicidal behavior. They believe, in general, that the genesis of suicidal behavior lies in the early years of life when the child picks up "Don't exist" injunctions from the parents and incorporates them into the script of the self (Woollams, at al., 1977).

Transactional analysis proposes that the mind is composed of three ego states: the child ego state, which resembles the state of mind the individual had as a child; the adult ego state, a mature, information-processing state of mind; and the parent ego state, which is a state of mind based on the individual's identification with his or her parents or parent substitutes. Orten (1974) noted that it is the suicidal client's child ego state that is feeling despair and hopelessness and suggested that the counselor attempt to get the client's adult ego state in control at times of suicidal preoccupation. Nurturing responses from the counselor's parent ego state will not accomplish this. Messages that convey "Somebody loves you," Promise me you won't kill yourself," or "I won't let you do it" simply reinforce the executive role of the client's child ego stage.

Asking questions designed to elicit information is the most effective method of getting the client's adult ego state to take control. The questions should be non-threatening, that is, unrelated at first to the problems causing the suicidal preoccupation (e.g., ascertaining the client's current life situation-job, marriage, living arrangements, etc.) Prematurely rushing into consideration of the client's problems strengthens the child ego state's position. Upon being firmly established in the adult ego state, the client may immediately feel relief, because in this ego state he or she sees the world differently and feels more capable of dealing with it.

The counselor then can decide whether it would be useful to begin discussing the problems confronting the client or whether to postpone such a discussion to the next visit. If the counselor begins an exploration of the personal problems, he or she must be alert for signs that the child ego state is taking control again. If this happens, the counselor should recontact the adult ego state by moving away from the topics that have elicited the child's ego state.

Behavior Therapy

Behavior therapy is a system of therapy in which the therapist manipulates rewards and punishments, primarily using the principles of classical and operant conditioning, to change the client's behavior. For example, clients may be led to associate undesirable behavior with pain or nausea (classical conditioning), or appropriate behavior on the part of the client may be rewarded while inappropriate behavior unrewarded (operant conditioning).

Behavior therapists have described how their techniques can be applied to suicidal clients. Stuart (1967) reported treatment of a suicidal client who was receiving inadequate reinforcement, and Jansson (1984) described a suicidal client with poor social skills. Bostock and Williams (1974) and O'Farrell, Goodenough, and Cutter (1981) have also reported treatment of suicidal clients with behavioral therapy.

Rosenthal (1986) outlined steps for treating clients who are suicidal within the context of a learned-helplessness syndrome. First, clients sign a written contract to call the therapist if they feel suicidal. This shows clients that their behavior has had an effect on at least one person, the therapist. There is some debate, however, as to the usefulness of such contracts and the extent to which they should be used with suicidal clients.

Second, it helps if the therapist intervenes in the client's environment. For example, perhaps the therapist can talk to a suicidal teenager's parents. This shows clients that the therapist is on their side and that they do not have to tackle their problems alone. It demonstrates that the situation, although undesirable, is not catastrophic and can be approached rationally.

Third, Rosenthal suggested having clients keep a log of self-defeating thoughts and feelings. Unlike cognitive therapists, Rosenthal did not advocate challenging these thoughts and changing them. He believed that simply tabulating the thoughts lessens their frequency and impact.

Fourth, the therapist can work on anger. Rosenthal believed that anger and suicide are closely related. Shy and timid people need to be taught assertiveness skills and how to express anger in socially acceptable ways. Aggressive clients need to be given homework assignments in which they practice more empathic ways of expressing their feelings.

Finally, Rosenthal suggested that the therapist hold out hope that solutions are possible. For example, a teenager ignored by her parents can be told that the therapist will talk to them or can teach the teenager ways of dealing with them. A physically abused wife can be told that tomorrow the therapist will take her to court to get a police protection order and then to a women's shelter.

Other Systems of Psychotherapy

In addition to psychoanalysis, cognitive therapy, transactional analysis, and behavior therapy, other systems of psychotherapy may be useful for suicidal clients. Lester (1991) has discussed the applicability of these systems for the treatment of suicidal clients, and this section briefly outlines a few of them.

Primal Therapy

Primal therapy is a derivative of psychoanalysis in which traumatic early events are re-experienced emotionally very quickly in the course of psychotherapy. This re-experiencing is assumed to be cathartic. The extreme emotions aroused during primal therapy might be thought to be too stressful for suicidal individuals. However, Janov (1974) has reported using primal therapy with suicidal clients with no adverse effects.

Gestalt Therapy

Gestalt therapy (Perls, et al., 1951), a more confrontive style of therapy than many other systems, seeks to increase the awareness of clients of their emotions and bodily sensations. Gestalt therapy might also be thought to be too stressful for suicidal clients. There is also perhaps a danger in having suicidal clients dwell too intensely and too experientially on the here and now of their feelings. However, some Gestalt therapists have worked through the current feelings of suicidal clients. Many psychotherapists may not feel comfortable with encouraging such re-encounters; of course, the psychotherapist must be very experienced in using such techniques so that he or she can monitor the client's psychological state carefully during the experiences and calm the client when necessary. In addition, when closing the therapy session with the suicidal client, the therapist should take greater care than usual to ensure that the client has achieved a temporary resolution of the conflicts and feelings just experienced.

Reality Therapy

Reality therapy focuses largely on the client's behavior and seeks to have the client label inappropriate behavior as irresponsible and to substitute responsible behavior. Adherents of reality therapy find that suicidal clients pose no particular problem and can be helped by its standard techniques (Wubbolding, 1989).

Person-centered Therapy

In person-centered therapy (Rogers, 1959), the therapist tries to come to an understanding of clients' experience by reflecting back what they say and encouraging them to explore their feelings and thoughts in greater depth. This system of counseling has long been the basis for the crisis of counseling of suicidal clients, and its usefulness has now been widely acknowledged. Person-centered therapy differs from other therapies in maintaining that simply listening emphatically to clients is sufficient for therapy; most psychotherapists would not accept this, however.

Existential Therapy

Existential psychotherapy (Yalom, 1980) and Jungian analysis (Stein, 1982) seem to fit together, with existential therapists seeing the search for meaning for one's life as a powerful force in human behavior and Jungian analysts believing that the meaning is there if the individual can perceive it. Although neither system of psychotherapy proposes techniques specifically for the suicidal client, both systems seem relevant for the long-term treatment of suicidal clients.

Discussion

The usefulness of systematically considering the major forms of psychotherapy for their applicability to the treatment of suicidal clients is that the theorists of each system take a rather narrow and extreme position about the rationale for, purpose of, and techniques of their system of psychotherapy, exploring their perspective to the full. This permits examination of the power of the system acting in isolation. For example, what can psychoanalysis or person-centered therapy achieve if either is used exclusively with a suicidal client? It also reveals where the system of therapy fails, for example, what issues it overlooks and for which types of suicidal clients it may not be appropriate.

The practicing psychotherapist, in contrast, is able to use whatever theory and techniques best fit the client, both in the long term and in each moment of therapy. Thus, despite their orientation, psychotherapists often need to be eclectic in their approach, drawing on whatever system of psychotherapy seems appropriate in the moment. For example, if the client experiences an acute suicidal crisis, the psychotherapist can use the short-term strategies suggested by transactional analysts and behavior therapists or can use a standard crisis-counseling approach. After the suicidal crisis has subsided, the psychotherapist can then switch to more long-term strategies, such as modifying dysfunctional patterns of thinking or undertaking a psychoanalytic exploration of the client's conflicts. Suicidal clients may thus be able to make use of all of the techniques discussed herein to leave the abyss of despair.

References

Beck, A. T. The core problem in depression. *Science & Psychoanalysis*, 1970, 17, 47-55.

______ . *Cognitive therapy and emotional disorders*. New York: International Universities Press, 1976.

Bostock, T., & Williams, C. L. Attempted suicide as an operant behavior. *Archives of General Psychiatry*, 1974, 31, 482-486.

Burns, D., & Persons, J. Hope and hopelessness. In L. E. Abt & I. R. Stuart (Eds.) *The newer therapies*, pp. 33-57. New York: Van Nostrand Reinhold, 1982..

Cautela, J. R. The modification of behaviors that influence the probability of suicide in elders. Paper presented at the 78th Annual Convention of the American Psychological Association, Miami, FL, September, 1970.

Clum, G. A., & Lerner, M. A problem solving approach to treating individuals at risk for suicide. In D. Lester (Ed.) *Current concepts of suicide*, pp. 194-202. Philadelphia: Charles Press, 1990.

Ellis, A. *Reason and emotion in psychotherapy*. Secaucus, NJ: Lyle Stuart, 1962.

______ . *Humanistic psychotherapy*. New York: Julian, 1973.

______ . Using rational-emotive therapy (RET) as crisis intervention. *Individual Psychology*, 1989, 45, 75-81.

Emery, G., Hollon, S. D., & Bedrosian, R. C. *New directions in cognitive therapy*. New York: Guilford Press, 1981.

Fremouw, W. J., de Perczel, M., & Ellis, T. E. *Suicide risk*. New York: Pergamon, 1990.

Hughes, S. L., & Neimeyer, R. A. A cognitive model of suicidal behavior. In D. Lester (Ed.) *Current concepts of suicide*, pp. 1-28. Philadelphia: Charles Press, 1990.

Jansson, I. Social skills training for unipolar depression. *Scandinavian Journal of Behavior Therapy*, 1984, 13, 237-241.

Janov, A. Further implications of "level of consciousness." *Journal of Primal Therapy*, 1974, 1, 193-212.

Leenaars, A. A. Suicide notes and their implications for intervention. *Crisis*, 1991, 12, 1-20.

Lester, D. *Suicide from a psychological perspective*. Springfield, IL: Charles C. Thomas, 1988.

______. *Psychotherapy for suicidal clients*. Springfield, IL: Charles Thomas, 1991.

______. *Why people kill themselves*. Springfield, IL.: Charles C. Thomas, 1992.

Linehan, M. M, Armstrong, H. E., Suarez, A., Allmon, D., & Heard, H. I. Cognitive-behavioral treatment of chronically parasuicidal borderline patients. *Archives of General Psychiatry*, 1991, 48, 1060-1064.

Litman, R. F. Sigmund Freud on suicide. In E. S. Shneidman (Ed.) *Essays in self-destruction*, pp. 324-344. New York: Science House, 1967.

Neuringer, C. The thinking processes in suicidal women. In D. Lester (Ed.) *Why women kill themselves*, pp. 43-52. Springfield, IL: Charles C. Thomas, 1988.

O'Farrell, T. J., Goodenough, D. S., & Cutter, H. S. G. Behavioral contracting for repeated suicide attempts. *Behavioral Modification*, 1981, 5, 255-272.

Orten, J. D. A transactional approach to suicide prevention. *Clinical Social Work Journal*, 1974, 2, 57-63.

Perls, F. S., Hefferline, R. F., & Goodman, P. *Gestalt therapy*. New York: Julian, 1951.

Plath, S. *Ariel*. New York: Harper & Row, 1986.

Revere, V. I. Treatment of suicidal patients. *Independent Practitioner*, 1985, 5, 17-18.

Richman, J., & Eyman, J. R. Psychotherapy of suicide. In D. Lester (Ed.) *Current concepts of suicide*, pp. 139-158. Philadelphia: Charles Press, 1990.

Rogers, C. R. A theory of therapy, personality, and interpersonal relationships, as developed in the client-centered framework. In S. Koch (Ed.) *Psychology: A study of a science*, volume 3, pp. 184-256. New York: McGraw-Hill, 1959.

Rosenthal, H. The learned helplessness syndrome. *Emotional First Aid*, 1986, 3(2), 5-8.

Rudestam, K. E. Suicide and the selfless patient. *Psychotherapy & the Patient*, 1985-1986, 2, 83-95.

Stein, M. *Jungian analysis*. LaSalle, IL: Open Court, 1982.

Stuart, R. B. Casework treatment of depression viewed as an interpersonal disturbance. *Social Work*, 1967, 12, 27-36.

Trexler, L. The suicidal person and the restoration of hope. *Rational Living*, 1973, 8(2), 19-23.

Woollams, S., Brown, M., & Huige, K. What transactional analysts clients to know. In G. Barnes (Ed.) *Transactional analysis after Eric Berne*, pp. 487-525. New York: Harper's College Press, 1977.

Wubbolding, R. E. Professional issues: Four stages of decision making in suicidal client recovery. *Journal of Reality Therapy*, 1989, 8(2), 57-61.

Yalom, I. D. *Existential psychotherapy*. New York: Basic Books, 1980.

INDEX

A

B

C

D

E

F

G

H

I

J

K

L

M

N

O

P

R

S

T